The Transgender Myth

The Transgender Myth

Through the Gender Looking Glass

Paula Mirare Overby

MIRARE PUBLISHING
EAGAN

Contents

Part VIII: Gender Rebellion: Sex, sexuality, gender, and gender roles

Part IX: Uncommon Origins: A two-family divide

Part X: Flowering Gardenia: Acceptance and triumph

Acknowledgements

This is the second printing. I want to thank everyone who provided their review of the text for final release.

I want to express my appreciation to all of my family for embracing my humanity even if the changes seemed incomprehensible. I am grateful for all of the suggestions and background I received from friends and family.

Thank you to my editor, Ellie Davis, who insisted on changes I was reluctant to make and my sister Sharon for her critical review.

I want to acknowledge the support of the Twin Cities Men's Center and my transgender community. I offer special thanks to June Remus for her excellent mentoring and my dear friend, Dani Austin, for sharing the unique intimacy of the transgender experience. I am especially grateful to Dani for the lovely art work that adorns the cover.

Finally, I offer thanks to all of the people in my life that have made my life experience such an amazing journey.

Thank you everyone

Foreword

This story examines the historical, social, political, economic, and legal impact of gender on my life as a transgender woman. It evolves within the context of the civil rights movement, feminism, the gay rights movement, and today's transgender movement. It is a journey from blissful innocence, through fear and isolation, past denial and defeat, into acceptance and triumph, examining the best and the worst of living in both genders.

The story encompasses my own transition, but it isn't a story about transition. Moving from one gender to the other was socially and economically devastating: not the result of transition but rather the cause of it. Society's gender norms wouldn't allow me to sustain a false gender presentation.

This book is written in an associative style in honor of my former spouse, Marie, who had an associative memory. People, places and events from vastly different times and locations could be linked together in a single memory. This confused me greatly until I began to understand it.

I have always been fascinated by memory studies and their inherent complexity. Memory isn't like a video that will replay itself exactly the same every time. If you have ever watched a movie or read a book more than once, you have probably recognized that you notice different things the second or third or even the fourth time. This is the nature of memory. It is a creative process. Memory helps us organize current events according to past experiences. If the relevance of those past experiences changes, the memory itself can change.

I can only speculate what Marie experienced around my gender, and I have tried to avoid such speculation. Still, I'm certain it was significant, and I will always admire her courage and her commitment to overcoming the enormous challenges we dealt with. I'd love, if someday, I could hear her side of the story.

A yardstick from the future is a process of interpreting the past according to some future knowledge. History is written this way. Circumstances, events, and relationships are defined by future outcomes. This idea propels the belief in natural law or the determinism of fate.

The transgender myth isn't a specification for some unconfirmed mystery like the mystical Unicorn. We know transgender people exist. Chances are you already know one. While we remain a mystery to many, transgender people marvel at the belief that there are but two distinct sexes, each with its own unique gender that defines specific abilities. That is a myth in our view, the transgender myth. To be free of that myth is to realize a deeper relationship to the diversity of the human experience.

I want to say thank you to thousands of people who respectfully engaged with me during this journey and for your forthright courage in asking difficult questions. I know there are hundreds of photographs of me out there all around the world. If you have one, I'd love to see it and hear your story about when we met.

Hugs!

Paula

Part I: Childhood Innocence: My life before sex and gender

It was 2008 when I first began writing some of the stories about my life that appear in this book. It was only a year after our first transgender march at a time when the transgender community was largely invisible to the general public. It was for many, their desire to remain stealth, to have a physical appearance that would allow them to pass imperceptibly.

The media represents transgender as boys becoming girls. It's dramatized by the statement: "a woman trapped in a man's body." I loathed hearing that statement, but it does comport well with the notion that the woman I am today has little to do with the sex I was assigned at birth.

In July of 2013 Laverne Cox, appearing in the hit series, *Orange Is the New Black*, pressed transgender women, in particular, transgender women of color, into the public spotlight with a new legitimacy. Laverne's eloquent pronouncement that womanhood is distinct from physical characteristics, buttressed a long-standing battle against the objectification and sexualization of women. In February the following year, her message was reinforced by Janet Mock's *New York Times* best-selling book, *Redefining Realness*. By May of 2014, Laverne Cox appeared on the cover of *Time Magazine* with the cover story "The Transgender Tipping Point."

It was an exciting time for the transgender community. In April of 2015, media focus took a decidedly different turn when Dianne Sawyer interviewed Bruce Jenner on *20/20*. The interview itself offered viewers a window into some of the challenges faced by transgender people. Then in July, in a manner reminiscent of the ugly duckling becoming a beautiful swan, the hapless male Jenner is suddenly transformed into a gorgeous cover girl model in a virgin white corset on the cover of *Vanity Fair*. It fulfilled the public perception of boys becoming girls and blatantly objectified women, contradicting the value of womanhood advanced by Laverne Cox and Janet Mock. It was exactly the kind of image transgender woman have fought against. Reactions were strained. It was impossible not to empathize, but accepting her as the self-anointed spokesperson for the transgender community was challenging.

In December of 2015, she appeared at the United Nations as a spokesperson for all women around the world. While Jenner is exploring what it means to be a woman, the focus is shifting to transgender children and youth.

In February of 2017, Katie Couric hosted the *National Geographic* Documentary, *Gender Revolution* in which she explains sex and gender this way: "Sex is who you go to bed with, and gender is who you go to bed as." It undermines the distinction between sex and gender, derailing the entire discussion with a suggestion that a person's sex is the same thing as their sexuality.

Naturally, there are intersections. For clarity in the discussion, sex and sexuality are about the gay community. Sex and gender are about the transgender community. That discussion is only now just beginning to emerge between the gay and the transgender communities.

The way the gender revolution is being presented reminds me of the hippie movement of my day or the goth movement of my oldest daughter's generation. Fashion has always been part of a youthful rebellion. Today's extreme gender morphing of makeup, hair, and fashion spotlights the "gender revolution" but does little to contribute to the broader discussion of gender roles and gender equity.

National Geographic's January, special edition, *Gender Revolution,* features a cover photo of nine-year-old Avery Jackson. Dressed in pink, reclined across the arm of a chair, with a sultry look on her face, the caption reads, "The best thing about being a girl, is not having to pretend you're a boy." She's a hero in the gender queer community.

Avery transitioned when she was four years old. She explains that her life was miserable living as a boy. It raises some intriguing questions about what children are learning about sex and gender that allows a three old child to have a deeply held belief that they are one sex and a different gender. In contemplation of that thought, my story begins at birth and explores some of my earliest memories, occurring well before the generally accepted average of 3.5 years. My mother provided information prior to that so that I might understand the consequences attached to these events even as I have no recollection.

I had a great childhood. I had loving parents and good friends. I went to a parochial school where I learned about a loving God. I lived in a peaceful neighborhood rich with activity. I was free to explore the world around me in its entire splendor. Every day was filled with new opportunities and new activities. It was everything childhood should be.

Yet, there were shadows of a different reality shrouded in secrecy that awakened suspicions of a more menacing existence. Like the tree of knowledge of good and evil in the Garden of Eden, I'd have to partake of its fruits to understand its secrets.

Chapter One: Start at the Beginning

"Begin at the beginning," the King said, very gravely, "and go on till you come to the end: then stop."

−Lewis Carroll, Alice in Wonderland

I was born just after midnight on Sunday, February 28, 1954, in Redwood Falls, Minnesota. With my footprints imprinted, I became Paul Stewart Overby, second male child of Luverne and Verna Overby.

At sixteen months I was in Cincinnati, Ohio. My father traded a teaching career for a more lucrative career in engineering. There, at the tender age of eighteen months, I discovered life's adversity, when I broke my right upper femur. It was a serious, greenstick fracture, where the bone bends and cracks instead of breaking completely. It's common for young children, but my case was unusually severe with the bone collapsing and protruding through my upper thigh. I'd spend the next six weeks in a hospital bed with my leg in traction.

Speculation—the how and why—was natural. My brother often claimed responsibility, saying he'd pushed me off the couch, but just as often Mom denied that story. I imagine; so he wouldn't feel responsible. It never mattered to me. I had no memory of it.

As a mother, I try to imagine my child lying in a hospital bed with their leg in traction for six weeks. I can't imagine it, so I call my own mother. For the first time in my life, I wanted to hear the story I'd always thought had no real significance in my life. It took awhilea while for the scene to solidify in my mind: a young mother in an unfamiliar city far from friends and family. Her husband is at the start of a new career, and money is scarce. Moving from rural farm life to a large city presents unexpected challenges. A co-worker paid their first few weeks of living expenses. In the first two months, my brother had already been to the hospital for a tonsillectomy. Suddenly, she hears crying and finds her baby on the floor with a broken leg, the bone visibly protruding. There's no 911, no thought of an ambulance, no driver's license; so she holds me and waits for dad to drive home from work.

To this I can relate, holding my baby in my arms unable to calm the hurt. When my daughter, Courtney, was close to the same age, she and I flew to New Hampshire for my brother's wedding. I made sure she'd be hungry when we took off. Nursing a bottle would help her ears adjust. The plane was full, but we found our seat and settled in for takeoff. As we neared the runway, I gave her a bottle.

Takeoff went fine, but as we ascended through the clouds, Courtney began to cry. She wasn't fussing the way babies communicate. She squalled like I imagine I had when I'd broken my leg. The bottle trick had failed. In the late eighties, it was rare to see a man traveling with a baby. People didn't see an inexperienced mother; they saw an incompetent dad. I went to the back of the plane where I stood and rocked her the entire flight.

As soon as we landed, I wanted to change her, but those days, there were no changing stations in the men's room. I eyed the women's room as I thought about a woman I'd seen on Johnny Carson who had been arrested for using a men's room. Perhaps if I got arrested in the women's room I might be on Johnny Carson myself. Who could fault me for changing a baby's diaper?

Fear dictated a secluded spot on the concourse where I changed her on the floor. Her diaper was blood red, and her bottom looked as if it had been skinned. I was horrified. I certainly couldn't rub Desitin on raw skin. I cleaned her and patted gently, sprinkled some baby powder, and put on a clean diaper. Courtney was strangely cooperative, and she didn't cry. I was relieved to see my mother: she'd certainly know what to do.

Back in Cincinnati, my own mother waits anxiously for Dad to get home. The details are sketchy. Did Mark go with to the hospital? Did they go to the doctor first or go straight to the emergency room? I wonder how Dad would remember it. In any case, I made it to Children's Hospital, where I laid in bed for six weeks with my leg in traction, stretching the bone back into position so it could heal properly.

Mom couldn't drive, so there weren't visits until after Dad got home from work. I try to imagine how he understood the challenge at the start of a new career. Mother told me there were nights when they couldn't come at all.

I am like an orphan without my mother. Life builds on these early experiences, even If I have no memory of it. Piecing together fragments of mom's recollections I try to imagine it. My bed is in a really, really big room. Sometimes I hear other babies crying. They are hungry or wet; sometimes they are lonely, and other times they are hurting real bad. Most of the moms look the same, and none of them are my Mom, but they take care of me anyway. I don't see any toys or colors, anything to stare at or reach for. Sometimes it's bright, and sometimes it's dark.

I'm excited when I hear Mom and Dad talking to one of the other moms. At my bedside I reach up to them, wanting them to pick me up, wanting them to hold me, but they never do. I offer my biggest smile and my most charming greeting "grapes?" I love grapes. Tonight Mommy reads to me, and her voice is soothing. I want her to stay, but the visit is short. It is always short. It is time for them to leave, and I am crying.

I returned home encased in plaster from the ankle of my right leg up past my hips and halfway down my other leg. Dad, being inventive, already had the solution: marvelous mobility came through a board with four wheels, allowing me to scoot about the floor using my hands. Dad was an engineer, but the form of his creations always exceeded the function. He was an artist, too. When the cast came off I had to start over, learning to sit up, stand, and walk.

With pride apparent, Dad showed me that board when I was in my teens. It truly was ingenious for its directional stability combined with radial turning ability at either end, but I had nothing to connect it to. Dad would have those memories, but they are now forever lost. I could ask a thousand questions today. While I have no memory of this time it doesn't mean memories don't exist. When I look in the mirror I slightly raise my right heel to level my hips. The leg I broke is a bit shorter than the other. There is a different person in the reflection who I will often ponder throughout my life.

Nine months later I was back in Minnesota staying with mom's sister, Borgney, awaiting the birth of my sister Lori. Mom, Mark, and I stayed with her while Dad took care of the move from Cincinnati to Milwaukee, Wisconsin.

Borgney would become a major inspiration in my life. I hoped that I'd live my life the same way. "Live till you die" was her style, always a plan for tomorrow. Her funeral was a sad day for me, the last person to take a rose off the top of her casket as they lowered it into the ground. It was one of her wishes that people take the flowers with them. That's how she was.

My older cousin Steven once recounted his own memory of my childhood charm. When dessert arrived, I said to my Uncle Selmer, "I like peaches too." Then I'd get to sit in his lap and eat his peaches. It was one of the softer ways men relate to children. I still love peaches.

Our new home in Milwaukee was across from Humbolt Park. Dad thought considerably about the needs of his family when selecting new locations. He often didn't understand those needs, but his intentions were good. Dad was the provider.

That's where my earliest memory unfolds at age two-and-a-half. I have images of a Christmas tree, two brothers in their pajamas and a shattered Christmas bulb. To share that memory with you I need information and verbal skills I acquired much later in life.

Mark and I received a pair of pump guns for Christmas, able to shoot small plastic balls. The tree was an attractive target, and one well-placed shot sent a Christmas bulb crashing to the floor. Even a three-year-old child knows this isn't a good thing. You can complete the story with a reaction from your own mother or perhaps how you as a parent might react. I'm guessing my mom just put things back in order. She was a loving mom, placing a positive construction on everything. Mom was the caretaker.

I have a photograph of Mark and me with our pump guns, standing in front of the Christmas tree. Perhaps the memory formed later in my life, invoked by that photograph. I believe that memory is legitimate because there is a visceral sensation of hearing the bulb breaking.

Sensory memories like sound or smell can have a profound impact on our life but can be difficult to articulate. Memory isn't like a photograph or a movie film that we can replay over and over forever, unchanging no matter how many times we view it.

Human memory is notoriously unreliable, even as we believe in the permanency and the accuracy of what we do remember. A memory is constructed with each recollection. It can change over time as new experiences alter the priority of past events. The evolution of memory creates distance in a relationship when memories are not shared. Talking about the "good old days" is more than an idle pastime. It is an essential part of strong relationships.

My time on Humbolt Avenue was brief, and my last memory of it came with sledding in the park. Mark sat in the back with his feet on the steering bar. Dad tucked me safely between Mark's knees and pushed us down the hill.

I remember screaming, as a tree loomed larger. Maybe the scream is one of those fill-in-the-blank kinds of memories, but I know we hit the tree. The image of the tree is clear in my mind. I remember I cried.

When I asked Mom about life on Humbolt Avenue she even asked me if I remembered when I almost ran into a tree out sledding. I said, "Mom . . . we did run into a tree." You could always depend on Mom to ensure that things were never as bad as they might seem.

Chapter Two: Boys and Girls

Imagination is the only weapon in the war against reality.

–Lewis Carroll, Alice in Wonderland

It was raining. Normally, one might describe that in more animated ways, but the rain wasn't that interesting. What was interesting was the mud covering expansive areas of new yards with no grass, no flowers, no trees. That's how I remember our arrival to Grafton, Wisconsin. At age three-and-a-half, it's where my childhood began.

My mom described it as a palace. A brand-new three-bedroom rambler, small by today's standards, less than half the size of an average home today.

It gives me pause to think about my first home purchase which was definitely not a palace. Approximately the same size as the house in Grafton with only two bedrooms. It had a lower-level walkout with a tuck-under garage devouring half of it. Wallpaper was falling off the walls, announcing serious neglect everywhere. The outside was badly in need of paint, and moss consumed the roof on the back porch. Railings were falling off the deck, as the whole deck was nearing collapse. The yard was overgrown with weeds, and the bushes were wildly out of control.

So I have to agree, the house in Grafton was a palace. Mark and I lay on our stuffed Scotty dogs in front of the TV. This is my first memory of Lori. She's there in her bouncy baby seat. Those Scotty dogs were black with red plaid saddles. Enshrined in my earliest memories, I have no idea where they came from or where they went.

I also remember a little red fire truck and a huge lake in our backyard. Jimmy, our next-door neighbor hurled that little red fire truck into the lake where it sank into the depths never to be seen again. I cried.

No one else remembers that little red fire truck, and the lake was just a puddle. A child's world is a fascinating place. That memory always reminds me how adults become isolated from a child's perceptions of time and space.

My childhood in Grafton forged the values that sustained me through life's adversities. There I learned the value of faith. We three kids attended Saint Paul's Elementary School, where I learned about a loving God through Bible stories, songs, and pageants. We had bible stories in our home and 78 LPs that told miraculous stories of popular biblical events. Every year the students of Saint Paul's performed the Christmas Story. Christmas was a special time.

One Christmas, Santa Claus brought me the Fighting Lady. The Fighting Lady was a battleship, a superior fighting force with motorized gun turrets, firing cannons, fighter jets that launched off the aft deck, and a horn that sounded the alarm. It was a pretty cool toy. Lori got Chatty Cathy that same Christmas. Chatty Cathy talked when you pulled the string. To me, that was way cooler.

I don't remember thinking I was a girl, but that's what I was. As a child, I had no conflict with gender. Grafton had two neighborhood groups: the girls and the boys. That seems natural to most people, but we weren't separated by gender; we were separated by age.

My brother Mark was older, and his friends in the neighborhood were his age. Jerry, Nibby, Steve, I can't remember all their names. They were the boys. They did boy stuff.

I was the same age as my best friend, LeeAnn, who lived across the street. LeeAnn's younger sister was the same age as Lori. That made me one of the girls. We did girl stuff.

The girls jumped rope and played hopscotch. We played house, modeling our future roles as homemakers and moms. Other times we went on magical adventures to the moon or to fabulous undersea worlds. When we played the Barbie Game, none of us ever wanted to get stuck with Poindexter.

The boys played marbles and captured honeybees in Mason jars.

They went out to the neighbor's farm to climb trees and down to the creek to torture frogs or hunt for crayfish. In the fall they threw sticks to knock down chestnuts in the park.

I learned many things from Mark about being a boy which helped me move fluidly around the world. While not enthralled by his activities myself, I totally enjoyed his enthusiasm. He loved our Lionel trains and strategy games like Civil War, Dogfight, and Summit. I was exceptionally good at strategy games and commonly victorious, but that only inspired him. We played again and again. He never seemed to tire of it.

Today I absolutely hate to fish. As a child, fish fomented the bond between my brother and I. I recall my first fishing trip when Mark took me to Mill Pond Park. The bullhead I caught, about the size of my thumb, remains to this day the largest fish I have ever caught. Mark was unimpressed with my catch, and fed my bullhead to a cat. That made me cry, but Mark never treated me like a sissy. A gallon jar of guppies we received from one of Dad's friends started a hobby that would become a central part of our relationship.

Dad created activities for Mark. Sometimes they included me. Mark was in Boy Scouts, and they went camping. There was Camp Jamboree in the summer and in the winter the Klondike Derby which was an outdoor activities course using dogsleds. There were kite-flying contests, and Dad designed monstrous kites. We built pinewood derby cars and assembled walkie-talkies. I enjoyed building balsa wood model airplanes. I realize now that Dad thought of me as his son and Mark and me as brothers. Naturally, he wanted to teach me boy stuff, but I never understood it that way.

Lori got a puppy, a registered toy poodle. I didn't understand why she got the puppy. Now I might assume my parents thought she was the only girl, but I know she got the puppy because she wanted one. Lori named that puppy Misty Mimi Lori Louise. Lori always had an air of sophistication that placed her above suspicion. I don't believe she ever got in trouble for anything, though she definitely knew how to have fun. Lori kept me anchored, and I can't imagine my life without her. I've wondered sometimes how she put up with me, but like any great sister, she says she remembers all the fun we had.

We girls went to the covered bridge for picnic lunches, to pick flowers and listen to the babbling brook. It was definitely our favorite spot. The four of us rode our bikes four miles to the covered bridge park. Four young girls, ages six and four, alone on Highway 60. I think about how that would be viewed today.

I imagined a boyfriend too. David was real, and he was a boy but certainly didn't know he was my boyfriend. Girls do a lot of relationship planning. At school, David and I were a team providing the entertainment. Teachers maybe didn't see it that way, as it seems as though I was always writing some sentence on some blackboard. I can't imagine how David managed to get himself stuck inside that trash can or why I was unable to free him. He lived out in the country, and I stayed at his house occasionally. He had cool boy toys that he enjoyed demonstrating for me. He was courageous, bold, and daring.

I saw David again when we were both in college. It was a shallow reunion, reality replacing the imaginary bonds of childhood.

As a young child, I liked wrestling with the boys. If people knew I was a girl, then certainly I was a tomboy. One winter in fourth grade, the boys and I came in from recess soaking wet. The teacher wanted us out of our wet pants so she made us put on the girls pedal pushers. It was the first time I ever wore girls' clothes. It made me feel special. It was also an embarrassment because I was wearing long johns that kept slipping below the pedal pushers down to my ankles. These conflicting feelings were familiar partners in my life.

LeeAnn and I were the leaders of our club, the Blue Eagles. We sponsored penny fairs, raising money for charities. We went on mercy missions rescuing injured birds and small animals. We were determined to save the world, scarcely aware of the fact that there was a world in need of saving.

LeeAnn's home had a small blackboard on the inside of the basement door. If one of the girls misbehaved, her name went on the blackboard with a declaration that they would get their punishment when Dad got home. Her dad used a belt, and my dad used his hand. It was perfectly normal to spank a child. In fact, it was considered essential.

Even as a young child, I felt something more sinister. Mark and I wet the bed. Mom had an old Maytag with double rollers on top that were used to ring out the clothes before they were hung on the line. Washing sheets and pajamas many times a week was hard work.

They tried everything: the doctor, the chiropractor, rewards, and gold stars on the calendar. In one moment of frustration Mom put me in a diaper. In pure desperation I'm sure, their most serious effort was also the last.

Each morning before Dad went to work he'd wake us up. If the bed was wet, we got a spanking. I'm sure Dad didn't enjoy it; there weren't many spankings.

I remember the mornings when I woke up while my Dad was getting ready. If my bed was wet, I laid there listening to Dad getting ready for work, waiting in fear for the moment he'd open the door, knowing there was no escape. Eventually, I'd hear his car pull out of the driveway, and I'd know I was safe for one more day

That's how I understood the blackboard in my neighbors' house. I felt the same fear the girls felt when their name went on the board. This was especially true for LeeAnn. As a child, I had no context for understanding these feelings crouched in secrecy. Many more years of my life will pass before that understanding emerges from those shadows.

In November of 1963, we got the news at school that the president had been shot. Three months later, in February of 1964, the Beatles made their first appearance in the U.S. on the Ed Sullivan show. The girls traded Beatles cards like the boys traded baseball cards. The Vietnam War moved into high gear. The baby boomers started to make their mark on the world. The world was changing, and my childhood reached an abrupt halt. We left Grafton for a new home in Cudahy, a suburb on the south side of Milwaukee.

I don't think I ever said goodbye to LeeAnn. Maybe it's not proper to ever say goodbye to your very best friend.

My first night in Cudahy I laid awake, and I cried. For a while, I sustained myself with fantasies about a helicopter that would magically keep me connected with Grafton while living in a foreign place, imagination being my only weapon in the war against reality. Grafton was the beginning of my childhood. Leaving Grafton was the end of it.

Chapter Three: One Part Country

–Lewis Carroll, Alice in Wonderland

Life in Cudahy left me feeling like a branch broken from a tree by a gale force wind. I was alone. But a branch will wither and die. I was more like the flower separated from the Gardenia bush. Though I was vulnerable to the elements, I was capable of growing new roots, to become a lovely plant, and bloom once again.

We lived in one end of a fourplex. Each unit was two stories with bedrooms and a bathroom upstairs. It was near the airport, and I'd walk to the fence at the end of the runway, and watch the planes take off. There under the intense noise of the airplanes was my quiet space, much like the cone of silence from the popular TV show of the day, *Get Smart*, where conversations were completely secret because conversations were impossible.

Mark remained with friends back in Grafton finishing his last year of school at Saint Paul's. Recalling that fact, I'd presume some level of jealousy, knowing he was where I wanted to be. Those feelings didn't exist, establishing that Mark and I lived in separate worlds, intersecting in brief moments of time.

We were just a couple of blocks from my new school, Parkview Elementary, which I remember best as the place I first met twins: two girls who were, to me, except for their appearance, as different as night and day. They were not friends of mine, only a reminder of how personally isolated I was during my two grades at Parkview Elementary.

Lots of kids move to new places, some of them many times. I wonder if they struggle in the same way I did. Is it harder for a transgender girl to find friends among other girls? For me, it took nearly two years.

As always, there was a boy. Keith wasn't the type I'd choose for a boyfriend, but he was kind and innocent and he liked me. He lived in a house just a few blocks away. He had a color television built into the wall made of fieldstone, which I guess was the coolest thing he had to show me. I did my best to protect him.

I learned an important survival skill at Park View from an altercation with a teacher in sixth grade. After another boy on the playground jumped on my back, we were both instructed to write sentences about our behavior. I wasn't averse to writing sentences; I'd done that plenty of times before. I was averse to the sentence itself, and I refused to do it, asserting my innocence. I sat there a long time before I said to the teacher, "I know you don't like me, and I don't like you either." He laughed. I can appreciate now why that amused him. I never did write a single sentence. Confronting teachers was a good way to maintain high visibility and garner a certain sense of esteem from fellow classmates.

Dad loved guns, though all he had were a couple of 22 rifles and an old Japanese rifle he'd brought home after World War II. He belonged to a rod and gun club. I went with him to his meetings. I can imagine nothing more boring for a fifth-grade girl than attending meetings of a rod and gun club, but I was happy to be with my father, riding in the car with him. It was a quiet ride. Sometimes I'd be falling asleep on the way home because of the late hour, but I went to every meeting.

Dad did get a handgun while he was in that club. He bought a 357 Magnum service revolver from a police officer. I was with him. He was happy, so I was happy. Dad had a great smile. To see him smile was to smile yourself. My favorite picture of Dad shows him holding my sister Sharon, who arrived just three months after our move to Cudahy. He's holding her in one outstretched hand, looking into her eyes; on his face the greatest smile you've ever seen. It is as if experiencing the miracle of life for the first time. Many times I've wondered if that picture of Sharon is the first time he ever really held a baby. It's a false memory. Sharon produced the picture. He is not smiling. There is an expression of slight bewilderment, as if it's the first time he's ever seen a baby.

Sharon was the only one of us born in Wisconsin. This made her unique, but then there were many things that made her unique. Sharon's arrival presented my first opportunity to be a mom. She couldn't imagine how precious she was to me. Her birth also rendered my first associative memory. I clearly remember Dad gathering us together in the living room at our house on Trinthammer to pray for Mom who was in the hospital delivering Sharon. I know it is a false memory because we didn't have that house when Sharon was born. It was Lori who was in the hospital. It was Lori we prayed for.

Minnesota relatives came for Sharon's baptism. It was unusual to have visits from Minnesota relatives. We always made the trip. Both sides of the family lived in Minnesota, and it was easier for us to go there. I loved those trips. I cherished family, and everywhere we went there were good things to eat. Mom had three sisters who seemed to love cooking. The kitchen was a comfortable place for me. It was central to the strong connection I felt with my mother and the role she maintained in our family. Milwaukee was city living. Minnesota was farm country.

My life split me between the city and the farm. The split started in Grafton in 1963, when the call came that Grandpa Overby had passed away from heart failure. I was with the Cub Scouts getting ready to march in the Memorial Day Parade. As it was explained to me, Grandpa went out in the morning to feed his animals, came back to the house, lay down, and passed on. It sounds peaceful and serene in a way.

At the funeral, my cousin Dianne and I stood by Grandpa's grave for an hour talking. She told me about Grandpa, a man I barely knew. We talked about life, about family and friends, about our own lives and our future lives. We were both nine years old, but her birthday was six months ahead of mine. She would become like an older sister, who enjoyed teasing me about being her younger cousin.

For Mark, it was a different story. He loved his Grandpa and spent summers on Uncle Jim's farm so he could be with Grandpa. Mark never returned, and I took his place that summer of 1963.

My first assignment that summer spun a story I retold many times because it was so unbelievable. Uncle Jim put me on an old John Deere D tractor. It was a small stocky tractor with a wide front end. There was a platform for the driver and a metal seat attached to the platform with a spring metal bar. It was completely bare bones and clearly not built with any thought of safety.

In order to start this machine, there were valves on either side of the engine called pit-cocks that had to be open. After the engine started, they whistled out a tremendous roar. Then, I had to go down by the engine and close the pit-cocks. It was terrifying, and I never got used to it. I hated shutting it off knowing I'd have to start it again.

My job was to disc a freshly plowed field. A disc was a piece of farm machinery with two rows of heavy steel discs that sliced through the chunks of dirt smoothing out the soil for planting. Had I fallen off that tractor those discs would have diced me up in a dozen slices like a hot knife through butter. I was too short to reach the steering wheel, so Uncle Jim gave me these instructions, "Don't try to steer it. Just hold on to the wheel."

Whenever that story came up I'd say to Uncle Jim, "Do you know that I was only nine years old?" He'd say, "No, I can't believe that."

At the end of the summer in 1963, I rode the Hiawatha rail line back home to Milwaukee. My uncle dropped me at the train station in Red Wing, Minnesota, and my parents picked me up at the depot in Milwaukee. I loved the exhilaration of going from car to car. You could see the tracks through the cracks. The noise of the wheels clacking across the rails was deafening. That one ride instilled in me a nostalgic passion for passenger trains.

I'd be back on the farm every summer until college. It was a safe place for me. I was close to Dianne. She had girlfriends, and that worked well for me.

Life in Cudahy was a different story, the other half of my life. Roots were slow to develop, and I'd run out of time long before there was any hope of a flowering Gardenia.

By seventh grade, we were living in a house on Trinthammer Avenue, on the other side of the tracks. Cudahy was situated between the airport on the west side and Lake Michigan to the east with railroad tracks down the middle. The bluffs along Lake Michigan were a beautiful place to go walking. I could sit by the lake and listen to the waves ripple on the shoreline. It was much better than the fence line at the airport.

By the time we moved to Trinthammer, I'd accepted that I wasn't going back, and it was time to move forward. My activities drew me away from my isolation. I was Boy Scout patrol leader, rising to first class scout within a year. I was the first chair in the band, winning multiple state competitions. I was chosen to perform in the high school play, *A Music Man*, representative of the seventy-six trombones. I rode my bike to school and walked if I couldn't ride because I hated the social hierarchy that existed on the school bus.

Mark and I found a common purpose in our tropical fish. That gallon jar of guppies we had gotten in Grafton expanded to nearly 200 gallons of twenty- and thirty-gallon tanks. We managed some difficult successes. We spawned Siamese fighting fish, raising them to adult specimens. We even managed to raise saltwater brine shrimp to adult size. In those days brine shrimp eggs were packaged and sold in comic book ads as the Amazing Sea Monkeys. Check it out online.

When I was at the farm, we communicated about fish catalogs and fish acquisitions and future expansions. For the two us, that year-and-a-half was the most quality time we ever had together.

Eventually, I found a couple girlfriends to hang out with. It was great to be one of the girls again with Debbie and Carol, but things were getting more complicated. At twelve years old, it wasn't clear to me there were significant anatomical differences between boys and girls.

There was a boy on the other side of town as well. He'd wrestle me in the unfinished space on the second story of our house. I don't even remember his name. Maybe I invented the whole thing in my fantasies. I believe it's a true memory because it's so physical.

The junior high had a pool, and swimming was part of the curriculum. I was terrified of the water from nearly drowning in a pool. Standing with a row of boys in a sport swimsuit next to that pool was an uncomfortable experience. Showering naked with the boys enhanced my sense of vulnerability. I learned to swim very quickly which avoided the teasing.

The relationship with my girlfriends was getting complicated as well. At Christmas time Carol gave me a red heart with the inscription, "good for one free kiss." I examined those words many times over the next few weeks until Carol finally took the initiative at a school dance. Debbie held the mistletoe. It wasn't an unpleasant experience. Carol knew how to French kiss. For me it was my first kiss.

So much happened during the short time we lived in Cudahy. Misty Mimi Lori Louise had her first litter of puppies. Sharon fell down the steps and knocked out her two front teeth. Mom became a nurse's aide at the hospital. She had always wanted to work, and I was beginning to understand those unfulfilled ambitions. With little advance warning, life in Cudahy ended abruptly the day we boarded the plane in Milwaukee destined for our new home in Nashua, New Hampshire.

I. We stood by Grandpa's grave for an hour talking. She told me about Grandpa, a man I barely knew. We talked about life, about family and friends, about our own lives and our future lives. I was nine years old. She was nine years old, but her birthday was in August, six months ahead of mine. She would become like an older sister, who enjoyed teasing me about being her younger cousin.

For Mark it was a different story. He loved his Grandpa and spent summers on Uncle Jim's farm so he could be with Grandpa. Mark never returned, and I took his place that summer of 1963.

My first assignment that summer spun a story I retold many times because it was so unbelievable. Uncle Jim put me on an old John Deere D tractor. It was a small stocky tractor with a wide front end. There was a platform for the driver and a metal seat attached to the platform with a spring metal bar. It was completely bare bones and clearly not built with any thought of safety.

In order to start this machine there were valves on either side of the engine called pit-cocks that had to be open. After the engine started, they whistled out a tremendous roar and you had to go down by the engine and close the pit-cocks. It was terrifying, and I never got used to it. I hated shutting it off knowing I'd have to start it again.

My job was to disc a freshly plowed field. A disc was a piece of farm machinery with two rows of heavy steel discs that sliced through the chunks of dirt smoothing out the soil for planting. Had I fallen off that tractor those discs would have diced me up in a dozen slices like a hot knife through butter. I was too short to reach the steering wheel, so Uncle Jim gave me these instructions, "Don't try to steer it. Just hold on to the wheel."

Whenever that story came up I'd say to Uncle Jim, "Do you know that I was only nine years old?" He'd say, "No, I can't believe that."

At the end of the summer in 1963, I rode the Hiawatha rail line back home to Milwaukee. My uncle dropped me at the train station in Red Wing, Minnesota, and my parents picked me up at the depot in Milwaukee. I loved the exhilaration of going from car to car. You could see the tracks through the cracks, and the noise of the wheels clacking across the rails was deafening. That one ride instilled in me a nostalgic passion for passenger trains.

I'd be back on the farm every summer until college. It was a safe place for me. I was close to Dianne. She had girlfriends, and that worked well for me.

Life in Cudahy was a different story, the other half of my life. Roots were slow to develop and I'd run out of time long before there was any hope of a flowering Gardenia.

By seventh grade we were living in a house on Trinthammer Avenue, on the other side of the tracks. Cudahy was situated between the airport on the west side and Lake Michigan to the east with railroad tracks down the middle. The bluffs along Lake Michigan were a beautiful place to go walking. I could sit by the lake and listen to the waves ripple on the shoreline. It was much better than the fence line at the airport.

By the time we moved to Trinthammer, I'd accepted that I wasn't going back, and it was time to move forward. My activities drew me away from my isolation. I was Boy Scout patrol leader, rising to first class scout within a year. I was first chair in the band, winning multiple state competitions. I was chosen to perform in the high school play, *A Music Man*, representative of the seventy-six trombones. I rode my bike to school and walked if I couldn't ride because I hated the social hierarchy that existed on the school bus.

Mark and I found a common purpose in our tropical fish. That gallon jar of guppies we had gotten in Grafton expanded to nearly 200 gallons of twenty and thirty gallon tanks. We managed some difficult successes. We spawned Siamese fighting fish, raising them to adult specimens. We even managed to raise saltwater brine shrimp to adult size. In those days brine shrimp eggs were packaged and sold in comic book ads as the Amazing Sea Monkeys. Check it out online.

When I was at the farm, we communicated about fish catalogs and fish acquisitions and future expansions. For the two us, that year and a half was the most quality time we ever had together.

Eventually I found a couple girlfriends to hang out with. It was great to be one of the girls again with Debbie and Carol, but things were getting more complicated. At twelve years old, it wasn't clear to me there were significant anatomical differences between boys and girls.

There was a boy on the other side of town as well. He'd wrestle me in the unfinished space on the second story of our house. I don't even remember his name. Maybe I invented the whole thing in my fantasies. I believe it's a true memory. Wrestling with a boy is one of those visceral memories a girl doesn't just make up.

The junior high had a pool, and swimming was part of the curriculum. I was terrified of the water from nearly drowning in a pool. Standing with a row of boys in a sport swimsuit next to that pool was an uncomfortable experience. Showering naked with the boys enhanced my sense of vulnerability. I learned to swim very quickly which avoided the teasing.

The relationship with my girlfriends was getting complicated as well. At Christmas time Carol gave me a red heart with the inscription, "good for one free kiss." I examined those words many times over the next few weeks until Carol finally took the initiative at a school dance. Debbie held the mistletoe. It wasn't an unpleasant experience. Carol knew how to French kiss. For me it was my first kiss.

So much happened during the short time we lived in Cudahy. Sharon's birth, Misty Mimi Lori Louise had her first litter of puppies, Sharon fell down the steps and knocked out her two front teeth, and Mom became a nurse's aid at the hospital. She had always wanted to work, and I was beginning to understand those unfulfilled ambitions. With little advance warning, life in Cudahy ended abruptly the day we boarded the plane in Milwaukee destined for our new home in Nashua, New Hampshire.

Part II: Adolescence: If there were only one sex, would we still have gender?

In transgender narratives it is common to hear, "I've known I was a girl since early childhood." They will recall wearing dresses. I never experienced this need. Dresses don't make you a girl. A girl dreams of becoming a woman. I know some girls dream about becoming a princess but familiar role models are more common, perhaps a teacher or a nurse. For me, the woman I wanted to be was my mom. As a child, there was never any doubt about that.

In any event, if there were only one sex, would we still have gender? I never thought of myself as a girl; I just was. It was embodied in all of my role-play as a child and reflected in my struggle to find female relationships. I had a powerful emotional sense of it, showering naked with the boys, though I knew nothing of sex or gender. The onset of puberty exaggerated those differences, making female relationships more difficult.

You are what people perceive you to be. Janet Mock in her book, *Redefining Realness*, expressed the problem bluntly when she explained, "...both our parents taught us that because the world would perceive us as black, we were black." In other words, if the world perceived me as a boy, I was a boy.

Ms. Mock, along with other transgender women of color, like Laverne Cox and Angelica Ross, instantiated the issue of intersectionality and ignited the transgender movement at the *Transgender Tipping Point*[1]. Women of color have always held pivotal roles advancing gender equity, but Ms. Mock never fully establishes that connection to the broader transgender movement. Grouping so many unique cultures under the heading "women of color" tends to reinforce an unbending social binary that there can only be two sides. You're white or you're not white. You're a man or you're a woman. In recognition of the non-trivial role of language, one could argue that white isn't a color. It is a socioeconomic class defined by wealthy white men.

By crossing class boundaries, the transgender movement emphasizes the impact inherent in that separation. It emphasizes the fallacy of identity politics that seeks to create inclusiveness or exclude classes according to some superficial characteristic like skin color or even gender. The transgender movement is a long way from achieving its potential for overcoming class segregation.

Puberty distinguishes male from female in a way that is profoundly different from early childhood. The intense polarity of gender identity was pressuring me to make a choice. By a skillful use of individualism, I was able to delay that choice for nearly a decade, but it left me feeling isolated and alone.

1 Steinmetz, Kathy, Time | US, Laverne Cox Talks to TIME About the Transgender Movement, May 29, 2014, accessed June 21, 2017, http://time.com/132769/transgender-orange-is-the-new-black-laverne-cox-interview/

Chapter Four: City Boy, Country Girl

It was this last argument that had everyone looking so nervous and uncomfortable.

–Lewis Carroll, Alice in Wonderland

I couldn't wait to return to the security of the farm that summer following our move to Nashua. That summer on the farm aided my transition from Cudahy to Nashua. I had a direct flight from Boston to Minneapolis on a "12 to 21" pass that allowed me to fly standby for $33. The only seat they had left was in first class. Only thirteen at the time, I was served wine with my meal. When people talk about freedom, I nostalgically recall this particular flight.

City life and country life are as different as male and female. I contemplate how people might interpret that comparison. Life on the farm was an escape from my world. My peers and I were becoming adults. They were transitioning into men and women. For me it was more complicated, challenging my relationships to those I'd known only as children. I thought about Carol's kiss.

Life on the farm gave me a few more years as one of the girls and helped me survive my high school years back in Nashua.

Cousin is a nice term because it is gender neutral; not at all like having to announce you're someone's brother. Just like it was in Grafton, I could be a girl and nobody noticed, well… almost nobody.

Uncle Jim was a dairy farmer. He loved his animals, but they were also his greatest source of frustration. I never saw him get angry except for one evening when he was introducing a new cow to milking machines.

This particular cow was having none of it. Her hind legs were tied. Uncle Jim sat next to her on a milking stool, resting on four short iron legs. That cow swung her hindquarter around knocking him to the floor. With a string of curse words like I'd never heard before, he got up with stool in hand, slamming those metal legs into the back of that poor animal. I was stunned, and I really felt sorry for that animal. I'm sure he hadn't intended for me to see that. We did what I expect a man to do, finish up and move on, not one word about it.

Milking cows taught me about people in general. Early on, Uncle Jim told me to look at the herd. He said, "They all look the same don't they?" They did all look the same. As you become familiar with them, it becomes obvious that each of them is unique, with their own personality.

Cows have beautiful brown eyes with long dark lashes that would make any girl envious. Auntie Pat used to tell me I had beautiful brown eyes just like cows' eyes. I felt like a princess.

Cows were also the main event at the summer's biggest attraction, the county fair. Dianne always had a Holstein to show. The one I remember best was Queeny because she had a mean kick that made me nervous around her. You don't want to get kicked by a cow. I kept my distance.

Cows eat hay, and baling hay was the job I enjoyed most. It was a great physical workout in the open air. I loved to see how high I could stack bales and how many bales I could get on the wagon. Sometimes our older cousin Dennis was around to help during hay season.

The farm could be a scary place for a young girl. Out fencing in grass as tall as me, it wasn't unusual to come across a garden spider as big as my hand staring me right in the eyes. One of my regular jobs was to feed the calves in the abandoned barn at Grandpa's old place. Grandpa was gone, and the place was deserted, creating a sense of eeriness. The barn door was open just wide enough to squeeze through. In the corner of that opening just above my head was a spider web tended by a huge wolf spider. Once inside you could hear the bees and the flies buzzing about. Once I got about the task of feeding the calves, my heart stopped racing. When I was done I'd squeeze through the door and race back to the tractor.

The absolute worst fear I ever conquered on the farm came when I was assigned to clean out the rotting silage at the bottom of a cement silo. It seemed doable at first until I climbed in through an access door about eighteen inches square and realized I was standing on an undulating floor, completely covered with every creepy crawly thing imaginable. Standing at the bottom of that cement silo, it was too late to panic. I would have to endure.

Life on the farm taught me how to confront my fears. I found inspiration in my Uncle Jim who could take on an entire hornet's nest armed with nothing but a baseball cap. As a child, I saw enormous courage each time I witnessed it. Gradually, I was inspired to expect no less of myself. Girls on the farm don't encounter these opportunities as often as boys.

For the most part, farming was freedom. Driving tractors or loading hay bales or chasing gophers and mice around the hayfields was just plain fun. Days when we couldn't do fieldwork, we did housework; washing dishes or hanging clothes on the line. Dennis was older, excused from housework, but did work with us a couple of times on the most dreaded chore of all: weeding the garden. This represents my earliest perceptions of gender segregation. Among Dennis, Dianne, and I it was unanimous: fieldwork was better than housework.

I felt a powerful connection with Dennis, not because he was a handsome older guy with an infectious smile and a great sense of humor. It wasn't because he was always kind and attentive and exuded an obvious passion in everything he did. He was all those things, and certainly the type of boy I'd choose for myself if he wasn't my cousin. My connection with Dennis was about living life in the shadows of greatness. It's about feeling transparent when there isn't enough attention to go around.

For my mother, that shadow was cast by my own father, and she never achieved her full potential. For Dennis, that shadow was cast by his older brother. Strong feelings of empathy, magnified by my own sense of isolation, compelled me to respond to that imbalance.

His older brother was named Ben. Stories of Ben's heroic feats abounded. He was a football hero playing for St. Olaf College. He later went on to become a fighter pilot and first lieutenant in the United States Air Force. The stories were all true.

Ben used to fly trainers up to the farm offering rides from his hayfield landing strip. I missed my turn because I had the mumps.

A couple weeks later, I missed my second chance as well because I had mumps on the other side. That's the kind of story they told about me.

While learning about responsibility, I prefaced my explanations with, "I thought—" Just as often Uncle Jim replied, "No! You didn't think."

The only exception I recall occurred when I returned empty-handed from an assignment to retrieve a flare box. He said to me, "So you looked around the flare box and under the flare box and inside the flare box, but you couldn't find the flare box." I didn't know a flare box is a large grain wagon. That's the kind of story they told about me.

Uncle Jim told different stories about Ben. One particular story he told often; about the time Ben got up early and had the milking done before Uncle Jim got up. Milking cows two hours ahead of schedule is not a particularly good idea.

I got tired of hearing the story so one morning I got up at four AM, put on my clothes, and went out to milk the cows. Normally, at milking time the cows would already be on their way to the barn because they anticipate it. In the pitch darkness, I couldn't see a cow anywhere. I had to search for them and getting them in the barn took longer than expected. Finally in their stalls, I put out the feed and the hay they were expecting. Queeny was in the barn that night. When it was her turn, anxiety overtook me. I approached her slowly, talking sweetly and petting her hind-quarter. We reached an understanding. We were both there for the same reason. An hour later the milking was done. That was an accomplishment at my age, but I wasn't impressed with myself. After all, my intention was to prove the story was not that impressive.

There were no accolades from anyone else either. Years later, Uncle Jim wouldn't even remember it, but I never had to listen to that story again. So many of us live in the shadows of greatness, convinced that we are somehow less because we are measured according to an arbitrarily prescribed standard. Even though nobody noticed, I was stepping out of the shadows and becoming me. It didn't need to be spectacular or dramatic.

My experience on the farm contrasted sharply with what was

happening in Nashua but remained intimately linked in terms of dramatic changes in my awareness of gender and sexuality during the onset of puberty. That understanding challenged my self-perception, separating me from the security of my early childhood, demanding new ways of relating to the world.

I was thirteen that summer when I decided to try on girls' clothes.[1] It seemed perfectly natural. It was a blue ruffled nightie belonging to my cousin that first attracted my interest. My cousin Dianne surprised me by taking a picture of the event. She seemed amused as much as anything, but I'm sure she must have understood that the picture would give her serious talk material. I wanted to see the picture, but I didn't want Dianne to have it, so I switched the film. She had one of those Kodak Instamatic cameras with the plastic film cartridges so it was easy to do. I hid the cartridge in a grain bin down in the machine shed, waiting for Friday to take the film into town.

When Friday came, the grain bin was empty, and the film was gone. My inquiries about the missing film naturally lead to revelations about what was on the film. The discussion focused on how stupid it was to hide it in the grain bin, nothing about why I was wearing a girl's nightie.

On the farm, I was one of the girls, but the sexual transformation of puberty was drawing closer scrutiny from the adults. Unofficially, Barb was my girlfriend. Barb's cousin Debbie was younger and teased about having a crush on me. My real attraction was Michelle, the daughter of another farm family in the area. I'm not sure either of us understood it, but I perceived it as a mature female relationship

It was my relationship to Michelle that had the adults looking so nervous and uncomfortable. I suspect, because of the age difference, they saw a sexual attraction between a young woman and since I was only thirteen, a boy.

I was losing the innocence of my youth. It was not at all like a fork in the road, where we diverge toward becoming men and women. For me, it was like a full stop when you suddenly realize the bridge is out. I was facing a choice between gender roles which I was unprepared to make. One does not choose to be transgender.

1 This story appears in a slightly modified form in a one-act play I later wrote and performed called *Confessions of a Crossdresser*. See Appendix A.

Chapter Five: Artistic Disguise

It was overcast when we arrived in Boston from General Mitchel Field. It was appropriate to the mood I was in. It was misting during the drive from Boston to Nashua New Hampshire. Lori carried the conversation. She was excited to be in New England, and her enthusiasm ultimately enabled my adjustment to Nashua.

Dad took us to Priscilla's Restaurant on Pearl Street. It must have been a Friday because we had to wait for a table. Eventually, our name was announced over the intercom, "Oh va Bee Potty." We heard it several times. The New England accent was so thick none of us recognized it. Finally, Dad revealed it, "Overby party, that's us."

After we were seated the waitress came and picked up Dad's handkerchief and wiped off the table. It was a perfectly innocent mistake, but it didn't help my perception that I'd been dropped off somewhere between Kansas and Oz without my ruby slippers.

Our new home consisted of two adjoining rooms at a modest motel on the outskirts of Nashua. From a house in Grafton to a fourplex in Cudahy to a motel in Nashua: we were homeless. No longer possessing the imagination necessary to protect me from reality, I slept well that night. As a single ray of hope, it was some serious family time, playing ball with Sharon, Lori, and Misty on the small strip of grass behind the motel. As usual, it was Mom who kept things running smoothly.

The real moment of truth came the first day of school. Perusing my class schedule I knew my life was over. There was not one glimmer of hope.

Junior high in Cudahy was like a college campus compared

to Fairgrounds Junior High in Nashua. In Cudahy, I was on the honor roll so we girls could skip study halls and go off campus. At Fairgrounds we walked single file around the outside of the hallways until we reached our next class. Traversing three spokes on a wheel, you could make a complete circle if your next class happened to be the room to the left. At lunch, the boys were separated from the girls. Students had fifteen minutes to eat and then they had to go outside and "play."

The boys got the playground on one side of the horseshoe drive, and the girls got the sidewalk on the other side. Watching the boys play was depressing. At that moment, I realized these are boys, and people believe I am one of them. For the first time in my life, I felt the despair of being a boy. I realized my birthright, my anatomy, was determining my place in society. I spent my lunch hours alone longing to be with my peers on the other side of the horseshoe drive.

By the time Mom picked me up that first day I felt totally humiliated. What could I have said to her? I was calculating my escape from Nashua.

They asked for "idears" and suggested you find the answer in an "encyclopeedeeeear." They ate strange fruits like "pahhhs" and "bananerrs." They did not know what a soda was. They had public schools but little evidence of education. I was spending half my school day with non-performing students learning absolutely nothing. Two of my teachers were clearly incompetent, a sense I generalized to all of my teachers. I challenged misinformation with a conspicuously mocking presentation. It's a skill I learned at Parkview Elementary in Cudahy. It was a safety mechanism that kept me isolated and revered at the same time.

Then came a glimmer of hope in the endemic field of desperation. In shop class, there was a boy named Glenn, also recently assimilated into this barren landscape. The teacher was empathetic and worked with Glenn and me to develop a syllabus and course materials for an electronics class he'd teach for us in the fall. Curiously, it was my first introduction to self-study concepts and undoubtedly the most important thing I learned at Fairgrounds.

Come fall, there was no shop teacher. Our mentor had transferred. The first two weeks, Glenn and I taught the class, trying to impart whatever knowledge we could to a largely unreceptive audience. Glenn and I became close compatriots in an intellectual void. To my advantage, he also knew how to treat a girl. Naturally, he viewed it as helping a fellow in need.

Not only was Nashua void of intellectual opportunities, it was also void of any cultural opportunities. There was football, basketball, and baseball for the boys and cheerleading for the girls. That was it: no band, no debate team, no drama club; no clubs at all.

Glenn persuaded me to try sports. Some subliminal awareness urged me to engage in more boy stuff. Growing up as a girl, I had no exposure to sports other than men watching football on Sunday afternoons. In 1969, girls' sports were virtually unheard of and certainly not in Nashua. That was before Title IX passed in 1972.

Glenn played all three sports. He recommended I try baseball and spent much of his time that summer teaching me to pitch. It was a futile effort but did boost my waning spirit. I tried out for the team. I actually hit one pitch in the batting tryouts, but my pitching was a laughing stock. The only significant outcome: I no longer throw like a girl.

Outside of school, I filled the isolation by staining woodwork and painting walls for our new home that dad had bought unfinished. It was productive, task-oriented behavior that kept my mind off my social situation. It also taught me a skill that later enabled me to rise above the minimum wage which was $1.70 at the time. Gas was 29 cents a gallon. Dad was a do-it-yourselfer; a condition he passed on to me. I was never certain if I should be grateful for that.

The roots of my ambition, cultivated in Cudahy, were ripped away, leaving little hope of a flowering gardenia. There was no band, no Boy Scouts, no theater arts, and no girlfriends. Along with this, I lost my passion for my hobbies. The most devastating collateral damage was my relationship with Mark. In Grafton, I was one of the girls, and he was one of the boys. The only connection I ever really had with him was our tropical fish. He wanted desperately to start over, to rebuild our tropical paradise. While I was in Minnesota, he sent tropical fish catalogs and wrote about the kind of fish we should pursue. He had ideas about raising Siamese fighting fish again, but my passion for it had completely evaporated.

My parents ensured my continuing religious education, but if God has answered any of my prayers it didn't happen in Nashua. It did provide some social connection through Walther League, the church youth group, but the loving God I'd learned about as a child had been replaced by a jealous God who destroyed entire civilizations like Sodom and Gomorrah with hellfire and brimstone. God had not yet taken a position on transgender people, but it was still clear to me I was on a fast track to hell.

If one word could describe Nashua, it was football. It was central to life in Nashua but for me, a love-hate relationship that kindled my disdain for its disproportionate cultural dominance. Glenn was a football hero so our paths separated.

A new hope arrived my junior year. Coach Biladeau was introducing the sport of wrestling, and anyone who tried out made the team. Wrestling with boys was already a favorite pastime. Though I lacked endurance, I was fast, and I was strong from my summer's bailing hay. I generally lost if I couldn't make a pin in the first round, but I was good enough to make it to regionals. Wrestling with boys presents an uncomfortable problem to the transgender community. Even as my gender was female my body was still male. Past puberty, males have a higher ratio of muscle to fat. Boys are stronger than girls in the same weight class. Weight classes would be an inadequate metric for co-ed wrestling, even if most female athletes could easily win against most boys. The exceptional case does not prove the rule.

The school refused to purchase a wrestling mat for us to practice on which amplified my resentment for football. They had a huge budget for football with new uniforms for both home and away games. We practiced on regular gym mats tied together. Early in my senior year, the mats separated during a practice, and I slammed my head against the floor. The coach was not happy, but I couldn't continue wrestling with the headaches.

I'm not sure I could articulate it then, but I was definitely learning that gender is more about perception than presentation.

Young scholars rated publications supposedly written by male scientists as higher quality than identical work identified with female authors.[1] Did Glenn ever notice that I threw like a girl?

Society allows for masculine behavior in girls. There's even a name for it: tomboy. We don't allow for feminine behaviors in boys. Gender perception worked in my favor by masking feminine behaviors which were readily reinterpreted. This is difficult to explain because people think of feminine behavior in boys as effeminate. It's also interpreted as being gay. But that behavior is considered "girly" even in girls. I wore extremely flamboyant fashions which made me a non-conformist, not a sissy. I was never bitchy. I was confident. The only behavior I deliberately concealed was crying. I wish I hadn't cried so much! It's okay for a man to cry but only in well-defined situations. Wrestling with boys fulfilled my physical needs while preserving the perception of a strong competitive male.

Lori cheered for the Nashua Giants, and the captain of the squad was my girlfriend. It was the perfect cover. I was the older brother and the protective boyfriend. For me, I was just one of the girls having fun.

My first test of faith came at one of the football after parties when my girlfriend's father engaged me. "You're Paul," he said. Perhaps he'd heard about me "dating" his daughter. He said, "Do you believe in God?" He was short with a powerful build and a competition level black belt in karate. I knew he had a temper. He was also drinking. "Yes," I replied. He continued with his next question. "Do you believe that a man can walk on water?" "Yes," I replied. He raised his fist to my face and said, "Do you really believe in God?" I could feel the tension in every muscle. "Yes," I replied.

Maybe it was his way of proving that a boy who couldn't play football could still be tough. He seemed to respect me for it because after that I was allowed to pick up his daughter at their home. We used to go to the Catholic service over in Hudson. I don't know if she believed in God or if she just needed the escape from her home life.

I had six girlfriends while I was in Nashua. Five of them had a strict, missing, or abusive father. These are the women I connected with. My relationships with the girls I dated revolved around the extreme issues in their lives.

The sixth was more high society. Her father had wealth, and she was a high rolling party girl. She showed me the anatomical differences between boys and girls when I was already 16. I am grateful for that, but sexual relationships continued to be difficult because sexuality conflicted with the emotional inherency of female relationships, creating an iconoclastic rebuttal of heterosexuality, where men want sex, and women want romance. It simply didn't play out that way for me in a sexual relationship with another girl.

Nashua had one major redeeming characteristic, that being it's geographical location: ocean with sandy beaches and the rocky coastline of Maine to the East; Mount Washington, the highest peak in the Appalachian mountains just a few hours to the north with lake Winnipesaukee nestled in between; Mount Monadnock less than an hour to the west; and of course Boston less than an hour to the south. We were surrounded by beautiful landscape, adventure, and history.

The best place to be for a group of teenage girls was definitely the beach. All you needed was the sun, a beach towel, and a bottle of tanning oil. You could always depend on the boys. The shops and the food stands completed the stroll from north beach to south beach. From the sidewalks along the beach, you could sometimes hear the sounds of bands like Chicago and Three Dog Night.

When I was fifteen, Dad gave me a 1961 Volkswagen that he had given up on. If there was anything on it that didn't need fixing I can't remember what it was. It became my project, consuming most of my income but having a car was freedom, and I was going to have it. Only a few of us had cars in my high school.

The boy in my life lived across the street from me. His name was Joe. I saw him frequently. I'm not sure if he liked me or just loved my Volkswagens. Brimming over with excitement, Joe came over one day with a record album. "You have got to hear this," he said. He put the record on the stereo, cranked it up, and played for me for the first time ever, Iron Butterfly's "In-A-Gadda-Da-Vida." I felt bad I couldn't share his enthusiasm, but it was my first introduction to rock music. Joe kept me up-to-date on pop culture. I never fully appreciated how much I depended on him. It took a long time to fully appreciate Joe, and we remain friends to this day.

I'd have four VWs before it was all said and done, including a cherry red convertible. During the muscle car heyday of Camaros, Chargers, and GTOs, I drove VW bugs. I had no need to impress the girls. Joe and I always talked about putting in a Corvair engine, a manly project indeed. Lori, being Lori, drove a Tempest convertible. She was a blond too. I had every right to be jealous, but she was my sister, and she had girlfriends. I could make exemptions.

In Nashua, there was a third boy in my life. There was something elusive about Bob[2]. His girlfriend was a close friend of mine too.

We organized the first official club at Nashua Senior High, the Spanish club. We were highly successful with fundraising, from bake sales to bringing in local bands for school dances. We brought new life to Nashua High. That success brought us to New York for our field trip: talk shows, Broadway, Empire State Building, Mama Leones, and 42nd Street.

We also organized a children's theater, struggling to fill the culture gap in Nashua. The only stage in town was in the high school where they wouldn't allow us to compete with the senior class play. There wasn't enough culture in all of Nashua to support more than one play a year.

The children's theater group was allowed one single-act play at a variety show held at the high school. The play was titled, "Why I Am a Bachelor." I played the part of the bachelor. Bob and I also performed an urban style ballet routine featuring leather vests, swaying hips, and swinging chains. We practiced for hours at a dance studio in town, which leaves me thinking maybe there was an underground subculture in Nashua where the arts survived their clandestine struggle.

The academic life at Nashua Senior High School never sufficiently engaged me. Our class of 1972 was the only class that endured four full years of split sessions while officials procrastinated about the need for a new high school. I took advanced placement chemistry but bowed out of pre-calculus having missed too many trigonometry classes enjoying breakfast at IHOP. I ranked in the top 2 percent in the nation on the National Merit Scholarship test but barely reached the top 25 percent of my class. At graduation, we sang "The Long and Winding Road," which was appropriately dismal and equally predictive. Had I garnered just a few more votes in the election for class president, graduation would have been different. We would have celebrated our anti-establishment agenda.

I've regretted leaving Nashua, having adjusted to its peculiarities. The Ivy League schools rejected me, I was suspicious of New Hampshire's public education, and my ticket to the University of Minnesota had already been booked. Unlike Grafton and Cudahy, already distant memories, Nashua would remain an integral part of my life. Though it hadn't flowered, the gardenia bush had taken root.

1 Grabmeier, Jeff, *Gender Bias Found in How Scholars Review Scientific Studies*, Ohio State University, April 3, 2013, Accessed May 20, 2017, http://researchnews.osu.edu/archive/matilda.html.

2 I reconnected with Bob after becoming Paula. He now identifies as Roberto, and, yes, he is gay. Roberto and Paula performing ballet for the culturally deprived citizens of Nashua. It all made sense now.

Part III Social Conscience: Is gender a civil rights issue?

We don't expect sexuality in young children, but we do expect consistent gender behavior. We intuitively understand that sexuality and gender are not the same thing but remain convinced they should align at puberty. Inter-sexed individuals have shown us that alignment may be impossible. In western culture there remains a strong presumption that a person's sex, sexuality, and gender are interchangeable, defining the notion of heteronormative. Separating these qualities is fundamental to understanding gender and the concept of transgender. At puberty my sexuality did not align with my sex: it aligned with my gender. The introduction of sexuality during puberty placed my female identity in conflict with people's perceptions. Eventual acceptance of my female gender was bolstered by understanding why my attraction to men was different than a man's attraction to men.

Alice Domurat Dreger authored several books on the subject of assigning a sex to newborns, including *Hermaphrodites and the Medical Invention of Sex*. In an article for the Intersex Society of North America titled "Ambiguous Sex or Ambivalent Medicine?," she concludes: "…any close study of sexual anatomy results in a loss of faith that there is a simple, 'natural' sex distinction that will not break down in the face of certain anatomical, behavioral, or philosophical challenges."

In the book *As Nature Made Him: The Boy Who Was Raised as a Girl*, John Colapinto chronicles a gender reassignment experiment[1] conducted by John Money at Hopkins University, where one of two twin boys is raised as a girl because of a botched circumcision. Even before Money's infamous John/Joan experiment, the medical community was assigning sex and gender to newborns. In a society unwilling to accept gender-neutral space, psychologists are now conducting similar experiments with children to enforce the transgender myth and maintain two distinct genders. Despite the compelling evidence presented by transgender children it also tends to contradict more gender fluid models of childhood development. Transition prior to puberty will be a totally different experience than transition after puberty.

Transition is presented as an alignment of one's physical and cognitive self. Consequences of transition are about aligning with social perceptions. Female impersonation is amply represented in our culture; these men don't claim to be women. Culturally, beauty validates transgender women as it does for all women. It was dramatized by Caitlyn Jenner in her first appearance as a woman, on the cover of Vanity Fair in a virgin white corset: the corset is a popular image for the containment of and gateway to female sexuality. It reinforces a perception of boys becoming girls. It is difficult to accept that there is a biological determinate for a culturally defined standard of beauty.

With exceptions for obvious displays of privilege like Caitlyn Jenner, transgender stories depict the awkwardness of puberty at a mature age, suggesting the importance of transition prior to puberty. If society can properly "gender" children before the natural transition of puberty than the whole issue of transgender will simply fade into history confirming the transgender myth. In a profound sense of irony, science will reclaim the ancient mythology of Adam and Eve. There is mounting evidence opposing that perspective.

I have examined many transitions in my life, from Grafton to Cudahy, from Cudahy to Nashua, from the city to the farm, from high school to college. None of these transitions impacted my identity, but all of them had a profound impact on my relationships and my relationship with society at large. We don't discuss gender transition this way, but there are significant parallels.

As a young teenager attending high school in Nashua, I thought deeply about other social issues, perhaps, in part because of the strong sense of isolation. I had lengthy debates with my father about the Cold War and the war in Vietnam.

I always enjoyed the company of old people, with so many

amazing stories and a calmness that soothed my restless soul. I never understood our culture's class separation between young and old. I loved the time spent with Grandma–except for her propensity to serve mush. To this day I couldn't really tell you what mush is, but it looked terrible, and it tasted terrible, and no amount of maple syrup could remedy the situation. My childhood imagination thrived on stories Grandma could tell about life on the farm. I loved her stories about horses, so much a central part of life back then

She spent the last few years of her life in a nursing home. It was hard for her, and I went to visit often. It was hard for me as well when I realized she no longer remembered who I was. On a good day, if I stayed long enough, memories would awaken, and we'd reminisce about the "good old days."

I often wondered about LeeAnn as I began to understand the abuse experienced by so many of my girlfriends. I know now, why we went to church on Saturday nights. I thought about the Women's Movement and the Civil Rights Movement and the politics of the day. The way I perceived the world seemed profoundly different from how others perceived it.

1 "Who Was David Reimer?," Intersex Society of North America, accessed: May 20, 2017, http://www.isna.org/faq/reimer.

Chapter Six: Freedom Fighter

"I shall be punished for it now, I suppose, by being drowned in my own tears!"

–Lewis Carroll, Alice in Wonderland

In 1970 the *USS John F. Kennedy* was the largest aircraft carrier in its class. Stationed in Boston, Massachusetts, the ship was christened in 1967 by Jacqueline Kennedy, widow of former president John F. Kennedy. It was also the only ship in its class, and seventeen feet shorter than the Kitty Hawk class carrier that was the original intended design. On a ship that size, seventeen feet is hardly noticeable, just room enough to park my Volkswagen beetle. Looking down the length of the flight deck from stem to stern was an emotionally captivating experience. The expansiveness of the hanger decks, void of aircraft at the time, stimulated the heighten arousal of an alien world, its purpose obscure and inexplicable.

How did I come to be standing on the hanger deck of one of the world's most powerful weapons systems? Just sixteen at the time, I was experiencing a dramatic demonstration of gender differentiation: war. I was there with my date, Phyllis. The setting was hardly inconsequential.

Her last name was Anglo-Saxon but her mother was clearly a matriarch in a large patriarchal Italian family. There was structure in out relationship enforced by brothers who instructed me on what my responsibilities and limitations were with respect to their sister. I also received instructions about the needs and the inconveniences of being a woman both by her mother and from my own mother. At sixteen we had adult privileges. We received regular instruction in proper courtship, and I was the man. She, of course, was the woman. We were always invited to accompany the adults, even to the piano lounge on Saturday nights, even a ritual sampling of wine to reinforce proper social etiquette.

As I once perceived gender segregation based on age I have always perceived age separation as the most disturbing class boundary in our culture. My TV view of the world always provided me with a romantic image of English and Irish pubs as multi-generational affairs with the entire family joining in the song and the dance. Age is a natural spectrum of polar opposites between impatient exuberance and cautious wisdom.

Phyllis was a perfect girlfriend for me. Sex before marriage wasn't even a consideration in her mind. We spent every opportunity making out in her basement. I loved the intimacy. I didn't really have any well-formed thoughts about the physiology of human sexuality. Words like gay or lesbian or even heterosexual were not even part of my vocabulary. In a legitimate way, my own introspection of gendered relationships was unencumbered by social contaminates because of how naive I was about those expectations. Making out with another girl was just as natural as wrestling with a boy. It was simply an obvious difference in the way boys and girls approached intimacy. I never met a boy who wanted to make out with me. Girls didn't seem to care for wrestling.

Though I just received my driver's license three weeks earlier, I was given the responsibility of driving their family car from Nashua to the USS Kennedy at the Boston Naval Shipyard. This meant driving through the city of Boston. Boston is still, to date, the most difficult city for driving of anywhere I have had that opportunity, and I've had a lot of opportunities. In my TV view of the world, I'm certain it can be no less challenging then Paris or Rome, perhaps a shade less difficult than Bangkok or Shanghai.

Naturally, we got lost and ended up following a cab driver to the shipyard. Like a Fast and Furious road rally competition, it was empowering. We all survived as did the car, and I was notably impressed with their faith in the benevolent will of God.

Phyllis' family had connections to the ship's captain. That's how I came to be standing on the hanger deck of the Navy's newest aircraft carrier. It was a privilege granted to me on the basis of my relationship with her daughter. It was an opportunity, but even at sixteen, I saw obvious reasons why that wouldn't work for me. I had long since given up on the domino theory of a communist global take over that I had written about in my seventh-grade social studies class. Now it seems quite incredulous that anyone actually believed it. I was fast approaching eligibility for the draft in a war that was becoming increasingly unpopular.

My views about war changed abruptly in December of 1969 when Captain Ben Danielson's F4 fighter was shot down over Laos. According to official government reports, we were not engaged in any military activity in Laos, so that information wasn't available to us. My cousin Ben was officially listed as missing in action, an obscure casualty of war in the military files but an instant national hero to those of us that knew him. It involved me in the POW/MIA movement in a personal way, but it also instilled in me an intense interest in military history and policies.

I was a peace activist during the Vietnam War. My father was a Cold War veteran. It generated some rather intense discussions. He served in the Navy and reached Japan after the war ended, after the atomic bombs dropped on Nagasaki and Hiroshima. He never talked about it, and I regret that I never asked. Dad always blamed his late arrival on his mother and the will of God. My grandmother was very religious, donating huge sums of money to Oral Roberts, a primary TV evangelist of the day. She prayed intently for God to spare her son from the war. Dad was in the brig the night his ship sailed to Japan. By the time he got a new assignment, the war was over. That was his war story.

Dad was also a spiritual man himself but he had little patience for religious doctrine. He asserted that peaceful negotiation demanded churches put their religious doctrine in their back pocket. Dad wasn't a warrior; Dad was more of a freedom fighter. Even in the 70's, he saw the failings of our political process and our criminal justice system. He referred to Washington as the Ivy League Club.

I know that my father cherished the time we had together, as I was one of the few people in his life, perhaps the only person in his life, that could really challenge him at his intellectual level. I regret that he never had the opportunity to know me as his daughter. It would have explained a lot for him, and I'm certain he'd be proud of me, as he was of my two sisters Lori and Sharon.

One of the last things he said to me before he died was for me emotionally overwhelming and intellectually challenging. He said, "if you had decided to go to Canada to escape the Vietnam War, I'd understand." To me, it meant that he finally understood.

My draft lottery number was 83 so I thought considerably about my choices. I couldn't say I was a girl, I had no proof. It didn't matter. "Transgender" did not exist in 1972. The word was transvestite. If I'd accept that designation then certainly I shall be punished for it now! It was a term synonymous with sexual perversion. I'd be classified a homosexual. The draft ended before I had to make that choice.

In 2007, Captain Benjamin Danielson came home, Just his dog tags and enough bone fragments to positively identify his DNA. I cannot begin to relate to you the depth of human emotion surrounding family and friends and community brought together by such an event. Even the funeral procession was lead by more than two hundred veterans from Minnesota's Patriot Guard. My daughter, Courtney, rode with a cousin on a motorcycle at the head of the procession.

Ben's son obtained permission to search for additional evidence of his father in Laos but nothing more was uncovered. The day of the funeral he shared the story of what happened that fateful day in December of 1969. Enemy ground fire disabled the F4, and Captain Danielson and his co-pilot ejected safely from the aircraft. They both made it to the ground where they had radio contact but they were on opposite sides of the river.

Efforts to rescue them lasted three days, becoming one of the largest air rescue missions in US history. During the day the rescue efforts were hampered by heavy enemy fire, and during the night the men lay in hiding, listening to enemy troops searching the area. On the third day, a rescue helicopter was able to retrieve the co-pilot. Another soldier was killed during the rescue. The co-pilot reported that he had heard shouts and gunfire the first night.

It is believed that Captain Danielson hadn't survived until the first dawn. Many years passed before his status was changed from MIA to KIA.

I had an opportunity to talk to the co-pilot following the funeral. It was a deeply moving experience which created for me an entirely different understanding of who are the real heroes of war. It was clear that no one recovers from an experience like that. To survive you find ways to cope with it.

I thought about the veterans I've known who never talked about the war. I understood the secrets they held contained. Not only did they fight and sacrifice for us; they came home and protected us from the horrors of what they had experienced.

In 2014, I posted an American Flag in honor of my father at the field of flags ceremony in Mazepa Minnesota. It was a moving experience, carrying the flag, escorted by a color guard, then standing in solitary honor of my father. I stood there a long time and I cried, knowing that I finally understood.

The family structure I had with Phyllis made a strong appeal to my fundamental family values. On the other hand, I was highly conflicted about the obvious link between male and military that seriously compromised my maternal instincts. At sixteen the other girls were not thinking about the draft; I was. There was one other problem no less complicated and just as compelling. I wasn't ready to give up on wrestling with boys.

Chapter Seven: Men 101

The Lory, who at last turned sulky, and would only say, "I am older than you, and must know better"

–Lewis Carroll, Alice in Wonderland

Yes, I'd have gone to Vietnam if I had been called. It is the most primal definition of gender there could be. Girls have the babies. Boys fight the wars. Masculinity is about strength, power, and control. Femininity is weak, passive, and dependent. It is the most basic and pervasive definition of gender we have. War creates war heroes. One cannot make the same argument for the woman's role in nurturing societies future generations.

Few people can abide that definition with such raw expression so we further define masculinity as a protective role. Men go to war to defend our freedom, the constitution, our way of life, and our women. From this emerges the romantic notion of gender with the knight in shining armor rescuing the poor helpless damsel in distress.

It's illustrated by traditional marriage, meaning one man and one woman according to the opponents of same-sex marriage. Up until the mid-1800s, women who married ceased to have any right to own property, sign contracts, keep her earnings or gain guardianship of her children. A married woman was for all intents and purposes the property of her husband. It is also not intuitively obvious how this separation of power is a natural determinant of gender.

In the 1840s and fifties, states began passing Married Women's Property Acts. Arguably, it was less about women's rights and more about protecting a household from economic crisis; just as a family business might place assets in the wife's name as protection from liability. By the time slavery was abolished, twenty-nine states had some form of Married Women's Property Law. Opponents of the Civil Rights Act of 1866, abolishing discrimination based on race or color, expressed concern that it would infringe upon a man's right to the service of his wife. During the Eugenics movement of the early 1900's, a woman could be institutionalized and sterilized for being feeble-minded, an imbecile, or a moron.

Born in 1954 I arrived right in the middle of the baby boom generation that resulted from the domestication of American women following World War II. Women in the 1930's and early forties were engaging new freedoms from the emancipation of women begun nearly a century early and following decades of women's suffrage that culminated in women's right to vote in 1920.

Whatever impact the WACs, WAVEs, and WASPs may have had on women's functional capacities in the military, it is certain, the most iconic image of female independence during the war years was Rosie the Riveter. Rosie the Riveter was the star of a government campaign aimed at recruiting female workers for the munitions industry.

American women entered the workforce in unprecedented numbers during World War II. The aviation industry saw the greatest increase in female workers, from one percent in the pre-war years to sixty-five percent by 1943. The munitions industry also heavily recruited women workers, as illustrated by the US government's Rosie the Riveter[1] propaganda campaign. Despite the crucial contribution of women to the war effort, female workers rarely earned more than fifty percent of male wages.

Following the war, the industrial capacity of Europe and Asia was severely depleted and America was uniquely positioned for strong economic growth. The GI bill provided a college education and housing loans that moved America into suburbia. Women were seduced back into the home to realize their natural role as mothers and homemakers.

The grand social experiment became the institutionalization of the American housewife. The advances made by women in the first half of the twentieth century were almost completely erased in a single decade following World War II.

While women were being endowed with the proclivity of their natural "nesting" instincts, men were enjoying an unprecedented technological expansion in science and industry, transportation, entertainment, and the new frontier of space exploration. Women were to experience fulfillment in the children and the home while men experienced free reign of the entire world outside the home. My parents fit well into this fifties' model of caretaker and provider.

Boys are raised to become men. That's not a simple process of maturing it is a deliberate filtering process that defines the type of social organization men create. It is a military style of hierarchical leadership: a hierarchy of power and control. I am older than you and must know better.

My introduction to this hierarchical structure began with Cub Scouts, progressed through Boy Scouts and ultimately halted with football, "no girls allowed" appears prominently on the clubhouse door. These are pathways to status and leadership in a man's world. Football is their team model, but it's a group following the orders of a quarterback, a captain, and a coach. It's a hierarchical model, not a distributed model of cooperative problem solving. There are places where that manner of leadership is valuable, but there are many places where it is totally dysfunctional.

It is easy to associate male and masculinity with the Boy Scouts. It is more difficult to associate female and femininity with the Girl Scouts. Girl Scouts is a distributed model of leadership based on cooperation and mentoring. Femininity is culturally defined as passive or weak but Girl Scouts are about empowering women. The Girl Scouts has long accepted transgender girls because women experience gender roles in a much broader context. The Boy Scouts policy on accepting transgender boys changed just recently while this book was in final review.

As a parent, the contrast was even more profound, as I engaged in both organizations on behalf of my children. As a child in Cub Scouts, my mother was my den mother. As a parent, I was my son's den leader. There is a certain irony in that. It certainly portends some evolution in gender roles but the progress is superficial. Performing as a den mother in the company of the cub scout fathers was a creative challenge that was sometimes awkward. Leadership activities in a patriarchal organization like the Boy Scouts was a conflicting challenge. Leadership activities in the girl scouts were never uncomfortable for me.

Unlike most of my girlfriends, I received extensive training on how to be a man. I learned about boy stuff through structured organizations like Cub Scouts and Boy Scouts. The majority of interaction with my father was through his leadership roles in those organizations. I rejected these hierarchical structures of masculine behavior from an early age. Identifying with my mother aligned with my rejection of "masculinity." Identifying as a girl might be less meaningful than my inability to identify as a boy. That inverse interpretation of gender assignment conflicts with the model of gender transition developed by a therapeutic community that remains tightly aligned with a binary gender model.

In the study of human behavior, the observation cannot be separated from the context of the observer. Theories of gender differentiation have always relied heavily on the assumption that there are two genders, which are innately distinct in their physiology and function. That's the transgender myth.

These theories originate within the context of an extremely patriarchal community. The transgender person defies the basic assumption and completely undermines all of the social theory developed upon that assumption. Therapy seeks to drive the individual toward their "natural" state. Paradoxically, the therapist, based largely on expert opinion, is defining what's natural.

That type of therapy was completely maladaptive for me. How I perceived my own gender was less significant compared to how others perceived my gender. Those social perceptions ultimately drove me to change my presentation. It was essential to align my presentation with my identity to address societies immutable perceptions.

The extreme role separation between the genders during the fifties played out in my own household between my mother and my father. It was obvious to me which side I was on. I had two sisters, but I was the only girl, the one that most identified with mother's capacities as a mother and homemaker. I learned to sew and to bake, carried on the traditional arts of coloring Easter eggs, preparing Thanksgiving dinner, and baking Christmas Cookies. My commitment was fully invested in my children and to the maximum extent possible, in the aesthetics of our home.

My mother like millions of other American homemakers began to realize how meaningless and unappreciated the role of housewife actually was. I began internalizing that conflict from early childhood in Grafton when mother was bringing home Elephant Ears following the night shift at the mill. I witnessed her dismay intensify over the years as she grew ever more insistent that the futility of her life was emphasized in her children because they all took after their father, and none acknowledged her sacrifice and commitment with any like sacrifice of their own.

My role as a provider overshadowed my primary role as a homemaker and mother. In my marriage, I assumed the roles of my parents, as both caretaker and provider. My parent's conflict had become my own internalized conflict.

Growing up in Grafton, Wisconsin in the early Sixties, LeeAnn and I were best friends. We were the oldest girls in the neighborhood. Even as young children we recognized the gender constraints. We were the future housewives of America. When we played Barbies, there were boyfriends; there was romance, but when we played house, there were no husbands. There was a mom, and there were children. Men were superfluous to family life in the sixties. We had no idea that we were preparing ourselves for a world that wouldn't be there for us when we arrived.

1 Rosie the Riveter is a cultural icon based in part on a real-life munitions worker. The strong, bandanna-clad Rosie became one of the most successful recruitment tools in American history. The classic image of Rosie the Riveter with the caption "We Can do it" adopted by the feminist movement in the sixties and seventies was actually a promotional campaign created prior to the government campaign by Westinghouse to boost morale.

Chapter Eight: Decade of My Youth

Well! I've often seen a cat without a grin, thought Alice; but a grin without a cat! It's the most curious thing I ever saw in my life!

– Lewis Carroll, Alice in Wonderland

Born in 1954 I was also at the beginning of the modern-day civil rights movement. Just nine months later on Dec 1, 1955, Rosa Parks, an African-American civil rights activist was arrested for refusing to give up her seat to a white passenger. The US Congress would later refer to her as "the first lady of civil rights" and "the mother of the freedom movement."

It was the case of Browder v. Galye that first prevailed in the courts but Rosa Parks became an iconic figure in the Montgomery Bus Boycott and the modern civil rights movement which produced the Civil Rights Act of 1964. The Civil Rights Act of 1964 outlawed school segregation but the Supreme Court had already ruled that segregated schools were unconstitutional ten years earlier, in 1954, when I was just two months old.

Scenes of nine African American students, known as The Little Rock Nine, entering school flanked by national guardsmen was a scene that shocked the nation. The violence that erupted in Little Rock became a hallmark of racial tension in the sixties.

Parks remained a strong civil rights activist and later became active in the "Black Power" movement, a slogan popularized by Stokely Carmichael. Black power was a solidarity movement that contrasted sharply with the "Freedom Now" slogan used by Martin Luther King. Stokely Carmichael insisted 'Black Power' means black people coming together to form a political force and either electing representatives or forcing their representatives to speak their needs.

Philp A. Randolph, founder of the Negro American Labor

Council (NALC) initiated the March on Washington in 1963 where Martin Luther King gave his infamous I Have a Dream speech. Neither of these groups felt women should be included in the Civil Rights Act. Black Women argued that black families were heavily dependent on women's income, and discrimination against women would be damaging to black families. The cause of black women was largely responsible for the inclusion of sex and gender in Title VII of the civil rights act of 1964.

Advocates of "Black Power" including Malcolm X, were critical of the nonviolence approach initiated by Rosa Parks. Malcolm X eventually supported voluntary integration but remained a strong advocate of black nationalism.

Martin Luther King was critical of the black power movement, stating in an August 1967 speech to the Southern Christian Leadership Conference, "Let us be dissatisfied until that day when nobody will shout 'White Power!'—when nobody will shout 'Black Power!'—but everybody will talk about God's power and human power."

What I emphasize in this sequence of events is the idea that rights guaranteed to us under the constitution are different than rights granted to us by law or executive order. President Lincoln freed the slaves by presidential proclamation but those rights were not guaranteed until the passage of the fourteenth amendment. The court relied on the fourteenth amendment to strike down school segregation which did not become law until the passage of the Civil Rights Act nearly ten years later. There is no law without someone to enforce it.

By the mid-sixties, the youth culture was starting to exert its own influence on the civil rights movement; long hair, Hippies, rock music, marijuana, peace and free love all became iconic symbols of the movement. The Anti-war movement began to crescendo with the Chicago Seven Conspiracy trial following the Democratic Convention in August of 1968. It was a year of extreme violence. Intense rioting in major cities across the US followed the Assassination of Martin Luther King on April fourth. Just one month prior to the Democratic National Convention, presidential hopeful Robert Kennedy was assassinated in Los Angeles.

Vice president Hubert Humphrey entered the race in March after President Johnson withdrew. Senator Eugene McCarthy was seen as the peace candidate. Even though 80 percent of primary voters had supported anti-war candidates, delegates overwhelmingly defeated Senator Eugene McCarty in favor of Hubert Humphrey who hadn't participated in any of the primaries. Humphrey delegates came from caucus states that were controlled by Democrat party leaders.

1,000 attended the protest and hundreds of police and protesters were injured in what the US National Commission on the Causes and Prevention of Violence characterized as a police riot. A federal grand jury indicted eight demonstrators and eight police officers. The Nixon administration's response to the anti-war movement was yet another war, "the War on Drugs."[1]

The eight became the "Chicago Seven," when Black Panther Party leader Bobby Seale was severed from the trial and sentenced to four years for contempt of court. Hippie leaders Abbie Hoffman and Jerry Rubin drew focus for their attacks on conservative US District Judge Julius J. Hoffman.

Abbie Hoffman described the purpose quite politely, "I pointed out that it was in the best interests of the City to have us in Lincoln Park ten miles away from the Convention hall. I said we had no intention of marching on the Convention hall, that I didn't particularly think that politics in America could be changed by marches and rallies, that what we were presenting was an alternative lifestyle, and we hoped that people of Chicago would come up and mingle in Lincoln Park and see what we were about."

Ron Kuby, in his eulogy to defense attorney William Moses Kunstler noted, "While defending the Chicago Seven, [Kunstler] put the war in Vietnam on trial, asking Judy Collins to sing 'Where Have All the Flowers Gone' from the witness stand, placing a Viet Cong flag on the defense table, and wearing a black armband to commemorate the war dead."

The *Chicago Tribune* offered this brief summary, "Eventually, all of the contempt sentences and the riot charges were either dismissed by higher courts or dropped by the government. At the time, it was the Trial of the Century, but in the end, the Chicago Seven Trial seemed to mean nothing at all.

I was watching the election returns with my father the night Richard M. Nixon defeated Hubert H. Humphrey. He supported Nixon, another of many things we disagreed on. It mattered little to me, as there was no peace candidate. Opposition to Johnson's war policies undoubtedly benefited the Republican candidate, but the war continued to escalate under Nixon.

One year later my cousin Ben Danielson disappeared in the jungles of Laos. A year after that, the National Guard gunned down four students at Kent State in Pennsylvania. A year after that I watched in disbelief as Nixon's presidential campaign assured us that victory was near, and we must stay the course or risk losing all that we had sacrificed. A year after that I became eligible for the draft. We all knew there wasn't going to be any victory. At the same time, we were watching men walk on the moon.

That was the decade of my youth. These are the things I remember. The Vietnam War, the assassination of President John F. Kennedy, Martin Luther King, and Senator Robert Kennedy, students gunned down on campus, riots in our cities, police in riot gear beating peace protesters. By the time we got to Woodstock in 1969, the youth movement was already nearing a close. It is an unfortunate characteristic of youth. It is far too fleeting. Some-times I wonder if I was the only one that noticed. When President Bush invaded Iraq in 2003, I thought to myself, *We are the Vietnam Generation, I can't believe we are doing this again.* It's the most curious thing I ever saw in my life!

A new feminist movement erupted in the mid-sixties following the publication of *The Feminine Mystique* by Betty Friedan in 1963 and the formation of the National Organization of Women in 1966. I was only twelve, but already, I was intensely interested in the feminist movement. It was intuitively obvious to me that any-thing that was good for women would be good for me.

Actress Jane Fonda entertained the troops in Vietnam and built a reputation around her anti-war sentiments, popularized with the title Hanoi Jane. She was also active in the feminist movement. She, along with Gloria Steinem and Robin Morgan, co-founded the Woman's Media Center in 2005. Gloria Steinem was a columnist for *New York Magazine* and a founder of *Ms.* magazine. The title Ms. was adopted at the urging of Ms. Shiela Michales, credited with popularizing its usage. Though the magazine's ideology did not reconcile well with commercial interests, the popularization of the title was hardly insignificant, freeing women from the obligation to divulge their marital status.

In 1969 Gloria Steinem published an article, "After Black Power, Women's Liberation." Her intent was to create a parallel between the feminist movement and the Black Power movement, but it also marked a transition from African American civil rights to feminism. It foreshadowed a division in the feminist movement that paralleled the divide between civil disobedience and black power. The feminist movement itself was already being overtaken by another movement that marked its beginning in 1968 with the Stonewall riots in New York City, the gay rights movement

The National Organization of Women was never intended to be a class war between men and women. It was a movement based on equality and basic human dignity. The organizers of NOW recognized that equality demanded economic independence for women, requiring a social restructuring that wouldn't simply create employment opportunity for women but create economic value for the work done by women. Community work and child-drearing would have to be shared more equally by husband, wife, and society.

The original statement of purpose stated, "…take action to bring women into full participation in the mainstream of American Society now, exercising all the privileges and responsibilities thereof, in truly equal partnership with men."

Media focused on the sensationalism of sex/class warfare, characterizing a "man hate" rebellion. Regardless of its legitimacy, it was a way to disrupt the movement and polarize the opposition.

While the sensationalism portrayed women protesting Miss America and Playboy bunnies, the feminist movement was being won in the courts. Title VII of the Civil Rights Act of 1964 prohibited employment discrimination on the basis of sex. One highly visible success was in the airline industry that was no longer able to dismiss stewardesses because of age or marital status.

The feminist arsenal expanded to include education with the passage of Title IX in 1972. Title IX is largely credited with the explosive growth of athletic opportunities for girls in the seventies, though sports isn't mentioned in the bill.

In his remarks on the Senate floor, coauthor Senator Birch Bayh of Indiana aptly described what Betty Friedan had described, "We are all familiar with the stereotype of women as pretty things who go to college to find a husband, go on to graduate school because they want a more interesting husband, and finally marry, have children, and never work again. The desire of many schools not to waste a 'man's place' on a woman stems from such stereotyped notions. But the facts absolutely contradict these myths about the 'weaker sex' and it is time to change our operating assumptions." Title IX was renamed the Patsy Mink Equal Opportunity in Education Act in 2002, after its House coauthor and sponsor Representative Patsy Mink of Hawaii.

Ironically the demise of the women's movement was the one piece of legislation fundamental to the concept of equality and basic human dignity, the Equal Rights Amendment. The ERA was a proposed amendment to the United States Constitution designed to guarantee equal rights for women. The National Woman's Party had introduced the Equal Rights Amendment to every Congress since 1923 until the feminist movement finally saw passage in the House in 1970 and the Senate in 1972.

The Republican Party included support of the ERA in its platform beginning in 1940, renewing the plank every four years until 1980. There was strong opposition in the democratic party from labor groups including the AFL-CIO, the American Federation of Teachers, and the American Nurses Association under the presumption that working-class women needed government protection. Eugene McCarthy, leader of the Anti-war movement in the Democratic Party, was also chief author of the ERA.

Initially, public support for the ERA was strong. Within a year after its passage in the Senate, the ERA had been ratified by thirty states. Opposition to the ERA quickly organized around the protection of women. Phyllis Schlafly became the spokesperson for the Stop ERA Movement emphasizing a threat to the security of middle-aged housewives. Organizers claimed women would lose their right to alimony and child custody. Perhaps the most effective tactic of the opposition movement threatened that women would lose their exemption from the draft.

Religious conservatives, Evangelical Christians, Mormons, Orthodox Jews, and Roman Catholics argued that the amendment would guarantee universal abortion rights, same-sex marriage, and eliminate single-sex bathrooms. By 1977 only five additional states had ratified the amendment, three short of the required thirty-eight. By 1996 men had reasserted the "traditional marriage," when Bill Clinton signed the Defense of Marriage Act.

Even today, opponents of gender equity focus the hysteria around bathroom issues.

It's women who are victimized by this type of messaging. These proposals require everyone to use public restrooms based on their biological sex. Even a team of doctors cannot always determine a persons "true" sex, so they specify "as designated on your birth certificate." This becomes problematic as more states adopt intersex designations on birth certificates when the sex is ambiguous.

Proponents are clearly not considering the consequences. Their claim is to protect women, but these proposals also require trans men to use women's bathrooms. Trans men are men, looking as strong and masculine as any man. How would requiring men to use women's bathrooms make women safer? These bills create a problem where none previously existed.

Women would continue fighting for equity in the courts, fighting for custody, fighting for alimony, and ultimately fighting for their very lives against the threat of domestic violence. In 1970 only 13 percent of families were headed by a single parent. By 1996 that number had doubled with 84 percent of these families headed by women. Dissolving family values fueled a divorce industry that would grow to fifty billion dollars by 2005.

The African American civil rights movement was split between civil disobedience and Black Power. The feminist movement was divided between empowerment and protectionism.

1 Baum, Dan, Washington Post, Smoke and Mirrors, 1996, Accessed June 23, 2017, http://www.washingtonpost.com/wp-srv/style/longterm/books/chap1/smoke.html.

Chapter Nine: My First Pregnancy

"If everybody minded their own business," the Duchess said in a hoarse growl, "the world would go round a deal faster than it does."

–Lewis Carroll, Alice in Wonderland

I wasn't surprised when Sue told me she was pregnant. She was open and adventuresome about sex. At seventeen I knew I was never going to have a period; I wouldn't have to worry about getting pregnant. Those were forbidden pleasures, even as most girls wouldn't describe it that way. Even as I knew I wasn't a boy, it was evident that I wasn't exactly a girl either.

I was more surprised when Sue asked me to take her to New York for an abortion. It was a frightening thought. In those days, at barely eighteen, abortion brought forth images of coat hangers and girls bleeding in back alleys. Every big city hospital had one: a septic abortion ward, for women who had nearly killed themselves trying to abort a pregnancy. We knew you could go to Sweden if you had the money. I didn't realize at the time how difficult it was to obtain contraception. In most states, it was illegal for an unmarried woman to receive contraceptives up until 1972.

In 1971 there were only two states in the US, where a woman could obtain a legal abortion. New York was one and only a few hours away from Nashua. We were quite relieved when Sue's period finally arrived. For two teenage girls, having a baby can be both a dream and a nightmare. For me, it was an early lesson about what it means to be a female.

While planning our trip to New York, the appeal of Roe v. Wade was reaching the Supreme Court. In 1973, the court deemed abortion to be a fundamental right under the constitution. The court defined it as a right to privacy according to the fourteenth amendment. Under the ruling, laws restricting abortion would have to define a compelling interest of the state following strict interpretation. The court presented a trimester framework in which a woman's right to choose was essentially unrestricted in the first trimester. If everybody minded their own business, the world would go around a great deal faster. It was the first time in history that American women had recognized control over the one thing that has defined females for centuries, childbirth.

In many respects, women's reproductive rights were central to women's equality, and the Roe v Wade decision was a major turning point. Its effect on the polarization of advocates and opponents of women's equity is perhaps no less significant than the manner in which the courts' decision on school desegregation polarized the African American civil rights movement.

One of the "compelling interests" allowed that the State could regulate the abortion procedure if the regulation "reasonably relate[d] to the preservation and protection of maternal health." How states defined maternal health continued to evolve around preemptive strategies that diminished women's choices in favor of the states' authority to determine her own best interests.

Just nine years later, back in Minneapolis, I was at Lake Nokomis, sitting in my car with Karen. She was crying, as she told me about the break up of her marriage. She was my only close girlfriend at the time. The time we spent together was intensely intimate.

The reason for the breakup was distressing. She was unable to bear children. It contradicted my experience with male expectations. She was beautiful. She was faithful. Wasn't that every man's dream girl. Femininity can exist in two states: sexual vivacity and maternal. Transgender women cannot bear children which leaves sexuality. Many women cannot or will not bear children, but that too has long been considered dysfunctional rather than a meaningful choice. If she cannot be a complete female because she cannot bear children, does she remain a woman? If she simply chooses to reject childbirth, what then? These questions wouldn't be evanescent.

The ERA ideology of equality was defeated by the ideology of protectionism. Social policy continued to evolve according to these principles, even as opportunities for women were expanding. The failure to domesticate women in the fifties demanded new approaches for defining women according to their reproductive responsibilities.

I'd discover the underpinnings of this movement during work on a suburban police officer job analysis while I was in college in the early seventies. I was hired as a data collector for Author Young & Company, who conducted the study on behalf of the Twin Cities Metropolitan Council and the Metropolitan Area Management Association. My role included recording actual police activities while on patrol.

The study gave me significant insights into the nature of police work. In my personal assessment, it involved long hours of routine activity punctuated by potentially life-threatening situations. The notion was reinforced by many of the officers I interviewed. Some of these officers had been fired upon or discharged a weapon while on duty. One had shot a suspect. I observed officers with weapons drawn during patrol.

I observed evening patrols, presenting some bias, but it was evident to me that the most frequent type of call I observed was domestic disputes. Officers despised these calls. They usually were repeat calls, and there was little hope of any meaningful solution. It could also be physically hazardous to the police officer.

One enlightening aspect of the report is simply the sheer volume of information dealt with by a police officer. Police training, at the time, included three hours of training for handling domestic disputes. I found it hopelessly inadequate by any standard and was dismayed that it primarily focused on officer safety in these volatile situations.

The experience was contributing to a broader understanding of dysfunctional family patterns I first saw written on the neighbor's blackboard that so terrified my best friend back in Grafton. It was evident society needed some type of meaningful response to this type of violence.

My knowledge of domestic abuse evolved through working with other women employed in battered women's shelters. The battered woman became the iconic representation of the movement that evolved into the Violence Against Women Act (VAWA) passed by Congress in 1994.

VAWA was a mixed blessing. It reinforced the oppositional relationship between men and women. It clearly defined women as the victim and created a presumption of male violence. VAWA accelerated the dissolution of family structure, exacerbated the issue of child welfare, and pushed poverty and homelessness deeper into the middle class.

The protections provided by VAWA are exceedingly reactionary, providing little initiative for the identification and treatment of underlying causes. It empowered police, attorneys, and judges but did little to empower women who are deemed incapable of making constructive choices about how to deal with the violence in their relationships. Women, having escaped from the legal dominance of husbands in the early nineteen hundreds, now find themselves under the control of social services, police, attorneys, and judges.

VAWA also provided generous funding for providing treatment services to women but little if any funding for early intervention and treatment. Harsh criminal penalties and familial consequences for men also preempted any meaningful intervention. A pound of treatment cannot overcome an ounce of prevention. By the time a woman is rescued from a hospital bed, there may be little hope of any meaningful recovery.

Despite claims that the law isn't gender specific in spite of the name, victim services for men are exceedingly rare. Treatment services for men generally follow a criminal conviction. While there is a steadfast presumption that women are the victim, violence against a male is naturally presumed to be self-defense. The reverse is also true. Self-defense by a man is naturally presumed to be an aggressive act of violence.

The World Health Organization describes one of the primary risk factors for domestic violence: Sexual violence, particularly during childhood, can lead to increased smoking, drug and alcohol misuse, and risky sexual behaviors in later life. It is also associated with perpetration of violence (for males) and being a victim of violence (for females).

The idea that childhood sexual abuse creates a perpetrator, if the child is male and a victim if the child is a female, is intuitively suspect and empirically emphasized by false assumptions created more by political agendas than sound social science. My own individual experience presented a profoundly different interpretation of domestic violence and its relationship to gender.

The social system and the judicial process that sustains it have institutionalized this model of domestic violence. That presumption confounds efforts to illuminate meaningful solutions. It becomes exceedingly problematic when both partners are of the same sex. It completely disrupts the fanciful notion of domestic tranquility perpetuated by the traditional family model of one prince and one princess.

Men are generally stronger and more aggressive, with women sustaining more frequent and more serious physical injuries. Beyond that, there is little to confirm claims that domestic abuse is something men do to women, particularly as the definition of domestic abuse has expanded to include emotional and psychological abuse. Prevention primarily involves the developmental environments of children: boys and girls. There are deeper issues of gender inequality; and emotional and economic dependence that are being completely omitted from the equation.

VAWA cemented the bond between women and children, like a right of ownership rather than a responsibility, and further alienated men from meaningful relationships with their children. There is something deeply insidious about a culture that objectifies women, defining them according to their sexuality while claiming to protect them from the vulnerability created by that identity.

Some of the benefits of VAWA are incontrovertible but examining VAWA within the context of ERA underscores a curious dichotomy in the status of women today. The National Organization of Women shifted its position on protectionism in favor of VAWA.

Phyllis Schlafly is quoted in the New York Times calling the Violence Against Women Act a slush fund "used to fill feminist coffers" and demanded that Republicans stand up against legislation that promotes "divorce, breakup of marriage and hatred of men." It is an enlightening exercise to contrast Phyllis Schlafly's position on the ERA with her subsequent position on VAWA.

I grew up in two different cultures, one of them male and one of them female. Many times I've been told that I couldn't be on both sides of the fence. During my divorce, I'd be forced to represent both sides: the perpetrator and the victim. That dichotomy redefines the entire discussion about what it means to be transgender. You don't need to be on both sides of the fence. You need to understand that the fence is an arbitrary designation.

All of that would happen to me before Vice President Joe Biden said transgender discrimination is "the civil rights issue of our time" during a campaign stop in Sarasota, Florida. in October of 2012.

Part IV: Lost Innocence: Where a story begins, depends on the story told.

Where a story begins, depends on what story is told. My story began with the birth of a baby boy. Others insist life begins at conception. Birth is an arbitrary designation. This is equally arbitrary.

Jeffrey Eugenides, in his widely acclaimed novel Middlesex, traces the beginning of his story back two generations, through a gene on the fifth chromosome, to the birth of Calliope Helen Stephanides, born with 5-alpha-reductase deficiency giving her the appearance of a female but actually having the chromosomes and sexual organs of a male. Puberty did not transform her into a woman. She was transformed into a man.

The co-joining of chromosomes doesn't guarantee birth. Many things have to happen before two cells develop into a new birth. Many of those cell unions will pass into obscurity without notice. History, however, is written with a yardstick from the future. We measure circumstances, events, and relationships according to our future knowledge of the outcomes. It propels the belief in natural law or the determinism of fate.

Many transgender women maintain that transition is simply affirming their born identity. They will insist that they are not transitioning from male to female. They object strenuously to any suggestion that they were ever a boy. The byline reads, "'born a boy, she now …" The desire to create a clear demarcation between a physical sex and a cognitive gender also suggests that transgender is simply a physical anomaly easily corrected by appropriate medical treatment.

This is the nature argument for gender, conforming to the classical notion that either we're men or we're women with the additional caveat that your sex can be female, and your gender can be male or vice versa. The erasure of transition from any meaningful cultural experience effectively assigns it to an illusionary invocation of the transgender myth.

I have never objected to the idea I was born a boy. It's my social reality, a reality that enlightens my perspectives of sexuality and gender and the broader themes of a social class structure. At puberty, I did not transition into a woman. My sex and gender were at odds. How I perceived society was in conflict with how society perceived me.

Presenting as a male was awkward as well because the transition of puberty was incomplete. failing to provide me a fully masculine appearance. I have gorgeous legs most women would envy. They are smooth, without shaving, because I have no hair. It isn't just my opinion. I've seen dozens of posts wondering if my legs were photo-shopped. I can compete in any hot legs contest … and I have.

I couldn't grow facial hair. I looked like Shaggy from Scooby-Doo. I also have no underarm hair. Not a problem: unless you're pretending to be a man and you don't have it.

When puberty failed me, I searched for other alternatives. I was desperate for a man who'd make me feel like a woman, but the tragic circumstances of those engagements betrayed me. I choose what seemed to be the only option available to me: be a man.

When I left Nashua in the fall of 1972 headed for the University of Minnesota I was excited about new opportunities. I was escaping from the limitless constraints I felt in Nashua. The promise of new freedoms become the abrupt ending to the genuine freedom of expression I enjoyed in childhood and adolescence.

Chapter Ten: College life

In September of 1972, I arrived at the University of Minnesota in Minneapolis with Jim, my good friend from high school. He had decided he wanted to get away from New England for a new experience, and the U of M was a good choice for his major. In the more liberal college atmosphere, I began to think that maybe I was gay. It was a peculiar interpretation. I didn't know anyone gay, but if they liked men, perhaps they identified with women as I did.

For years I've pondered the consequences of telling what happens next. I want to leave it out, believe it's tangential, an irrelevant sideline, but it isn't. It is an integral part of the story. I first mentioned it publicly in 2013 to the reporter, Jessica Harper of the local *Sun Thisweek newspaper*[1]. During the interview about my life story, I described it as a rape. When the story was published she described it simply as an abusive relationship. I was grateful at the time, but it doesn't begin to encompass what really happened.

It is difficult to tell this experience. There is an intense degree of disassociation that tends to invalidate the experience. The emotional and sensory responses burrowed deep into my subconscious, creating triggers to dysfunctional feelings I couldn't define. The memories don't validate the experience. I don't remember the pain though I know for certain there were times when the pain must have been intense and prolonged.

There are vivid images, but I am reluctant to verbalize them in a way that might publicly validate them. I perceive it as the out of body experience survivors sometimes use to describe a traumatic event. I visualized what was happening, as if a bystander watching the scene rather than experiencing it. It was conspicuous in the context of when I was blindfolded. I imagined what was happening, and that visualization is what I remember. It isn't a valid memory. The disassociation, visualization, anxiety, and uncertainty are difficult to place into a relatable context. Few people really understand what they are asking for by expecting a rape survivor to verbalize their experience.

I internalized a cultural value that it was my own choice. When a co-facilitator for a group for male survivors of child sexual abuse once asked if I could ever forgive that guy; I realized that I had never considered the question. I blamed myself. I refused to acknowledge my vulnerability, so it was apparent that I must be responsible. People can't imagine why I didn't report the crime. I can't imagine how I could possibly share this story with a police officer. It's hard enough to just to write the words.

In various forms, it's an experience shared by millions of women, and it's a serious cultural problem that needs a broader dialogue. I want to avoid gruesome details, but it was violent.

He is the first man I dated outside of my own fantasies. I was working the counter at the Big Ten Bar and Grill on the University of Minnesota campus in Minneapolis my freshman year. He came in the evening for pizza takeout. The conversations were brief and flattering. He didn't want to drive downtown to Spalachi's. Our pizza recipe came from Spalachi's. I had trained there to make the same famous pizza. Just knowing that, gave him a familiarity. He was older and better dressed than our regular clientele.

His pizza was usually ready when he arrived. He always complimented my appearance which must have been dreadful, working in the kitchen half the night. He would pay for his pizza, thank me kindly with a beautiful smile, and he'd leave. After a few visits, I recognized his name on the order slip and I could feel the anticipation. It was an uncomfortable feeling because I knew what I was anticipating, and I was far from believing that was okay.

One night he invited me to dinner, and I accepted. I agreed for him to meet me at my dorm. He told me to wear something nice. I had no idea what to do with that request. I was really excited and super nervous. For me, it really was my first date.

When the night came I decided to wear my white suede baggies, high heeled platform shoes, and a blue satin shirt. There was a brief period in 1972 when a guy could wear baggies and platform shoes. I was hopeful of more feminine fashions. I loved those high heeled shoes, but they were the only pair I ever found. My hope for feminine fashions didn't last long, similar to the Nehru craze in 1970. I don't know how many were sold, but I'm certain I was the only one that ever wore one.

We had dinner at the Nankin in Downtown Minneapolis. There were flowers on the table which didn't seem odd to me. "Would you like some wine?" he offered. I was eighteen, and the drinking age in Minnesota would soon change to eighteen, but that evening I was still under-age. No one checked my ID. Before dinner, he removed a silver bracelet from its jewelry box and placed it on my wrist. It was clearly a woman's bracelet. It would be the only night I ever wore it. The conversation carries the haziness of too much wine, but I know we spent the whole evening talking about me. After dinner, I accepted his invitation to go to his house.

A sudden moment of truth was like standing at the bottom of that cement silo. It was too late to panic I'd have to endure. I didn't struggle against a rope around my neck. I accepted it the same way I accepted that silver bracelet around my wrist, with total innocence.

Standing naked in a doorway with the calves of my legs bound together, my hands restrained behind my back, and that rope around my neck tethered to the top of the doorway, I was completely vulnerable, completely available. The beard stubble that framed his masculinity felt rough and abrasive against my face when he pressed his lips against mine. I refused to open my mouth. It was my initial level of defiance which no doubt is what he was hoping for. It was a training session.

He held out a gag in front of my face and told me to open my mouth. I started crying. It is probably what he was hoping for. He tethered my hands to the top of the doorway so that I was bent over facing the floor. He paddled my behind till it bled. Being made to sit served as a reminder of what I could expect if I disobeyed. When he was done he put the gag in my mouth, and that's how I spent the rest of the night.

There were two rules much like a game of Simon Says. If I was given a command then I was required to beg for that privilege until it was approved. If he told me to suck his cock, my response was, "Baby can I suck your cock, please?" After a hundred repetitions, you're ready to do it. After one repetition, you're ready to do it because you know you're not being given a choice.

If it was a question then I was required to give a positive response. If he said, "does that feel good?", my response was, "Oh baby, that feels so good!" It never felt good. Certainly, I was already in excruciating pain before he even asked the question.

Those two rules are burned into my memory because they were repeated with every exercise, Even so, I couldn't tell you how many times I said, "Oh baby, that feels so good." The images that remain in my mind, are the ones when I was left with my own thoughts, anticipating his return, and of course, when blindfolded with nothing but my own thoughts.

I was given two opportunities to leave. On my first opportunity I didn't think to say "baby, may I leave please." This too was probably the response he wanted, and my disobedience was severely punished.

I did not want to return to the dorm, but I did not know where else to go either. Nobody ever asked where I had been for four days. I'm not sure how I was able to make it to class the following day. I suppose it was an essential part of the denial. A part of you shuts down. Pretending was a way of life for me.

I couldn't use the group showers in the dorm. It was a couple of weeks before I could shower again. I felt like everyone knew I was different now.

It is painful to tell this experience. It is a painful memory. I experience both self-incrimination and empathy at the same time.

I know people will judge. Just as society will judge me, I can blame her, even as she and I are the same person. I can say I am not that person today. I can tell myself she broke the rules, she dated a man, she drank the wine, she went to his house. I had no say in what she did. These feelings invoked by the memory of this experience underscores the disassociation. It's a natural coping mechanism for segregating the trauma, repressing bad memories. Somehow, a separate gender presentation seemed to support that separation.

But it was me, and it brings tears to my eyes to see myself at that young age of innocence: to understand her desperation, her passion, her desires for something that was forbidden. The choices she made decided our future choices.

It could have been different. What if he had been the man of our dreams? Then I'd be thanking her for her courage, her willingness to take risks, and venture outside herself. I'd be praising her willingness to trust in the outcomes. Life isn't about guaranteed outcomes. Life is about making better choices. We learn from experience, and our fear of the outcomes can paralyze and thwart our personal growth.

Like many forms of trauma, you don't really get over it, you find new ways of coping. It wasn't until 2011 at the first annual SlutWalk in Minneapolis that I first shared my experience with another survivor. It was a profound catharsis.

I did not return home to Nashua the following summer. I stayed on the farm, and drove a truck for my uncle. I returned to college in the fall hoping that Rod, my new roommate, would be a stabilizing influence. Rod was the perfect model of academic performance during freshman year. Concentrating on school work was difficult. When Rod dropped out during the first quarter so did I. He went to work at Toro Manufacturing, and I followed suit. We rented an apartment at Driftwood Estates. For a brief period, I enjoyed picking out furniture and playing house. I found female friendships, Barb and Janet, roommates who lived next door to us. Barb became my girlfriend in another of a long string of failed relationships.

In a desperate attempt to continue my education, I took a correspondence class in abnormal psychology. The first assignment was a paper in which we were to define abnormal. That paper would be different if I wrote it today. I live in a culture that defines normal as average or commonplace. Things that are rare are completely normal. We appreciate the extraordinary value in rare elements like gold. The same principle doesn't apply to people.

None of it could restore my self-worth. I started hanging out with a guy named JM from Toro, Every night we closed the bars and ended with a couple more at home. Then I'd get up for work the next day to do it all over again. Saturday's overtime ended with drinking scotch out in the parking lot.

There's little else to tell about those two years following that one date at the Nankin. I was little more than a gutter drunk, burying the past. I was wasting my life away, and I knew it. I regret the chaos I created in Barb's life, so I respect her departure when her patience finally ran out. She went off to school. Her abrupt departure did enable me to climb out of the drowning pool and head back to school myself.

I shared a place with JM and Bob: a basement apartment with three bedrooms for $100 a month. $35 was cheap rent, even then. I walked two miles to class. I remember well the winter of 1977 when the temperature never got above zero for six weeks. The Ohio River was frozen over, and factories shut down. People were going to their churches praying for warmer weather.

During most of my remaining two years at the University of Minnesota, I went to school during the day and worked third shift, as a security guard. I never went to bed. I took naps, most of them at the library before or after class. It was a solitary existence, but it kept me sober, more or less. By the spring of 1978, I had enough credits for my degree in psychology. I didn't go to graduation. I went to Germany.

Bob and I remained casual friends. In fact, we both bought homes in Eagan, little more than a mile apart, and our girls played basketball together in junior high. JM dropped out of my life. Years later I saw him one time at JJ's bar over in North Minneapolis. It was a short and painful reunion. He was angry with me for leaving him behind and not saving him. *Save you?* I thought to myself, *I barely got out.*

I'd learn to understand alcoholism as alcohol remained one of my best friends during periods of extreme isolation. It was an escape, but also a barrier to confronting the challenges of being female in a man's world.

1 Harper, Jessica, SUN Thisweek, Candidate for 2nd District endorsement Paula Overby spent a lifetime searching for her identity, January 24, 2014, accessed June 23, 2017, http://sunthisweek.com/2014/01/24/candidate-for-2nd-district-endorsement-paula-overby-spent-a-lifetime-searching-for-her-identity/

Chapter Eleven: Cultural Transition

"No wise fish would go anywhere without a porpoise." "Don't you mean 'purpose?'" said Alice.

–Lewis Carroll, Alice in Wonderland

In the spring of 1978, while completing my final quarter of college, I received a letter from Germany for an assignment at the Gravenbruch Hotel in New Isenberg as a *pool mit arbiter:* pool worker. I might imagine a gorgeous man with toned biceps and washboard abs wearing little more than a deep tan, skimming leafy flotillas off the surface of the pool while I, die *schöne fräulein* lounge about the pool.

I arrived at the Frankfurt Airport in Germany late in the evening with little more than a lightly loaded backpack and a phone number. What struck me immediately was the heavily armed Polizei.

I reflect on one night back in the states, returning to Nashua from the Merrimack drive-in. The 61 VW bug was comfortable on a winding back road until the blue lights flashed in the rearview mirror. "Where are you going?" the officer asked. He said, "Three people in the car looks suspicious." I didn't understand. There were only two of us.

How often I recall Mother saying, "Paul, you have a guardian angel. God has a plan for you." *Don't you mean purpose? What purpose would God have for someone like me?* I thought to myself. "Three times your life has been spared," she continued on one occasion, "so, of course, you have a purpose."

Perhaps the third person that night was my guardian angel. What possible reason could there be for making herself visible? Police have always complicated my life. They enforce the boundaries between the mainstream society and people like me, marginalized through no choice of our own. The police are the frontlines of a chaotic system of rules and regulations Americans choose to impose upon one another. Political agendas are often disguised as valuable social reforms.

It was rumored at the time, that Nashua had more police per capita than any other city in the nation. They were compelled to shake down teenagers in search of small baggies containing fragments of weed. They were diligent about this task. In Nashua, just being a teenager made you part of an undesirable subculture. That earned me traffic citations because of an error on my license that required glasses to drive. The judges refused to correct it. It primed my distrust for our criminal justice system. Affixed to the rear of that Volkswagen bug was a license plate with the motto, "Live Free or Die." In my mind, it lacked credibility.

Unlike the Nashua police, the German officers had far more important things to worry about than shaking down teenagers. The manner of their presence left me with a sense of safety and security. I could move freely through this space and pursue my destination.

There was no bus or rail transport to the hotel so I dialed the number, and they graciously arranged a cab to pick me up from the airport. Riding through the streets of Frankfort, I felt more like a dignitary than a migrant worker.

We were migrant workers, living in a dormitory and serving Europe's high society. We were served two meals a day: *brod und marmalade mit spritz wasser für frühstück und wurst mit kartoffeln und ein bier für abendessen.* We worked six days a week. Angelo was my roommate, a handsome Italian man who spoke several languages, but English wasn't one of them. Conversation was inconvenient and therefore non-existent. Communication between the sexes is strained enough without additional language barriers. If I had been naturally possessed of the kind of female body I desired, we may have overcome that minor inconvenience.

I wanted to work on my German, but most of the staff wanted my help with their English. I spent much of my free time in my room with 501 German verbs. Truthfully, my German was inadequate for the kind of conversations I might enjoy in English. It helped me understand how creative language actually is. A couple of beers was helpful to express myself in German rather than translate from English thoughts. By summer's end, I'd begin to have dreams in German.

There were five of us Americans at the hotel: two boys and three girls. I'm counting myself as one of the boys because that's how people perceived me. The boys were hotel porters, greeting guests, escorting them to their rooms, arranging the delivery of their luggage. It was a tipped position, so the pay was actually pretty good. The girls were the maids, cleaning the toilets, restocking the tissues, and cleaning up the remaining essence of romance and personal indulgence.

Statistically, five is a small sample size and one could argue the assignments were random. The argument would be irrelevant. All three women knew it was specific to gender. This wasn't a single experiment but one they had seen repeated many times. For me, it was an uncomfortable thought. Internally, I thought like a girl, socialized as a girl, and generally acted like a girl. Externally, I was a boy. That's all that mattered.

I began to experience gender identity from the privilege of my birthright, which according to the Hebrew ancestry of my faith always belonged to the first-born son. According to the same traditions, daughters fetched a price.

The men traveled by cab to the Irish pub in Sachsenhausen or the brothels of Frankfurt on Thursday nights. It seemed like an authentic Irish pub without the children and grandparents I imagined in my televised view of Irish culture. The place was packed with many nationalities speaking native languages. It was prime people watching. I drank my share of warm Guinness stout to fit in properly. It was a comfortable space for me. Anyplace where no one fits in is a place I feel comfortable.

The brothel was an entirely different story. Observing this raw physical interplay of the sexes left me with an inescapable realization that I was at that moment standing on the wrong side of the fence. Even omitting the emotional triggers, I was struck with how inappropriate my gender presentation seemed.

Angelo approached me with a simple request, *"Haben sie funfzig mark?"*

"Für was?" I replied.

"Zu liebe das madchen mit den blonden haaren," he responded, nodding toward the woman he had chosen.

"Wird mir es wieder sehen?" I queried.

"Ya stimmt! Bitte." he pleaded.

Three months I shared a room with Angelo, and that was the longest conversation we ever had. Who was I to deny the authority of natural law of which I myself was in profound violation? I didn't expect to see the money again. There is a masculine code of monetary flow to which women are seldom privy.

It was the last time I traveled with the men. I found a new relationship with Bernd, the hotel butcher. That's how he referred to himself: "The Butcher." He was a culinary artist preparing elegant banquets for visiting dignitaries arriving in government limousines and military helicopters. Non-essential staff was sometimes restricted to the dorm. Bernd loved his job, loved life, and loved that fine German beer. He also loved having a driver. He was everything I could hope for in a partner. I discounted any jealousy I felt over his frequent requests for me to smooth things out with his girlfriend. I couldn't overlook the fact that he found me well suited to interceding with his girlfriend.

Sampling the wares of local breweries around Frankfurt was a great pastime. Occasionally, we drove over to the enlisted men's club in Hanover where they served Budweiser. It was cheap, and it would get you drunk. Why else would you drink it, surrounded by all of those fine German brews? Bernd loved Buddy Holly, which is all we listened to on his car stereo. It was the summer of "Baker Street" by Jerry Rafferty which left me a little homesick. They also don't celebrate Independence Day in Deutschland.

Following my servitude at Hotel Gravenbruch, I traveled about Europe for another three weeks.. I took a broad sampling of Europe: Hamburg, Copenhagen, Stockholm, Amsterdam, Paris, Munich. In Switzerland, I had the privilege of staying with relatives of friends back in the US. I stayed a full three days, the maximum of any proper welcome. On the last day, I took the cog railway to the top of the Matterhorn which in retrospect was much too close to the Sun. Traveling to Rome the following day I thought about little else besides my sunburn. My television knowledge of Rome hadn't prepared me for the extreme poverty I saw surrounding the train station. The temperature was approaching 100 degrees. From the train station, I walked to the Coliseum, which I found to be totally unimpressive. It is likely nothing could have impressed me under the circumstances.

As soon as I heard there was going to be a rail strike I headed back to the train station hoping to make it to the French Riviera. I got as far as Genoa, a harbor town fully prepared to consume my diminutive spirit. My travel companions incessant talking was driving me crazy. I finally went to the markets down by the docks. I feasted on Italian sausage, and got drunk on Mateus wine. Alcohol will never abandon you in a time of need.

I'd had enough. I decided to cut short my tour of Europe and head back to the familiar surroundings of Germany and my dear friend Bernd. I managed to get out of Genoa that night riding a vacant boxcar on a cargo train. Twice I switched trains and was searched by Swiss customs before I reached stable connections in Zurich. Finally seeing the familiar sites and sounds of Deutschland was a welcome relief.

On my final day in Germany, I stood at the end of the drive leading to the Hotel Gravenbruch waiting for a cab to take me to the airport. Angelo appeared from the doorway of our summer dormitory and walked down the drive to where I was standing. He took my hand in his and with the other placed fifty Deutsch marks in my hand. He looked into my eyes with one final word, *"Aufwiedersehen."*

"Danke," I replied, and turning back toward the street to conceal the tears welling up in my eyes, *"Aufwiedersehen."* I cried most of the way to the airport.

Back in the states, there was an airline strike in progress at JFK International Airport in New York and no connecting flights to Boston. The only available flight that evening was leaving from LaGuardia in two hours. My wallet was running light by that time, and I couldn't afford the cab fare so I opted for bus transportation. There was no express route, so a transfer occurred somewhere in the north end of Harlem. That's not completely accurate. I was in Queens but at the time, my televised view of inner-city New York was synonymous with Harlem, and that's where I decided I was.

Standing on a desolate corner of New York City late at night I really had no idea where I was. A lone individual stood on the opposite side of the street leaning against a brick stone building. I didn't want to attract his attention but I could have been an aerial floodlight, and I'd not have been any more conspicuous. After a few minutes, he began crossing the street directly toward me. My pulse quickened, my body tensed, and I thought to myself, *This is it.* Like standing at the bottom of that cement silo, it was too late to panic. He came directly to me. With an air of formality in his posture, he stood there in front of me. "Are you waiting for the bus to LaGuardia?" he queried.

"Yes," I replied.

"You need to be on that corner," he said, pointing kitty-corner to the opposite side of the intersection.

"Thank you, sir," I replied as he moved past me and walked back into the night.

Thanks to that chance encounter of two cultures on a desolate city street in New York, I arrived at LaGuardia in time to make my flight to Boston. Standing before the departure sign next to a young couple toting backpacks, another cultural experience unfolded. They wanted to dispense with several hash chocolate chip cookies to avoid any inconvenience with customs. I wasn't enthused about the hash but certainly reacted well to the thought of chocolate.

I never cared for marijuana because it is completely inconsistent with my concept of a recreational drug. It's great for relaxing, which I have never been good at. Anxiety was essential for me to maintain competitive masculine behavior. Alcohol was much better suited to that purpose.

The hash thoroughly engaged with my body's natural chemistry just about the time we reached cruising altitude. The moon was full, reflecting itself in the pitch-black darkness of the Atlantic

Ocean. I lay back in my chair and listened to the soothing hum of the jet engines. I was relaxed. I understood, for the first time, why people smoke pot and just as certainly understood why I couldn't.

Chapter Twelve: The Hour Glass

Not having planned for my return from Germany, I was homeless, jobless, and penniless by the time I got back to Minneapolis. In need of immediate employment, I took a management training position with Sambos Restaurants. They were offering an apartment, paid training, and an all-expenses-paid trip to Chicago.

I trained at Sambos on White Bear Avenue in St. Paul, where I was glad to have a female manager. I felt a strong connection to a black woman in training with me, perhaps because she too understood what it was like to be the most conspicuous person in the room. I wish I could have known her better. She was beautiful, she was intelligent, and she was passionate. Our assignments drew us apart, and I quickly lost contact with her.

My Assignment was in Sioux City, Iowa. My memory of the restaurant is like a movie with no sound. I see the faces of all of my staff. I see the setups on the tables and the Hershey syrup by the waitress station. I see the booths lining the front of the restaurant and the windows above them with the view of the city behind them, looking like a mural on the wall. I see a menu on the counter, the cash register behind it, and the hallway to the restrooms behind that.

With a good forensic artist I could create the entire scene in vivid detail, but it is surreal as if I have somehow shifted into a parallel universe. Two booths from the end wall a woman is seated by herself. As I continue to stare at this scene, I see myself sitting across from her. It is another out of body experience. As my view pans to the other side of the room, I see her face and recognize Wanda, the woman who is about to enter my life with a mysterious impact.

She isn't like any of my previous girlfriends. She has come there to find me. She is a guide. Her influence in my life will be brief, tragic, and profound.

Sioux City is a depressed community, a cowboy town, still struggling with high unemployment from the recent demise of the major stockyards. The Sambos restaurant is equally run down, poorly staffed, losing customers, and losing money. With little more than three months of management training, I am there to turn it around. With little more than three months of experience, the restaurant is starting to turn a profit, but I'm earning less per hour than my lowest paid employee. The bonuses I've been promised will never materialize. Within two years the whole company will be in bankruptcy.

Wanda wanted a husband. I wanted to prove to myself that I could be a husband. What follows is a play. People would perceive a real relationship, in the same way they perceived me as a man. During the brief six months I was there, Wanda and I played house. I reenacted fantasies from my childhood, and she acted out fantasies of a childhood she never had. All of the scenes were reenactments but the actions were real. We shopped, furnished the new apartment, and picked out a new car, a 1976 Ford Cobra. We had dinner together and turned out the lights when it was time to go to bed. Like a dream flashing through random images, we were soon picking out an engagement ring.

I was experimenting with my childhood memory of the appropriate family model, where I'd be the husband, a role for which I felt unqualified. Society would wait patiently to expose the insolence of my deception.

On the last night I was in Sioux City I went down to the Long Branch Bar to meet Wanda. I never met up with her that night. I was assaulted in the entryway to the Long Branch. There is a significant gap in my memory. According to Wanda, I had been back at the restaurant late that evening. They had sent me to the hospital, where they kept me overnight for observation. The next day I was back in Minneapolis but it is unclear to me how I got there. That's how my career with Sambo's ended.

I could blame the concussion for the surreal nature of this time period but it doesn't explain the fact that I wasn't the only one who experienced the shift. While I was in Sioux City, my parents, along with my sister Sharon, had moved to St. Louis, Missouri. At the time there was no way to measure the significance of these events. There was no future yet to interpret them.

Mother called it divine guidance. She was convinced she was in St. Louis to care for me: explain all that. She was a mother above all else, and she overlooked what these changes meant in her own life. She also found relief in St. Louis, in the form of a doctor there able to deal with the complex health issues presented by the female anatomy.

It was my father who came to visit me in Sioux City to assess the situation. There was little he could offer. His career and his role as provider had taken him far away from his capacity as a parent. We went out to the club. It was appropriate for a father and son. How could he know that I wasn't really his son? It contradicted my commitment to being a husband. He encouraged me to dance. Dancing has always lifted my soul but boys don't dance alone.

Dad found a nice home in St. Louis and put a pool in the backyard. For him these trappings of daily living created continuity, but they couldn't sustain the family's heart and soul. Mom and Sharon failed to thrive, and my father started coming to grips with that.

I can trace the trail of mom's disappointments. Elephant Ears: that's what I remember of Mom's first job. She worked third shift at the mill in Grafton. In the morning she brought home Elephants Ears from the local bakery. They were a substitute for her home-baked goods. Dad would check on her in the middle of the night leaving her feeling embarrassed. The Elephant Ears didn't last long.

Mom also sold Avon when we were in Grafton. She loved it, and I looked forward to the arrival of each order with the opportunity to bag the orders and check out the new samples. It was the most fun I can remember having with my mother. I also remember the arguments from my parent's bedroom. Very soon the orders stopped arriving.

Mom often told me she wanted to be a nurse, "but Dad wanted me to be a professional secretary," she often added. Her nursing assistant job in Cudahy was the best compromise she could manage. The move to Nashua ended that fledgling career. In Nashua, she took a job doing injection molding, a clear convert of Betty Friedan's Feminine Mystique.

There was some comfort to the inexplicable fabric of distant relationships assembled around Sioux City as if passing through the waist of an hourglass. LeeAnn's sister was living in Sioux City with her husband while I was there, but her husband wouldn't allow me to see her. That type of control suggested an abusive husband as I thought back to the blackboard in Grafton. Future husbands and wives converged on St. Louis. My best friend from Nashua moved to Minneapolis. By the time the convergence ended, I was back in Minneapolis; Mom, Dad, and Sharon were back in Nashua; LeeAnn's sister was back in Wisconsin. The black hole created a slingshot back to our own universe.

Wanda came to Minneapolis with me. The play continued with introductions to the parents. We drove to her parent's home in Mississippi, stopping to see my folks in St. Louis on the way.

I can't envision how my parents must have felt about this performance. We ourselves hadn't discussed the realities of this experiment. Wanda was part of the inexplicable fabric of relationships passing through the hourglass. To suggest it would invalidate the experiment. The next day before leaving for Mississippi, we met with the pastor at my parent's church to discuss our wedding. I'm not clear he was agreeing to marry us, but we had a church and a minister chosen for a proper wedding.

At Wanda's home in Mississippi, I spent the first day alone with her family, helping with the farm work and sharing meals. The following day we looked at houses for rent. When we found one that was suitable, we went back to her parent's home, said good-bye, and headed back to Minneapolis, skipping any further amenities.

Back in Minneapolis, we shopped for a wedding dress. We picked out a date and sent out wedding invitations. The morning after we mailed the invitations Wanda was gone. Her note was brief. "I have to be with Jim. He needs me." The curtain came down on the final act. The play was over.

Mom took care of notifying the guests and canceling any arrangements. She always took care of me when chaos overwhelmed me. If ever I was completely alone, she was always there.

I left for Mississippi the following day. Leaving the Cobra there, I planned to hitchhike to Portland with some ill-formed plan about starting over or simply giving up if that didn't work out. A trucker picked me up out outside a truck stop somewhere west of Memphis. He was passing through St. Louis, which seemed to suggest I ought to stop off there. In 1979, we were in the midst of a militant truckers strike which was precipitated by the OPEC oil embargo in the early seventies.

The trip from Memphis to St. Louis took us through the Ozark Mountains which was a dangerous place to be. "I picked you up because I thought you were another trucker," he said. Then he handed me a shotgun as he went on, "As long as you're here, we need to protect ourselves." I assume the shotgun was loaded. I suspect boy scout gun safety rules didn't apply in the Ozarks. It was too late to panic. I rode shotgun all the way through to St. Louis.

Dawn was breaking through clear skies when we arrived in St. Louis. I slid the shotgun under a blanket behind the seat before we climbed out of the cab. It was another awkward moment for me. I thanked him for the ride. I watched him walk away until he disappeared into the truck stop. Then I headed off to find my parent's home.

I didn't have the courage to face my parents. I didn't have any explanations to offer them. The experiment was over but the results were inconclusive. When I got to their house, it was foreign to me. I left my embarrassment behind in a note. I walked back down the driveway and headed over to I55.

Hitching was common in the seventies, but hitching the interstates was chancy. You had to hope for a ride before you encountered a passing state patrol. To make it doubly so, my parents had contacted the state patrol. Within minutes I had a ride. The state patrol would never find me.

Random rules of engagement being what they are, the guy was going to Fargo, North Dakota. By the time we got to Kansas City, he had decided that going up I35 through Minneapolis would be better than the more direct route up I29. It wasn't difficult to recognize he enjoyed my company, and I was enjoying the attention. He was a perfect gentleman If he had any designs on me they never materialized. The consequence, however, was that I never made it to Portland. I don't know what awaited me in Portland, but that short relationship on I35 punctuated the reasons I never arrived. Portland has no place in the story except to mark a point where two possibilities diverged.

One doesn't choose to be transgender. It doesn't mean that we don't have choices but the choices are not usually attractive. I wanted a family, according to my own family model that was so much a part of my entire life experience. I did not have the same choices most women have. According to that family model, I'd have to be the husband. At age twenty-six I could already recount a long string of failed relationships suggesting a family was impossible. My relationship with Wanda was about proving to myself that I could commit to the impossible. It didn't quite work out that way but the rules of random engagement were drawing me closer to what I really wanted: to be a mother.

I met up with Wanda one last time at the Long Branch in Sioux City. She was standing behind the bar when I arrived. The place was completely empty. I sat down at a table opposite from the bar slightly shaded from the lights of the stage. There was an endless moment before she came out from behind the bar and joined me at the table. We reminisced for a while about our life together until we got to the point where it was time to say good-bye. I embraced her and we kissed. We gazed briefly at each other through tearful eyes and said our goodbye. That memory is clear in my mind as real as any of the experiences we had shared together but it was a dream. When I awoke I felt an enormous calm, and I knew that I was back in my own universe.

Chapter Thirteen: End of Men

"Who am I then? Tell me that first, and then, if I like being that person, I'll come up: if not, I'll stay down here till I'm somebody else"

–Lewis Carroll, Alice in Wonderland

When I'd returned to Minneapolis, I went to work for Sharing Life in the Community (SLIC) where I had been an intern while at the University of Minnesota. SLIC was a grant-funded pilot project intended to provide community living support for clients with mental health issues. The program evolved out of pressures to reduce the cost of the mental health hospital system and ostensibly improve the quality of life for mental health clients. Cutting cost was an obvious objective. The second part was more obfuscated. It was a pilot project so we only accepted chronic mental health patients, defined as three or more hospitalizations. Schizophrenia, manic-depressive disorder (now known as bipolar disorder), and clinical depression were the most common diagnoses.

The role of the community based mental health counselor was about teaching daily living skills; establishing structure in their lives; advocating for them with social services, employers, community services, and medical professionals; establishing goals and activities; and charting their progress. There was always a profound sense of inadequacy. Few of them were capable of maintaining gainful employment. Those with supplemental security income (SSI) generally received a livable income, but most were on general assistance which was inadequate for an independent living arrangement that was conducive to anyone's mental health.

We were their lifeline. I respected their tenacity and their perseverance. The two client suicides were tragic but understandable. Experiencing life within this community was profoundly different than reading about it or studying it in a classroom.

We were working with a largely invisible subculture of American society. The staff at SLIC was, in others ways, another largely invisible subculture. There was a natural imperative that required an ability to function in the majority culture and still relate to the fringes of our society. There were backgrounds in domestic violence and cultural studies. Three of the staff members were gay men.

This connection to the gay community presented a path to a transgender community, but I did not recognize it because I'm not gay. It was merely a decade after the 1969 Stonewall riots, which generally marks the beginning of the gay movement. Transgender women were a pivotal influence in that uprising but are seldom recognized for their role. Women are always at the forefront of major social change. Transgender women prefer to mark the beginning of the LGBT civil rights movement in 1966 with the Compton's Cafeteria riot in San Francisco, which was exclusively transgender women. It holds little notice in the history of the gay movement. The first symptoms of the AIDS epidemic are just beginning to mystify doctors across the country.

Stringing letters together doesn't create a cohesive community. Even today it is difficult to recognize any substantial connection between the gay community and the transgender community.

The gay movement remains largely a white male middle-class movement, more of an economic success than a major social victory. In 1969, gay rights were about freedom from persecution and sexual oppression. In time, the movement evolved toward gaining status as a protected identity. Hate crimes legislation empowered the institutions of oppression we rebelled against. Even today, in 2016, the criminalization of male sexuality remains profoundly intact, and solutions to Minnesota's Sexual Offenders Program are remote.

The transgender civil rights movement is infinitely more complex The challenge for transgender women is completely different from being gay. I feel more welcome in the general population than I do in the gay community, where there remains a strong association between transgender women and female impersonation: drag performance.

I was a guest at the wedding of one of my gay coworkers. Their home-style marriage ceremony wouldn't be recognized by society for another thirty-three years. Even cross-dressing was illegal. It was a beautiful ceremony; I felt deeply moved, but it was also clear this family model wasn't going to work for me.

My time at SLIC also represented a period of sexual exploration that, for me, was really about gender. In 1979 I dressed up as a woman for the first time ever, to attend a Halloween party. I remember the outfit well. It all came from a thrift store so it wasn't totally elegant, but that short red pleated skirt was stunning, a perfect accent to my legs. I experienced a positive feeling and noticed the mirror was, for the first time, presenting a reflection of me in a way I had never felt before. I wore that outfit all weekend.

By January of 1980, I slipped into a mild depression brought on by or perhaps accompanied by a brief drinking binge. The darkness of winter has always been one of my worst adversaries. I'm fond of saying I should have been an Egyptian princess around 4000 BC. That would have been perfect for me.

I took the Cobra down to New Orleans for Mardi Gras. It was a horrible trip. A huge snowstorm blanketed the entire Midwest. The interstate was single lane through most of Missouri with drifting and blowing snow, and there were two hundred miles of washboard ice through the Ozarks. When I got to New Orleans, it was snowing. "First time I've ever seen snow," was repeated everywhere I stopped. I never saw the sun.

Bourbon Street and the parades were somewhat passé in my opinion. The female impersonators intrigued me. I found myself a table near the stage and watched with quiet introspection, as one showgirl after another performed her routine. It's the first drag show I'd ever seen. I don't know if I had ever heard the term. No one would ever guess these girls might be men. With a yardstick from the future, I'd have known they were not a typical gay men's troupe. They were trans girls. I had no idea of the complex intermingling of needs and desires that overwhelmed the atmosphere in that establishment.

At the time, transgender was an obscure word and wasn't used to describe women like myself that have surgical transformations. Virginia Prince was promoting the word transgender as a replacement for transvestite to describe male cross-dressers. Tri-Ess, the Society for the Second Self, an organization of male, heterosexual cross-dressers was only a few years into its formation.

I had a close relationship with one of my coworkers at SLIC. He was a man, and he allowed me to feel like a woman. That emotional connection with a gay man filled the loneliness, awakening new possibilities I felt compelled to explore further.

This exploration happened one evening at the lake. I don't know how it came to be that this man and I were alone in front of the glowing embers in the fireplace. Wine glasses and beer bottles on the coffee table made up the jury of a reckless encounter. The physical stirrings of human passion, normally kept tightly constrained were suddenly uninhibited. I positioned myself on the couch next to him with my legs tucked under me and my arm extended across the couch above his shoulders. My lips were positioned seductively close to his cheek. I flirted with him. I praised him. I touched him. With subtle suggestions, I offered myself to him. He did not resist, but he did not accept my offer either. When he finally got up and went into the kitchen to get another beer the pulsing energy in my body subsided, and I felt suddenly overwhelmed with embarrassment. I said a clipped good night, as I passed by the kitchen.

He committed suicide the very next day. It was a violent conclusion. I didn't attend the funeral. Overwhelmed by guilt, I couldn't face the situation. I felt certain he was gay. I knew he wasn't out, not even to himself. I should have understood the complexities from my own experience in mental health. I should have known better. I should have anticipated the potential consequences. I let my passions run unrestrained. I had done what no woman should ever do to a man.

This time I couldn't blame the desires of a naive young girl. It dramatized the choice between family and romance. Within three months, I'd have a family of my own. I'll remain there till I'm somebody else. Like the planets in the house of the Zodiac, everything was aligned: my sex, my gender, my presentation, my future, or so I thought.

Part V: Uncommon Bonds: A conflict of sex and gender

The rape, the wedding play, the suicide, the realities of gay marriage, all overstated the harsh conflict between my sex and my gender. I saw no resolution to the dysphoria defined by the person I was and the person reflected in the mirror. Even though my commitment to marriage was accompanied by depression and agitation, it was clearly less threatening than the alternative. Becoming a mother was more desirable than the devastation that accompanied romance.

That choice created a mantle of denial that sustained me through twenty-eight years of marriage and brought to me, three lovely children. In dealing with my gender dysphoria, I used denial in much the same way I used it to cope with the rape. It is a useful coping mechanism when reality fails to offer you meaningful choices.

Chapter Fourteen: We're a Family

I had begun to think that very few things indeed were really impossible. Dad provided me with a powerful template for the provider role. I accepted that role, but I still identified with my mother for her role as caretaker. Assuming my father's role made my female identity substantially less manageable by the additional constraints of a traditional family model. Conversely, there were unexpected opportunities to express my femininity.

The first time I saw Marie was a picture of her presented to me by her mother, a coworker at Sharing Life in the Community (SLIC). She encouraged me to call Marie, but the girl in the picture looked twelve years old, and I never did.

I had recently purchased a mobile home in Emerald Hills Mobile Home Park in Inver Grove Heights. Dad assured me it was a good place to start, with interest rates on auto loans at the time hovering around 17 percent. The economy was still reeling from the OPEC oil embargo, and Reagan was preparing the nation for trickle-down economics.

I was visiting friends in St. Croix Beach on the St. Croix River in Minnesota, when I got a call from Marie in early November of 1980. Presumably, she got the number from her matchmaking mother.

I was instantly enamored by her direct approach. She announced she was coming into town for Brad's funeral. Before I could respond, she asked me if I had a girlfriend.

"No," I replied.

Certainly, Marie was nervous. She apologized for being so direct. I added, "I'm not dating anyone right now," curious to hear more. I learned she had an apartment in South Saint Paul but was currently visiting her mom at their farm in Wisconsin. Brad was a high school friend, and she was coming back to town for the funeral. We agreed to a meeting the next day.

The first time I saw Marie was at her apartment on November 13, 1980. I remember it was the thirteenth because of the superstition surrounding it. For the same reason, I knew it wasn't a Friday. The first thing I'd notice, seeing her from behind, was how great she looked in tight white jeans. For a man that might be a normal twinge of arousal, but for me, it was a subtle twinge of jealousy. These feelings were always uncomfortable.

Applying the yardstick from the future, I could easily measure some major problems right from the start, but the excitement, challenge, and chaos of those early years kept those issues at bay for a long time.

The first thing I discovered at Marie's apartment was her daughter, Jamie. She was extemporaneously shy when I arrived to meet her mom and wouldn't talk to me.

The evening at Wells Fargo Lanes went well. I'm thinking she was drinking a Black Russian. I was drinking beer, still possessed of the idea that beer was a guy thing that somehow made me more masculine. It humors me today to think of some of the ridiculous perceptions I subscribed to. Marie and I had a lot in common, but there were many other things we weren't sharing: things that we would never share.

Jamie had apparently prepared herself while we were out. When we returned to Marie's apartment, she was ready to meet me. Jamie was extremely loquacious and checked off each item on her list as she scrutinized whether I was suitable for her mom. She was barely three. I was instantly infatuated with her inordinate charm.

Following an old episode of the *Twilight Zone,* I excused myself for the evening agreeing to call her. There was no kiss that first date. Marie later told me she was impressed by how reserved I was. Extremely insecure might be more accurate, or nervous or confused as hell.

Outside, a police officer was putting a parking ticket on my car.

Insignificant perhaps, except that the officer apologized. It's the only apology I've gotten from law enforcement, and I responded, "It's okay, I had a really great evening."

I had plans to spend the weekend with LeeAnn's parents at their home overlooking Lake Baraboo in Wisconsin. The first time I called Marie I was asking her to spend the weekend with me. Despite her assertive introduction I never expected her to accept, but she did.

LeeAnn's parents were gracious hosts. No one ever believed our story of how we had just met a week ago. Believing it ourselves was difficult enough.

Saturday night was a beautiful clear autumn evening as we stood above the bluffs. The air was cool and refreshing, and the sun over the lake was settling into the horizon. She slipped her hands between my waist and my jacket, wrapped her arms around me, and rested her head on my shoulder. In a soft low voice, she spoke into my chest, "You don't know what you do to me."

In a low quiet voice, I replied, "I love you."

Young love is such a beautiful thing, so much passion and innocence, so much hope and faith. Marie often smiled in disbelief remembering that moment.

Sunday night we returned to Marie's apartment like any couple returning from a weekend at the lake. There was only one bed for the two of us, and we already knew the sleeping arrangements. Of course, there was exploration, an exchange of emotional passion, and fulfillment of physical desires. I'd be more surprised by that knowledge than you. What I found unusual was the conversation. We talked for hours. Our bed was always the soul of our relationship, pillow talk, the life-blood. Our bed was the chapel of intimacy, a private space sheltered from the prying judgments of the outside world.

That night we talked about skipping a few chapters, as we both had a sense things were moving a little too fast. This was something completely different from anything either of us had known before, so it seemed perfectly acceptable to throw caution to the wind.

In the morning, we were still in bed talking. Jamie dashed into the room and jumped on the bed. She looked at Marie and said, "We're a family right, Mom?"

Marie's eyes opened in clear disbelief. From the expression on her face, I'm certain she thought she was never going to see me again. She hadn't noticed the intense joy radiating through me from the depths of my heart. Jamie had only confirmed what I wanted to believe.

Almost as quickly as Jamie dashed into the room, Marie dashed out, taking Jamie with her to the kitchen, ostensibly to help with the cooking. Three people came together into our extemporaneous family, sharing breakfast together, playing make-believe: something that would continue for twenty-eight years.

Jamie was right though; we were a real family, but like millions of other families, we were not the ideal family. Like millions of other families, we invested too much energy in acting out an ideal that did not belong to us. Societies ideal family ordinance would eventually win out.

Chapter Fifteen: First Family Christmas

Marie and I were living together from the moment we returned from Lake Baraboo. I was moving into their routine. I never felt like an outsider, but also had little responsibility.

I was really in awe of Marie's abilities as a single mother raising a daughter by herself. She was much more mature than the girl I imagined in the high school photograph. She was passionate and compassionate, and she possessed a certain wisdom that only became familiar to me as some of the secrets of our relationship emerged in rather obscure and sometimes unmanageable ways.

Marie and I spent that first couple of months discovering things about each other. Even with all of the things that we couldn't or wouldn't share, we had long conversations. It is difficult to separate sexuality and gender in relationships. It seemed my romantic relationships with men were based on sexual attraction. My relationships with women were based on emotional attraction. It does, for me, explain the difficulty of romantic relationships with women, where they related to me sexually.

It is just as difficult to separate sex from sexuality, sexuality from sensuality, sensuality from sensitivity and sensitivity from sensibility. Like gender, it is a spectrum that is hard to decipher.

During our first phone call, Marie had posed the question, "Are you going with anyone?" I never thought to ask the same question to her. There was another man in Marie's life at the time. I could hardly be jealous, even as I felt disappointment. She identified him as her lawyer. It is true that he was handling her personal injury case from an auto accident. It is also true that she had been to Hawaii with him. I'm not certain about the wisdom or professional ethics of an attorney dating his client, but Hawaii is a pretty romantic destination. I believed her when she explained how she was put off by his aggressiveness. Wasn't it my lack of aggressiveness, after all, that attracted her to me?

She had concerns about Wanda. I told her about the dream and assured her that it was over. Her story was certainly more convincing than mine, but she accepted it. From all that disclosure so early in our relationship, it appeared to be an open and honest relationship. Perhaps there was no way to know what issues might lie below repressed memories.

I don't know exactly how much money Marie got from that insurance settlement, but I know she gave all of it to her mom. To me it seemed odd that she hadn't invested a portion of it in her own daughter and the needs she had as a single mom. Her relationship with money was completely different than mine. A yardstick from the future would measure major problems right from the start.

In a month's time, I had become intimately familiar with the three most indelible themes in our relationship: men, attorneys, and money. A gender-specific mix in my mind.

There is no universal agreement on what actually constitutes feminine qualities. They are often defined as opposite to masculine qualities. There is even less agreement about whether those qualities are genetically innate or culturally constructed. We rely on popular themes from literature and media.

All of the great male heroes of romantic lore are endowed with special characteristics that cloak the masculine core making them acceptable to feminine sensibilities. We want to believe in these fairy tales: the knight in shining armor and the helpless damsel in distress united in everlasting love. I didn't fit that model. In the beginning, my connection with Marie felt like a feminine relationship.

Marie and I first met on a Thursday. Two weeks later we were having Thanksgiving dinner with her parents and younger siblings, all three girls. I thought I knew her mom quite well from working together. Their home did not match my impressions of Marie. The house was in total disarray, overwhelmed with clutter, and desperately in need of cleaning. Marie and I were from completely different cultures despite the incredible bond of some common needs.

We met at a remarkably convenient time for skipping chapters in the natural course of a relationship. It is imperative to random rules of engagement that many seemingly improbable circumstances be present at the same time. This defines the perception that it could never have happened without some type of divine intervention, like star-crossed lovers. Sometimes I've believed as many as six impossible things before breakfast.

Holidays emphasize the differences in family traditions. Our first Christmas together emphasized an independence from family traditions. Ours was an intimate family Christmas, the type one might desire from a holiday meant to bring peace on earth and goodwill to all.

There was a complete universe separating me from the year before when I spent the holiday by myself attempting to bolster my Christmas spirit with a Norfolk Island pine and a few Christmas bulbs. Everything confirmed for me that Christmas was Marie's favorite holiday. It radiated from her excitement and enthusiasm and the beautiful way she decorated the apartment for the season.

The microwave I bought for Marie still sits on my kitchen countertop, outlasting the marriage already by a full six years. Any guy ought to know you don't give appliances for Christmas, birthdays, or any other holiday, especially anniversaries. It's anecdotal, of course. It's not representative of any innate characteristic of masculinity. The simplistic nature of this observation emphasizes something about transgender people that seems fairly universal. We spend an inordinate amount of time pondering the question of gender, considering issues that never engage most people. As a transgender woman, I was constantly struggling to emulate male behavior in all of its subtleties, no matter how absurd they might seem.

As the separation between the sexes increased through puberty, marriage, and parenting, I became increasingly mindful of gender approaching the level of obsession. I had an acute awareness of when I was acting like a "man," and when I was acting like a "girl." The use of "girl" in place of "woman" is deliberate. Females are segmented into attributes. Nowhere does woman hold the same level of completeness as a whole person the way it does for a man. Woman is presented as more respectful than girl, but realistically, the subtleties of any meaningful distinction are lost in the translation.

If memory serves me correctly, Marie gave me dress pants and a shirt. You really can't go wrong buying clothes for a man. Left to my own devices, I'd buy things like velvet baggies and platform shoes. Back then, you could be nearly certain anything I was wearing was probably a Christmas present.

The only thing worse than wearing men's clothes was shopping for them. Fashion is one of the more powerful affirmations of gender in our culture. That, along with hairstyles, creates a clear delineation between the genders that isn't possible strictly on the basis of secondary sex characteristics. Young children especially would be nearly impossible to distinguish if we didn't emphasize gender with specific clothes and hairstyles.

Shopping is also a stereotypical confirmation of gender. Men don't shop. They go to the store and get what they need. Christmas is certainly the shopping season. I have little doubt that men are far less enamored with it than women. I also know that women certainly feel overburdened, at times, by all of the holiday preparation. I certainly do.

Our first Christmas together, I met two more of Marie's sisters. It introduces the most difficult challenge I faced as a transgender woman presenting as a husband. It was easy to present as a man around other men. Men have simple social patterns and focused, task-oriented behaviors, which are easy to replicate. The challenge was understanding how to act like a man around other women.

Marie was a girl, right? She'd have girlfriends, right? Not quite. Marie had sisters. Sisters are in-laws. Sisters have a protective bond. This was particularly true in Marie's family. It wasn't possible for me to share in those female relationships in the same way I had with my sister or my cousin. Lori and Diane provided a connection. They didn't mind including me in their relationships. I could have female relationships with them as friends, sisters, and cousins. As a husband, I couldn't have female relationships with her sisters, and I certainly couldn't have my own girlfriends. That created a growing isolation from the female companionship that I desperately needed. My eventual solution to that dilemma would become a fascinating period of my life that also delayed the inevitable.

I've digressed from the spirit of the season. It will always stand as my most joyous Christmas holiday season, blessed with something we perhaps once thought to be impossible. We were celebrating the true spirit of Christmas as part of a loving family. We were establishing our own tradition, suitable to our own situation, independent of our past.

Chapter Sixteen: My First Child

Jamie brought our family together. She will always be my daughter and my first child. I view parenting as a responsibility, so I have never thought of my children as belonging to me as a right of ownership, but there were unique challenges associated with raising a child who wasn't legally recognized as my child. I wanted to adopt her, but Marie felt it was inappropriate to deny Jamie the experience and knowledge of her birth father.

In the eighties, there was a paranoia sweeping the nation that seriously compromised my parenting relationship with Jamie. I referred to it as the child abuse witch hunts, alluding to the witch trials of Salem Massachusetts in the late 1600's. The media referred to it as ritualized sexual abuse of children or even satanic ritual abuse.

The McMartin Preschool Trial was the most publicized case of childhood sexual abuse. As of 2006, it is the longest and most expensive criminal trial in the history of the United States. Judy Johnson, the mother of a two-and-one-half-year-old boy, reported to the police that Raymond Buckey at the McMartin Preschool in Manhattan Beach, California abused her son. After seven years of criminal trials, no convictions were obtained, and all charges were dropped. The accusations involved hidden tunnels, killing animals, Satan worship, and orgies. The entire property was excavated. Not a single shred of physical evidence was found. Judy Johnson was diagnosed with acute schizophrenia. In 1986, she was found dead in her home from complications of chronic alcoholism. Buckey and his mother, Peggy McMartin, were eventually released without any charges.

Jordan in Scott County, Minnesota was right next door to us. In all, twenty-four adults of this community of 2,700 were arrested and charged. It was sensationalized in the media as the "Jordan Sex Ring." Ultimately, there was only one conviction. It harmed the entire community, everyone viewed with fear and suspicion, wondering who would be next. The term "witch hunt" gradually emerged. There was talk of parents reluctant to bathe or even cuddle their children for fear of being charged with molesting them. These were the same anxieties I felt with Jamie.

Parents were going to jail based on false allegations, the overzealous efforts of prosecutors seeking notoriety, and misguided interrogations by detectives and social workers. Many of these cases were overturned, but the damage inflicted on families and even entire communities is painfully unmistakable. If you have never been falsely accused, you cannot begin to imagine how vulnerable you are. Any perception that innocent people are never charged is completely naive. That's how I began my role as a parent. It was hard enough being a step-father and transgender; living with the fear of reckless allegations of sexual misconduct was unnerving. That anxiety was one of many secrets Marie and I kept from each other, fearful of upsetting domestic tranquility.

I felt vulnerable as a male caring for a female child I wasn't legally related to. Female presentation could also be fatal, easily interpreted as sexual perversion. This wasn't at all like standing at the bottom of the concrete silo. This involved my entire family.

I was as naive about parenting as I had been about sex in my teens. Jamie was already three when I met her. I hadn't experienced the intense mother-child bonding occurring in infancy. From my own observations, fathers share little of that bonding experience. I was intensely aware of the false charges being filed against parents. In some respects, it made it easier to play the father role. I could tell you my adventures–beginning from this morning. I could teach her to ride a bike or fly a kite, but fears of being branded a pedophile isolated her from an affectionate relationship. I'm certain this negatively impacted her self-esteem.

Jamie was aware of my artificial status. Frequently she'd retort, "You can't tell me what to do. You're not my real dad." Even allowing for the innocence of childhood it was painful to hear it. She couldn't possibly realize just how accurate she really was.

Incredibly perhaps, Jamie and I shared some uniquely intimate experiences. She and I traveled by car to visit family and relatives in New Hampshire on two occasions. These trips included stops at Ed's parent's house in NJ. Ed was my roommate freshman year in college. He lived with us for a time, and Jamie was close to him. Ed's mom was an artist. On one of our trips, she created a pencil sketch of Jamie's heartthrob from New Kids on the Block.

In 1986, Marie's Christmas present to me was a pair of airline tickets for Jamie and me to fly to Boston to be with my family. Marie hated surprises, but she loved gift giving and loved to surprise me.

I felt obligated to express excitement, but I was completely stressed by it. The tickets were non-refundable. I knew we couldn't afford them. Just the year before I had taken the Greyhound bus to New Hampshire to avoid the cost of airfare. It wasn't entirely clear to me why she felt Jamie should go with me. I was also scheduled to be on call during the Christmas holiday. Finding someone to work for me was a burdensome request. I did get things arranged, so Jamie and I took off again on another of our great adventures.

Jamie sometimes rode to work with me on the back of my motorcycle when I was a night manager in a mental health care residence. The residents loved her. One in particular always brought out a special doll for Jamie.

Jamie came to me with a costume idea one Halloween. The costume of Frankenstein carrying a girl in a cage won her a trip for two to Florida to be extras in the filming of a Super Boy TV episode. I went with her. It was a great trip but not without its peculiar moments. Ironically, I was the only one who actually appeared in the episode, just the back of my head, sitting on a Kissimmee Courthouse bench. Super Boy was on trial.

We spent two days on the set in Kissimmee. The days were long and boring, but we were treated like special guests. Jamie was her exceedingly shy self, so I had to make arrangements for

Super Boy to create the photo op. I love that photo. She acted all embarrassed, but I know it made her feel special.

Jamie and I shared a room, which felt a little awkward for me. The second night we were there, the adults wanted to go out on the town, so we left Jamie and the only other teenager, David, at the hotel to watch movies. She wasn't too happy about it. When I left that night she followed me to the door, and I turned to kiss her goodbye as if it was Marie and me, rather than mother and daughter. That brief transposition was upsetting, engulfing all of my anxieties about the possibility that anyone might perceive I loved her as anything other than my daughter.

We spent the last day at Universal Studios theme park where Jamie enjoyed her first visit to Hard Rock Cafe.

My relationship with Jamie grew slowly, unpredictably. There were many shifts and challenges to the bonds between us. In fairness, providing for the family left me precious little time to invest in understanding the challenges she faced. She had the unfortunate privilege of providing the experience for young parents. She herself described her condition quite matter-of-factly, "I had a young mom."

Chapter Seventeen: Full Catastrophe Living

In February of 1981, we moved to the mobile home, just three months after I met Marie. I bought the place, after all, in preparation for some future family before I knew that there was going to be a family.

Marie started working as a nurse's aid in the children's burn unit at Saint Paul Ramsey Hospital. It was stressful for her; I know. Saint Paul Ramsey was a teaching hospital, so Marie had a story for me every night about interns poking, prodding, and disturbing the children she was responsible for.

I was still at SLIC working days, while Marie worked evenings. This gave me plenty of time with Jamie and plenty of responsibility as a parent.

It seems odd that I hadn't experienced the same anxiety working with female clients at SLIC. One of the young female clients became infatuated with me. I was terminated for failing to give the client clear and explicit instructions about dating clients. How I perceived my relationship to women conflicted with how others perceived that relationship. These are boundaries not really taught to boys It was an early illustration of the vulnerability men can experience.

I still doubt the legitimacy of the complaint. I had a bachelor's degree, and they were replacing us with master's degrees to upgrade the professional credibility of the organization, competing for tight funding.

I challenged the decision, hoping to secure unemployment benefits. During that process, I agreed to a Minnesota Multiphasic Personality Inventory, which is the most widely used and researched standardized psychometric test of adult personality. My results came back uninterpretable, despite taking it twice. As I understood it, the test had never attempted to define someone like me.

When I told Marie I had been fired, she had her own surprise. She told me she had resigned at the hospital. I didn't want to believe it, but faith in random models of engagement has its benefits. The timing was perfect to attend my sister Lori's wedding in New Hampshire in August. Rather than look for employment, we went on vacation. In hindsight, I believe it was a great decision because the next three years were a grueling test of endurance for both of us.

Mom, Dad, and Sharon had just moved back from St. Louis, but they weren't in their new house yet. The whole weekend took place at the Sheraton Tara in South Nashua. I love weddings, and Lori's wedding was no exception. It was an extravagant affair.

Marie and I traveled to New Hampshire many times over the years. Leaving was always difficult. Often I found myself wishing I had stayed. I've wondered how much different things might have been dealing with my family versus dealing with Marie's family. I wonder how my gender expression would have developed living in close proximity to my own family. It's useless speculation, of course. In the model of random engagement, it simply didn't happen that way, and probably wouldn't prevent the issue from coming to a full boil when the time was right.

I was facing two to four years of school for a master's or doctorate in psychology, more internships, and jobs that would be less attractive than what I had at SLIC. With a family to support, I decided to change careers and registered for computer programming classes at Brown Institute in Minneapolis. I also found a job with People, Inc. as a night manager at a residential care facility for mental health clients.

I worked full-time nights and attended school full-time days. It was only a nine-month course, but jobs were scarce when I graduated, and I returned to the University of Minnesota to earn my degree in computer science. Three years I maintained that schedule. I never slept. I took naps, often times in a chair at the library between classes. It was hard for Marie, waking me at night to go to work.

Marie and I saw little of each other. When Marie returned to work, Jamie often ended up alone in the house while I slept. Marie took classes at the Minnesota School of Bartending. She found her first position at Toner's Bar and Grill in Saint Paul, not too far from where I worked.

After she finished her shift, she'd stop by with coffee and donuts for me. It was thoughtful of her, but I became horribly dependent on it. I was intensely aware of it and fearful of it because of how my mother had responded to my father's own emotional dependence on her. Managing that dependency would be my biggest challenge. It goes back to the idea of how to act like a man around a woman, especially when that woman is your wife. This is one of those complications I had not anticipated.

I had few male friends and little interest in most of the things we did. It was hard to have any kind of an emotional connection. Even with the aid of alcohol, there was only a superficial sense of emotional connection.

In the midst of all that chaos, emerged one of our longest standing traditions, Halloween costumes. Marie dressed up as a biker dude on Halloween. Not a soul recognized her with the long hair and full beard. I have to say except for the beer belly, I found her rather attractive. I never told her that. If I had, I'd just be playing a part, even if the feeling was authentic. I played that part the next night when I was a female cop with a biker as my prisoner. We attended a Halloween contest at Peabody's, a huge cowboy bar with a mechanical bull. It wasn't exactly the type of relationship I'd romanticize about. It felt quite strange at first, but I embraced it anyway, feeling a certain degree of authenticity.

First prize for best costume was $1000. That kind of money and the costumes we saw that night sparked a creative note in both of us. The following year, we had our own first place costume, the infamous Aquarium Lady which won thousands of dollars over the years. Wearing a complex costume can be uncomfortable and making it come to life can be difficult. You have to visualize what people are seeing when you can't see it yourself. It's a performance, something both Marie and I were exceptionally good at.

Chapter Eighteen: The Proposal

In the early eighties, transgender people in Minnesota gained political recognition within the gay civil rights movement.

Anita Bryant is leading the charge to repeal gay civil rights. The campaign, Save Our Children, like so many morality crusades, created hysteria about the safety of our children. Jerry Falwell is organizing the Moral Majority which marks the first major inclusion of religious organizations in political organizing.

Transgender issues remained largely invisible to the general public. People called the police. I was questioned multiple times by the police for wearing a dress. Creating an imaginary threat against children has always been a popular tactic among the denizens of moral persecution and sexual abstinence. Transgender women are vulnerable to it. It's not paranoia: I've been accused of being a pedophile.

Even in 2015, the Child Protection League resorted to this tactic when the Minnesota High School League adopted a policy that would allow transgender girls to play on teams with other girls. The Child Protection League ran a full-page ad in major Minnesota newspapers depicting a locker room shower asking parents if they were okay with a male showering with their fourteen-year-old girls. There is the suggestion that the policy would allow adult male predators into the locker rooms of teenage girls. The imagery is effective because of a cruel cultural double standard that makes girls responsible for chastity while allowing that boys simply have no control over their behavior.

It didn't seem like it at the time, but wearing dresses in public was for me, not all that infrequent. Marie's mom gave me dresses,

I can think of half a dozen different outfits. I know I wore them more than once. As Robin Williams once said. "If you've worn a dress more than once you have to admit you enjoy it." Marie was generally supportive. She once took me dress shopping for my birthday, sometimes bought me lingerie on Valentine's Day, and even accompanied me in public on multiple occasions.

Dresses weren't my only form of feminine expression. With my legs, I was easily enticed by hot legs contests and bikini contests. It seemed quite dull and stupid for life to go on in the common way. Marie was always in attendance if I competed in hot legs or bikini contests though at times kept a discreet distance as if she wasn't really with me. She worried about someone assaulting me. These contests were a pressure relief for me, allowing me to feel a little like part of the female gender. People accepted it as theatrical, much like drag performance, I suppose. It was all in good fun, and I never challenged the idea, so naturally, no one ever knew how I really felt about the opportunity for this emotionally intimate experience with other girls.

In dozens of times I dressed or participated in girl contests I never felt threatened. Only once was I ever assaulted. I'd like to leave out this story too, but it does emphasize the range of intense emotional conflict that develops the perspicacity of transgender women.

Hawaiian Tropic sponsored a series of bikini contests looking for hot models for their promotions. Few women could compete with advertising's imagery of beach body models. If you're not a beach body model, you rely on personality.

Promoters were never quite certain how to deal with me in a bikini contest. These contests were really just a free show for the guys. In this particular case, they created a special category for me, so I was first in my category.

These contests were held in bars. I never felt any need for liquid courage, feeling totally liberated by the experience. It remained an important part of the performance to have a few drinks, as a social justification. This evening was extreme. When you're the center of attention and people are buying you drinks, it is easy to get carried away. In fact, posing as female for attention was a popular allegation I never challenged either.

We were there until closing time. When the bar closed, they directed everyone out of a side entrance. I was out in the parking lot with no idea where Marie was, or the car.

Not having taken the time to change, I am still wearing a bikini, standing in a parking lot, completely lost, talking to four or five other women. To complete the absurdity of this scene I have balloons cascading above my shoulders. The girls are concerned about me, and they are talking about taking me home with them when suddenly a fist connects with the side of my face and knocks me out. Certainly not a fair fight. I never saw it coming.

I could claim I was attacked for being transgender with a certain amount of validity since I'd not have been there otherwise. That would be absurd under the circumstances. I had engaged myself in the middle of a love affair, talking to his girlfriend. It was an aggressive act driven by anger, jealousy, and emotional dependence. I was fearful about how his girlfriend might become a subject of that aggression along with me. She was powerless to assist me after the assault.

Women are far too familiar with these situations. There are major differences between a group of girls standing together on a stage in bikinis in front of a packed bar and being at the beach with a couple of girlfriends. There was a certain camaraderie in the knowledge we were doing something good girls don't. There is a complex mix of feelings: vulnerability, excitement, defiance. Sharing those feelings with other girls felt natural. During this moment, the unifying force of those emotions was completely independent of our birth records. It is the quintessential example of why it is so difficult to explain the transgender experience to someone who has only known one gender.

The next day I'd go to work displaying my battle scars, leaving out the part about the bikini. The other girls would still be girls. These insights developed slowly over a long period of time.

The assault increased Marie's fear and anxiety. She'd gradually come to focus on my female gender presentation as the primary cause of her anxiety, but if it was that simple I wouldn't be telling this story. My transgender identity would eventually take center stage in Minnesota's First Judicial District Court.

It was risky behavior which conflicted with my anxiety about the child abuse witch hunts that were also going on at the time. Public appearances helped to legitimize it for me, minimizing the threat of an undisclosed secret. I was careful to associate the dressing with events or performances, in essence portraying it as costuming in a way that would be socially acceptable as entertainment. There was always the suggestion that it was the only time. Getting caught in a social faux pas seemed much safer than being discovered in private wearing a bra or panties, though I never actually wore panties. I preferred bikini swimsuit bottoms.

I also kept a clear distance from children, playgrounds, and childcare centers. I feel an intense empathy for one of my good friends who is a transgender man when he talks about having to maintain greater distance with children. Still, he is happy about being a father. I'm certain it's a common anxiety for men, an unfortunate loss for our children, and a threat to core family values.

I finished school nearly four years into our relationship which seemed like a good time to ask Marie to marry me. I was wearing a dress when I proposed to Marie, knowing it would make the proposal memorable. I sewed the dress myself.

I proposed to her at the Italian Pie Shoppe, in Eagan. That may not seem horribly romantic, but it had special significance in our relationship.

The restrooms were identified as the Library for men and the Powder Room for girls. Removing the D from powder created POWER. I gave the D to Marie. Marie called me her Letter Man, not the most enviable super-power but a super-hero just the same.

When I later went to return the D, it had already been replaced. With two doors, one marked for Knowledge and one marked for Power, where were the girls suppose to go? I was excited about the strong women's movement during the late sixties and early seventies. I wanted equity in my relationship with Marie that did not exist in my parent's marriage.

We had a church wedding. Jamie was the flower girl. It was a beautiful wedding followed by a horse-drawn carriage ride through the countryside with a reception at my uncle's farm, but it definitely wasn't a traditional wedding. Nearly all of the guests were from my friends and family. The matron of honor was Marie's younger sister, Tony. The other two were my sister, Sharon, and a friend of mine. It was a conspicuous reminder of the fact that Marie didn't have girlfriends.

Marie's sister had a beautiful singing voice. She was invited to sing a solo. Her accompaniment missed the dress rehearsal and was late for the wedding, so Tony was nervous. Tony burst into tears at the beginning of her solo, and nobody knew what to do. I finally walked over to her, and brought her back to complete the ceremony. It was the most touching part of the entire wedding.

It was a beautiful wedding, despite the low cost. I sewed all of the bridesmaid's dresses, Jamie's flower girl dress, and Marie's wedding dress. I gave Marie everything I wanted, including the dress. It was awkward really. When relatives discovered I sewed the dress, they were more interested in the construction of the dress than the bride.

Marie later told me she disliked the wedding and wanted a Las Vegas wedding. It was common to learn these things after the fact. She'd made her point by spending much of the day with the groomsmen at a strip club called the Belmont in Saint Paul. They never made an appearance at the reception. Marie knew what pleased the men.

I was hurt and uncertain about what to share with guests. Little did I realize how much that would be a trademark of our relationship, or what significance it had. We spent the night at a historic bed and breakfast in Hastings. We didn't drink the complimentary wine, and there wasn't any sex. We'd made it through the motions, and I suppose we were both glad to be done with it.

There was never a wedding album, though I do still love the photo of Marie and I standing next to the horse and carriage. It captures all of the things I want to remember about the relationship: all of the good intentions, the love, and the commitment.

There is one other photo in my personal wedding album. Friends and relatives spent the evening before the wedding at a motel in neighboring Cannon Falls. At the church the next day there was no bride. She and my sister Sharon, one of the bridesmaids, were still back at the hotel. When we got back to the hotel to retrieve the bride, Marie and Sharon were sitting on their suitcases in front of the hotel wearing dark sunglasses, looking every bit as independent as Thelma and Louise. I recall that Louise shoots and kills Thelma's attacker. This is where a man might start thinking he needs more to offer than an apology. Hell hath no fury like a woman scorned.

Love is certainly the capacity to care for someone and commit to them, but it doesn't guarantee us the ability. I have no reservations about the love that existed between Marie and me. What I failed to recognize and later accommodated with denial was the intense fear that existed between us. The power of raw female emotion is the antithesis of female innocence. I suspect it's what men fear most.

Marie and I struggled with difficult issues during our years together. The love and the commitment did not fail us. It remained steadfast to the end. We were overwhelmed by our vulnerability. The shroud of secrecy about past traumas, intended to protect us from the harsh social judgments, left us defenseless when the mechanisms of social management decided to intervene according to their own standards of an appropriate family model.

Chapter Nineteen: Like Father, Like Son

The wedding did little to legitimize our unique little family. What changed in 1984 was my career. In early December, I was requesting time off from my night manager post at Central Manor to visit my family in New Hampshire over Christmas. They refused to grant the time off. Next day I filled out an application at a company named Comten that manufactured specialized computers for communications. The company was the principal competitor of IBM in the area of communications. I had two interviews and an offer the same day. In two years of job applications, it is the only interview I'd had.

Thinking back to a young girl sitting next to her Daddy on the way to another boring meeting of the Rod and Gun Club, I realize how much I loved my father, but what I wanted was a man like my father. Isn't that what every girl wants at some point in her life.

I also had resentments toward my father. The family adjusted to his needs as a provider. None of us ever had a voice in the choices he made about where we lived, went to church and school, what activities we engaged in, and where we went on vacation. His involvement with the family was often superficial, and it was always abiding by his plan. It was exceedingly difficult for me to establish new female relationships after each move.

When I choose to marry Marie, I chose to be a husband. I chose to be a father. The matter of choice is endemic to any discussion about transgender. Who else would say I chose to be a man or I chose to be a woman? The most conspicuous attribute of a transgender person is a realization that such a choice exists. Transgender people are mystified by the majority's immutable understanding of sex and gender.

Marie chose to be a mom. She had been a single mom for three years by the time I met her. She was confident and determined. My relationship with Marie created options that neither of us thought possible in the beginning. Those opportunities would move us further and further apart.

I love Marie. Love is a word like transgender. It has so many uses it ceases to have meaning without further context. Men love football. As a child, I remember well, Thanksgiving with the men in front of the TV watching the Green Bay Packers. Who remembers Vince Lombardi and Bart Starr, my only real memory of football's greatest heroes. My sister Sharon was born in Wisconsin, and she is proud of that distinction within the family. Sharon loves the Green Bay Packers. You might just as well say, "I breathe when I sleep is the same thing as I sleep when I breathe!"

Marie hated the word as much as I hate football. I regret that it took so many years for me to understand why. In my television view of the world, I was convinced that these are the words a woman wants to hear from a man. For Marie, the language of love wasn't founded in words.

When I took the job at Comten I also secured my role as the provider in the image of the most important male role model I ever knew, my father. Just as my father had given up teaching to become an engineer I left psychology to become an IT professional because it was a financially advantageous decision. I never wanted to be like my father.

My father totally dominated the conversation at the dinner table talking about his day at work. Nobody had any idea what he was talking about. Mother frequently lamented that obvious fact. I took the opposite approach. I did not talk about my job at all. That left Marie completely incapable of relating to the most consuming part of my life.

I gravitated toward roles of individual responsibility consistent with the belief that there was no one else like me. There was only one other person dedicated to mainframe support.

In 1984 when I started at Comten, the US was at the beginning of another severe economic recession resulting in multiple waves of layoffs. Surviving those layoffs was a serious testament to the kind of talent that remained.

One of those layoffs involved my associate in the mainframe support. His departure created a serious challenge for me. It wasn't allowable for me to withdraw from any challenge. To do so would threaten my masculine presentation. It was exactly what my father would have done.

Assuming support for both systems literally doubled my workload. The first month after my associate's departure I was chosen as the employee of the month. I earned it. I recognized my value to the company, but it left me with little sense of security. As it would be for any woman, it was difficult to realize the benefits of the old boy network.

My new position at Comten also doubled my income. It created a fundamental shift in the equity of my marriage. In choosing to be a man, I wasn't defining my gender, I was choosing a role, a role in which I could never feel comfortable. Being a mother came naturally to me but also presented a uniquely different set of challenges.

Some women want careers. They want the freedom, the sense of individual accomplishment, and economic independence that is readily granted to men. Other women want to be mothers: nurturing members of the family and community. For many women, it is a common reality that they will end up being both. It seems they arrive at that point without much prior forethought in much the same way that I became a full time working mother.

Part VI: Married Life: Where love challenges reality

In our chronological view of life we think of young couples falling in love; over time the passion fades; the problems intensify; they gradually grow apart, and in half of all marriages they divorce. I see the world differently. In my view, most couples are incompatible from the start, drawn together by circumstance, chemistry, and social order. If there are a supportive family, community, and culture, successful couples will overcome those incompatibilities and develop mutually beneficial relationships. It suggests why arranged marriages may outlast romantic relationships.

In the beginning, Marie and I had that opportunity, despite some obvious incompatibilities. We came together from mutual backgrounds of intense isolation and failed relationships. Not exactly an arranged marriage, but certainly, Marie's mom brought us together. There was safety in the relationship that we both cherished.

Whimsically, I sometimes likened our relationship to the Island of Misfit Toys where an abandoned elf aspires to become a dentist in a world that doesn't allow elves to be dentists. I had an unfailing belief that we could overcome any obstacle in a world that denied us entry to the concert hall of social norms.

Despite the depth of our commitment and the intensity of our effort, we never overcame a fundamental reality that persisted. I wasn't the man Marie wanted. Truth be told, she wasn't the man I wanted either. Beneath the heteronormative perception of our relationship, existed a female relationship that neither of us could reconcile. There was an intense competition of female desires. Still, it was not the most difficult challenge we faced.

Chapter Twenty: Transgender Sexuality

"Tut, tut, child!" said the Duchess. "Everything's got a moral, if only you can find it."

– Lewis Carroll, Alice in Wonderland

If I could think of one thing that truly captured all of Marie's heart and imagination, it was a horse. I'd not be able to count the number of times she shared her story about summer camp caring for the horses. It fascinated me too that each time she told the story, she recounted her experience with a Stillwater prison inmate there on work release to help care for the camp horses. He had indigenous heritage and his stature must have been pretty imposing. That Marie wasn't intimidated by him must be a testament to their mutual love of horses. Naturally, I wanted to give Marie a horse. If I had, I'd be telling a different story.

One year after Marie and I were married, the new Canterbury Downs horse racing track opened in Shakopee, just twenty minutes from our home. We were there! Where else would we be? Marie loved horses, and she loved horse racing.

There was an opening day promotion which included a tour of the stables: something Marie was excited about. We went early to participate in the promotion. We were too early, much too early. Discovering that the gates wouldn't open for several hours, we opted to go into Shakopee for a cocktail and come back later. Upon our return, we found a long line of cars at a total stand-still. Unable to get into the park, we pulled off into a wooded area where we remained during the event.

I imagine two women at Churchill Downs for the Kentucky Derby in fine outfits lavishly accessorized with large, elaborate hats, sipping Mint Juleps." Now, imagine two young lovers in a small grove of trees outside the gates of Canterbury Downs sitting on a blanket sipping peach schnapps. The race announcer is barely audible in the background; a helicopter is hovering over-head; a bright red blanket is highly visible amongst the small grove of trees. A lack of inhibition, the gentleness of a warm sunny day, the intimacy of the moment combined to create an erotic sexual encounter filled with passion, reckless abandon, and defiance.

A passionate romantic encounter suddenly seems quite inap-propriate when a police officer arrives. To our favor, the police were probably busy doing crowd control and I am happy to report they never showed up for our private affair. There will be many police encounters in this story but this day wouldn't be one of them

Sexuality is a perfect target for disciplinary models of power and control. We learn how our bodies, actions, and behaviors make us into certain types of people. Individuals generally inter-nalize those values and adapt themselves to fit the model. The gay struggle against sexual oppression eventually resolved into a fight for civil rights. No longer are they supporting the diversity of sex-ual expression but simply the identity of being "gay." The notion denies the fluid boundaries of sexuality. A woman may perceive herself as heterosexual, attracted to men, but few women are attracted to all men. Sexuality is bounded by many factors other than one's physical sex.

The transgender movement has been guided down the same path, claiming a "gender identity", theorizing a "female brain," rather than supporting the diversity of gender expression. The gender queer movement takes the opposite extreme that there is no biological basis for gender. Either position is problematic because of the infinite array of law and policy around protection and support, totally segregated by sex.

Transgender 101 always emphasizes the idea that your sex is physical characteristics and your gender is cognitive (intellect, emotions, behaviors). Sex and gender are not the same things.

The analogy, "a woman trapped in a man's body," may improve understanding of transgender people but it's an oversimplifica-tion. In another way, a rather trite observation. If we didn't have sex could we still have gender? Would some people be more feminine and some people more masculine if everyone was the same sex? Who would ponder such a question in the first place?

The confusion comes from attempting to correlate sexuality and gender to physical sex. Physical sex is a highly bi-modal distribution, whereas sexuality and gender exist on a broad continuum. Physical sex is tightly linked to genetics, whereas sexuality and gender are far more susceptible to environmental influences.

Sexual fidelity is one of the type characteristics for "marriage" or "monogamous relationship" Sexual fidelity is proof of one's commitment. Forgiveness of sexual infidelity is also proof of one's commitment. Strangely, sex in a relationship generally outlasts the commitment. Marie frequently reminded me of my sexual infidelity though I will never know to what she was referring. It was always punctuated with the opposing assertion that she had never been unfaithful. I accepted that, though I certainly had ample evidence to believe otherwise.

Marie and I had an intensely intimate and sexual relationship for many years. Sexuality for a transgender or intersex individual can be extremely difficult. I assumed, naturally enough, that Marie really enjoyed sex. It never occurred to me that she too might be playing a role, just as I was. I wanted to please her. It is equally true that she wanted to please me, even if we might have differing motives. The underlying expectations were never communicated. Everything's got a moral if only you can find it. Neither of us was willing to acknowledge the fear and anxiety that existed between us. Isn't sex a healthy part of any successful marriage. It was exciting. It was fun. It was physical. It was lacking in most of the communication and emotional connection necessary for healthy sexual relationships.

Two more years after opening day at Canterbury Downs I was suggesting to Marie that I was going to get her a horse. We started looking at properties around our home in Inver Grove Heights. Moving wasn't an option for me. The one time I considered it, Marie told me I'd be going by myself.

In 1987, Eagan was still a rural community, but land prices were already rising sharply due to urban expansion. Many places with enough land had a dwelling that was uninhabitable. We couldn't afford to buy land and build a house.

Then we discovered a place in the southeastern corner of Eagan with one and one-half acres of land on a wooded lot surrounded by parkland. The previous renter had boarded her horse there, and the property was zoned agricultural. The next door neighbors had three horses. The house was definitely no palace as I've previously described it, but it was livable. If I had my yardstick from the future I'd have known that the visual disintegration of the property suggested other problems that were not visible. None of that really mattered. It was a great place to have a horse.

Somehow, getting a horse seemed reasonable at the time. Jamie was already ten years old, and Marie didn't seem interested in another child. I was already feeling somewhat inadequate to the task of providing for our family with just the three of us. Had I applied the same logic to caring for a horse, I'd have had a more sensible perspective. In time, Marie would make the case that I never wanted children. To me, it was the other way around. That again emphasizes the lack of communication about significant issues.

Given the questionable nature of our intention and my naive perceptions of the condition, the house actually was a good investment. It was fundamentally a well-built house that could probably withstand gale force winds. It had beautiful hardwood flooring and lovely brick fireplaces on both floors. The kitchen was large with plenty of cupboard space. Finally, there was the yard. The Oak Pond neighborhood in Eagan was a mini ecosystem with a wide range of birds including great horned owls. Other wildlife included deer, raccoon, and fox, including one sighting of a silver fox.

Finally, there was one groundhog. I started many a morning sipping my coffee staring out the window, watching him foraging in the backyard. After many years of watching that groundhog, it finally became apparent that he was a female with seven pups following after her. That memory of him makes me smile.

Marie was passionate about her sexuality and very creative. She liked Anne Rice, and suggested soft porn titles for us to watch. Lusty pornographic prose is better suited to fiction than it is here in the context of this story but my most sensual image of Marie appeared outdoors one cold winter night in January.

This encounter was a far more private and intimate affair, not beneath the starlit night sky but snug inside an Igloo. Never has Marie looked so beautiful and so sexy as she did with the camera lens peering through the tunnel entrance of the Igloo at a woman smiling softly, lying beneath a snow background, partially wrapped in a fur blanket. The soft intimacy of a cold winter night struck in bold contrast to the raw passion of a hot summer day.

Chapter Twenty-one: Infidelity

The housing market was weak in the early eighties with mortgage rates peaking around 15 percent, but by 1987, rates had dipped below 8 percent. When we signed the purchase agreement that spring, the rate was 7.78 percent with zero points. This is where Marie's sixth sister enters the story.

Marie's sister, Randi was returning from Hawaii, and she was staying with us. Marie had encouraged her to go there several years earlier. Having left rather suddenly, it was Marie and I that cleaned out her apartment and her belongings were still stored away in our shed.

What I thought would be a short-term visit became an entire summer of revelry. In the 17th century, French philosopher, René Descartes advanced a philosophical proof of existence. That summer, René Descartes' simple proof, "I think, therefore I am," was transformed into a more observable form of existence; "I am, therefore I party." It's the oldest rule in the book. The crest of alcohol abuse became several broken bottles of St Pauli Girl left in the freezer too long. Presenting as a man around other men was never difficult. Men are exceedingly task oriented. Their goals are invariably defined in terms of task completion whether it be fixing a faucet or sending a man to the moon. Women's lives are infinitely more complicated by the fact that they nurture the family, community and social infrastructure that allows men to focus on their tasks.

Perhaps Descartes could have postulated a proof about gender with "I stand on the moon, therefore I am male." It would be punctuated by the first woman in space, Sharon Christa Corrigan

McAuliffe, a teacher from Concord, New Hampshire, who was killed tragically in a cataclysmic failure of man's technology when the space shuttle Challenger exploded seventy-three seconds after launch.

There will be an instantaneous rebuttal from knowledgeable experts who will point out that Sally Ride was the first woman in space, proceeding Ms. McAuliffe's flight by nearly two years. Others will point out that Russian Cosmonaut, Valentina Vladimirovna Tereshkova was actually the first woman in space, preceding Sally Ride by nearly two decades.

The rebuttal underscores the fundamental fallacy of defining men and women according to some rudimentary examination of body parts. Sally Ride was performing in a distinctly male role. She has in fact been lauded for her composure, "a competent engineer who was cool under stress." I'm half expecting the caveat "for a woman." Her entry into an exclusively male domain is applauded as continuing proof of the gender equity in our society.

Christa McAuliffe, on the other hand, was performing in a traditionally feminine role. She was in fact chosen for her well-rounded appeal, "the perfect woman." NASA Psychiatrist, Dr. Terrence McGuire, told New Woman magazine, "In my opinion, she was the most broad-based, best-balanced person of the ten." Her participation emphasizes the value of women's roles in our society but she was not applauded as continuing proof of the gender equity in our society.

I don't wish to minimize the role that all of these women played toward inspiring girls to pursue ambitious goals or participate in traditionally masculine pursuits. I'd, however, argue that women don't feel profoundly enlightened by the idea that a woman can do a man's job. Women might prefer to see some legitimate proof that a man can do a woman's job.

The traditional roles of women are increasingly capitalized at an economic level far below the prevailing standard of living. In many ways, examining gender in the context of wealth or technological accomplishments is a rather trivial pursuit. Patriarchal models of power and control have minimized the essential role of women in creating civilized societies. It is difficult to make convincing arguments that maximizing profits has had positive impact on the social and emotional health of our nation.

Classifying and categorizing are essential elements of developing public policy and creating a nation-state. It allows for strategies of disciplinary rules and population management that define who is part of the protected class, who represents a potential threat or drain on the state, and who should be entitled to benefits or protections.

Transgender people have never been classified by our society. There is no checkbox for us on the US census. There is no consensus on how many transgender people exist or what social norms they should conform to. Transgender women have frequently been classified as men with sexually inappropriate behavior. From this perspective trans women had a common purpose with the early gay rights movement because, at the start, the movement was challenging societies right to murder us, beat us, or imprison us because of our sexuality. In the extreme case, fundamentalist groups and politicians seek to classify transgender women as sexual predators, dressing up to prey on innocent children.

Transgender women are still widely associated with the female impersonation of drag queen performers. I myself have been classified in therapy notes and medical records as a cross-dresser. Even if not perceived as a social threat, it would later have major consequences according to the legal and psychiatric perceptions of how it impacted family values. Societies model family ordinance did not allow for a transgender woman to be a mother.

The summer of 1987, became the first major challenge to my assumed presentation as husband and father. It was the first threat to our marriage..

Four years of full time working nights and full-time days going to school couldn't hold a candle to the exhausting schedule of working full-time day's and partying full-time nights. Though I tried, for a time at least, I couldn't keep up with their party schedule. I started feeling intensely isolated. Marie didn't object if I joined them, but I was never invited. Often times I didn't know where they were. I worried about how it was impacting Jamie when picking her up from various locations. I felt overwhelmed by the responsibility.

At times I felt intensely minimized. Imagine a man coming home drunk in the middle of the night, smelling like the bottom of an old whiskey barrel having sex with his wife while she's barely awake. That's how I felt, knowing too that I'd have to get up for work in a couple of hours. I didn't complain. I accepted it as part of my commitment to our marriage. One therapist would later make light of it with a remark about how lucky I was to be "getting it at all."

There was a growing sense of resentment while balancing the checkbook, clearing checks from places I'd never heard of, seeing the enormous cost of their nightly escapades. Daily I checked the mortgage rates watching them gradually creeping upward, recognizing the hopes of home ownership fading away. I recall asking Marie if she wanted to party or buy the house but her response lacked any commitment. I was alone.

Eventually, there was another offer on the house. Any sane person would have backed out at that point but a sense of commitment and a sense of denial made it impossible for me. I dropped the contingency in our offer, committing a deposit that we could scarcely afford to lose.

Marie was a man magnet. She was beautiful, blond, and socially aggressive. She was also elusive which can make a woman attractive prey. There was a certain safety in my presence making her unavailable, and she always made it clear that she was with me. I was drawn between the protective husband and the overly possessive male. Playing those roles, I was constantly assessing my presentation.

A different problem arose when she was not with me. A total test of insecurity came one night around three in the morning when I got a call from Marie. She wanted me to come and get her. She and Randi had gone home with a couple of guys. She was regretting it and she wanted me to rescue her. Resentment and relief battled each other in my mind. She wasn't exactly sure where she was. At 3:30 in the morning I was wandering around some neighborhood in Saint Paul peering in windows trying to locate them. Commitment was morphing into responsibility. I have to remind readers, this was before cell phones. Marie often reminded me that she never cheated on me. I always wondered what she meant exactly.

Relief came one day in the form of a man who started dating Randi. Greg was a real man, the kind of man Marie wanted. I know that. He was exactly the kind of man I wanted too. It changed the whole dynamic. No longer was I the intrusive spouse, imposing on Marie's relationship with her sister. I was a partner again, no longer the third wheel. Randi was spending more time with Greg and I was seeing more of Marie. There was an immediate relief to our budget.

Towards the end of the summer, Randi returned to Hawaii. That's not the final note but it was an important transition. Marie and I closed on the house. The financial consequences were painful.. The adjustable-rate mortgage would increase 1 percent a year for two more years going to 11.5 percent. The emotional debit, however, would never be paid back.

The closing took place at a law office on Hwy 52 in Hastings. I remember it as a happy day for the two us. As we were leaving the parking lot a car backed out into the side of our car. With literary license, I could offer it as a foreshadowing of a looming disaster. In truth, it is simply an irrelevant detail that can occur in any story.

Chapter Twenty-two: Common Ground

"No, I give up," Alice replied. "What's the answer?" "I haven't the slightest idea," said the Hatter.

-Lewis Carroll, Alice in Wonderland

From the beginning the house had a life of its own. Perhaps it is true of all old houses shrouding a mystery of an unknown past, tempting us with the promise of delightful future. The house wasn't merely a setting for the story; it entwined with the lives of its inhabitants helping to craft the story.

It was a difficult transition for Jamie. She lost all of her neighborhood friends. Her life became rather sedentary, and she put on weight. Still charming, but not the slender active girl she had been at the trailer park. I'd broken my rule about moving.

After Randi went back to Hawaii, things settled into a fairly workable routine. Greg actually came to stay with us for a while. It was comforting to have him there though there was some jealousy over all the time Marie and Greg were out together.

In our new home, Marie and I discovered another common interest. She was a pyro. She laid proud claim to starting her parents' home on fire and once burning down a boy friend's couch.

For several years we attended conventions of the Pyro Techniques Guild International in Fargo North Dakota and Appleton, Wisconsin. Our yard was perfect for bonfires. There was plenty of wood. There was the definite feeling of being out in the woods. Some years it was emphasized by an abundance of mosquitoes but the night was usually accented with the lovely twinkle of fire flies. After we got the spa, hot tub parties and bonfires were a common social event for a number of years.

Marie started working at the Minneapolis International Airport as a bartender, a goal she had pursued since the time she attended bartending school. I loved to visit her there just to see her work. My visits to the airport replaced the time when she came to have lunch with me while working at Central Manor.

It was impressive how well she controlled the space and engaged the customers. She enjoyed talking about her work, giving us some connection, but working evenings and weekends left us little time together. She was often out with her friends after work. Still I enjoyed her friends from the airport. It was for a brief time like having girl friends again.

That first year the house placed overwhelming demands on my time. There was clogged plumbing, broken appliances, a leaking water heater and the old oil burning furnace that went the first year. A small explosion convinced me it was time for a replacement.

I remember listening to Otto Titsling from the Beeches sound track by Bette Midler a thousand times. Jamie loved that song and that was how she choose to memorize it. We were still ten years away from our first home computer, mobile phones were the size of a small suitcase, even the CD she was listening to was new to the music industry.

Jamie and I were also brought together by another mysterious connection. I had an inexplicable sense that there was something fundamentally different living in that house. Jamie and I discovered it together though we might never come to understand it.

The first time it happened was very frightening. One evening Marie simply disappeared. Jamie and I started looking for her. We searched the whole house and called out for her but there was no answer. I was confused and worried. We finally located her tucked tightly into the very corner of one of the bedroom closets completely surrounded by boxes and pillows. It was difficult persuading her to retreat from her hiding place.

Before long Marie took to leaving the house suddenly, usually late at night. I never understood why she left, where she was going or when she would be back; or even if she would be back. I felt a sense of compassion wanting desperately to know what she was experiencing, but I also feared engaging the topic. Soon she was seeing a therapist. It was for many years her private side of our relationship. Beside the occasional disappearances everything else seemed pretty normal.

Barely more than a year after we moved into our new home, during a freezing rain, Marie sustained a whiplash when she was rear ended in a car accident on the Lafayette bridge in St Paul. I'd like to tell you it was just an irrelevant detail that can happen in any story but it's not. This is the chronological time frame of the event. The full significance comes later.

Then one day around Easter time in the spring of 1989 I received a small card from Marie. She handed it to me after we sat down on the floor next to the coffee table in our living room. It was a rare intimate moment. Outside of our pillow talk we never had each other's undivided attention. I remember a cute baby chick on the cover which was appropriate to the season but it wasn't an Easter card. The message was simple, "We're pregnant."

I'm not certain how a man would respond to that since I never heard it in male conversation. I passed through at least a half a dozen emotional states before I actually had a conscious thought. The lack of response wasn't reassuring. I must have hesitated a long time. It is the nature of shock: time passes that you're unaware of.

Even after I regained consciousness I had to assess how a man should react. Acting like a man during an intensely female situation like this was exceedingly difficult. It dramatizes the internal conflict that I hadn't anticipated. It was totally opposite when Sue asked me to take her to New York. That felt like a shared experience. I could be honest about how I was feeling. There was no role to play.

It was totally unexpected. Marie hadn't told me that she stopped taking birth control, believing it was no longer possible to become pregnant. The explanation held little comfort knowing it couldn't be shared with me. I also was the last person to know about the pregnancy.

"We're pregnant" is supposed to denote a shared experience. I have a sense the whole concept is completely lost on most men. I wanted desperately to feel like part of the experience but the circumstances left me with a profound sense that she was pregnant and I wasn't. I couldn't acknowledge that even to myself. I was jealous. I was anxious as well. I was already feeling overwhelmed and a baby would be an added level of responsibility. It emphasized the separation of roles. It did not bring me closer to Marie or her experience.

Recalling all the men in my life that never were; I remember the excitement, the desire, the longing in my heart and the pain in my soul watching each of them pass in and out of my life. Acting like a man around other men was easy. What was impossible was acting like a woman. Be it a single night together passing through the Ozarks or an entire summer as roommates I couldn't share these desires. Maybe they knew that. Maybe I didn't conceal it so well. What's the answer? I haven't the slightest idea. I could only deny it. To do otherwise would leave me vulnerable. I couldn't allow myself to feel vulnerable or trust in my own desires. I had been taught that lesson only too well.

I begin to realize that perhaps I wasn't the only one who understood that lesson. Perhaps Marie and I had something else in common: presenting a well rehearsed role to protect a vulnerable soul.

Part VII: Motherhood: A woman's transition

When a woman has children, she becomes a mom. If she has a husband, he becomes the Dad. You're thinking, "So what's your point?" The point is that we are so imbued with this idea; few people ever consider what it means. I didn't have that luxury.

A man gains social status when his wife bears children. No matter how much we attempt to promote childbirth as a shared experience with concepts like "we're pregnant," when you examine who gets custody; it's women, nearly 90 percent of the time. A woman gains social responsibility, even if initially, she enjoys greater attention. For a woman, their identity shifts to mom. For men, regardless of how much they invest in parenting their career remains their primary identity. A woman's change of identity is, hypothetically, a choice: a choice that men don't have.

I believe it is largely what betrayed my female identity in my career. Before Courtney was born I had a presentation that was consistent with man and father. After Courtney was born I became a mom. It was difficult to disguise that shift. The primacy of my focus shifted from provider to caretaker. Even I failed to recognize just how transparent that transition was to people. This perception is still used to exclude women from promotions and positions of meaningful authority.

My spouse was also identified as the mom. It didn't have the same impact on our children that it might have for children of a lesbian couple where both women are perceived as moms.

I could assume the role of father, and generally, it seemed pretty normative. Even if I identified as mom, some were compelled to correct me; "you mean father." The issue manifested itself in my relationship with Marie, not in the impact on our children. Even as I did most of the parenting chores, she expected the identity of mom. There was conflict in presenting a normal family dynamic. She wasn't willing to challenge social prejudices. I had little choice.

For most women, becoming a mom starts with delivering a baby. For me, it was a little more complicated. It does not seem right that the joy of becoming a mother should begin with the tragedy of facing my own mortality but that's how it happened.

Chapter Twenty-three: New Mom

–Lewis Carroll, Alice in Wonderland

I knew about the frightening ordeal Marie had been through when Jamie was born. I knew that she had been alone during that experience; in the next room was a woman suffering a breach birth. Marie had every right to feel anxious. I wanted to reassure her. My own anxiety wasn't at all helpful.

I missed her ultrasound appointment. She had asked me to be there. It upset me too, but not nearly so much as the disappointment in her voice when she told me about it.

It was a long hot summer, not a blistering hot record heat but uncomfortable for certain. We had no air conditioning in the house yet. Marie continued working right up until the due date. The delivery was still several weeks away. There were other sacrifices as well. She was meant to be matron-of-honor at her best friend's wedding but decided to withdraw because she'd be nearly nine months pregnant. We attended the wedding, but it was disappointing that she wasn't in it.

The due date was in early September, but Courtney wouldn't arrive until October 1. Courtney always had an indifference to too much structure. September 30 was Marie's golden birthday. She'd looked forward to it for a long time. In place of a grand celebration, the two of us had a quiet dinner at home. These intimate moments are some of my best memories.

True to her disposition, when Marie told me she thought it might be time to go to the hospital there was no sense of urgency. On the positive side, Courtney was born on a Sunday which means I wasn't at work.

Marie insisted on natural childbirth. opting out of any anesthesia which again reinforced my perceptions of her remarkable courage. It was clearly a painful delivery. Courtney was already ten pounds. Marie finally asked for painkillers at the very end, but it was too late to administer anything. I was proud of her. I cut the umbilical cord. I wonder if that really leaves men feeling engaged. It is something else I have never heard in any male conversation.

I'm certain Marie could have used more time to recuperate. I'm certain too that I should have taken some time off from work. Understanding my own vulnerability I had an unnatural fear of anything that might compromise my position at work.

Marie took three months of maternity leave: something not available to me. Courtney's crib was in our bedroom because we only had two bedrooms, and Jamie had the other one. I assumed many middle of the night feedings. Courtney was a good baby. She loved her pacifier, her swing, and riding in the car. Sometimes taking her for a ride was the last resort for getting her to sleep. Caring for a newborn baby consumed my entire focus while other issues seemed to disappear. Be what you would seem to be.

At Christmas time we went to New Hampshire to visit my parents so they could meet the new grandchild. It was the first time we didn't drive. We flew to New York and took a small commuter plane to Boston. Courtney and Jamie took their first plane ride together.

I thought a break for Marie might be helpful so I made arrangements to go to Atlantic City with our friend Ed who was at his parent's home in New Jersey. Lori was gracious about watching Courtney but perturbed about the glass baby bottles. I can visualize the scene with that glass bottle crashing to the tile floor. My relationship with Marie created a one-way flow between our families.

It was late when we arrived at Ed's house, and we spent the night there before driving to Atlantic City in the morning. There is a reason why nursing mothers need to be close to their infants. We had no spare batteries for her breast pump. Marie suggested a creative solution that shouldn't have seemed unnatural. My discomfort reflects on the challenge of separating sex from sexuality, sexuality from sensuality, sensuality from sensitivity and sensitivity from sensibility. Providing relief to my partner was nothing more than personal care.

Atlantic city reminded me of my experience in Rome, obscene wealth surrounded by abject poverty. There were warning signs about not leaving the strip. It would be difficult to imagine that the person who created such an unpleasant contrast would one day be president of the United States.

We stayed in the casinos for the most part. The place really seemed to have little atmosphere, not at all like Las Vegas. I'm not fond of gambling, but I did extremely well at the blackjack tables that afternoon, and we spent the evening doing shots in one of the hotel lounges. The next day we were back in Nashua, in time for old fashions: Dad's favorite holiday offering.

All in all, it was a great trip. Anytime I had with Marie was always precious to me, but it was more than a simple getaway from life's routines. It had more pervasive undertones of a particular lifestyle established when Marie's sister stayed with us for the summer.

Chapter Twenty-four: Bear the Cross

"Mine is a long and a sad tale!" said the Mouse, "It is a long tail, certainly," said Alice, looking down with wonder at the mouse's tail. "But why do you call it sad?"

–Lewis Carroll, Alice in Wonderland

Remembering the past is a creative process. Reviewing my experiences as a young woman, I can evaluate her choices and make judgments about the outcomes utilizing knowledge and experience that she didn't have. I can imagine her as a different person, even as I know I am talking about myself. The choices available to me now weren't choices available to her and not the same choices my own daughters have today.

How those experiences are selected, assembled, and arranged isn't fully independent of the present. I am reminded of that this past Christmas in 2016. A dear friend of the family passed away suddenly. Terri was far too young and her life far from complete. Many lives were touched by her bravery, her audacity, her uncommon wisdom, and her enduring selflessness. Terri was for me both the protagonist and the antagonist.

She was Marie's most trusted confidant. They identified as sisters, making her the seventh sister. Terri embraced my unique gender presentation. She orchestrated photo shoots, doing my hair and makeup, and arranging the fashions and poses. For Christmas, she often gave me women's accessories. We shared a karaoke business for several years, and I often portrayed female artists.

She encouraged me to do a strip routine at the Non-Commissioned Officer's club for a birthday celebration. I enjoyed doing it, but I also felt like I should not be doing it. Isolated from meaningful peer relationships with other females, I find transgender women often internalize the cultural objectification of women. For me, escaping those internalized images was part of transition.

It may suggest the reason trans women want to disassociate themselves from the hypersexualized femininity of drag.

It was impossible to escape the dissonance of feeling like I was engaged in something uniquely female while also feeling minimized, or exploited. It seems like an experience shared by many women. Terri and Marie gave me the permission to do things I'd never have done on my own. In retrospect, I appreciated this, but often I felt I was being teased or ridiculed.

Terri's funeral at Christmas time caused me to reflect on another Christmas back in 1989, the year Courtney was born. The day we returned from our trip to see my family, I came down with a high fever. I slept for three days round the clock before I recovered enough to go to work. Health maintenance organizations were the latest innovation, and our family doctor wasn't part of the network. The illusion was a team of doctors managing your care. I experienced a different reality. The doctor I saw failed to recognize a bacterial infection causing the fever. They tested for some obscure possibilities like AIDS. At my third visit, the doctor suggested it was a virus that may clear up on its own. Though a month had passed, he recommended waiting four weeks.

Mine is a long and a sad tale! It's hard to imagine those eight weeks or how I lived them. Marie had returned to work. The plan was to split shifts caring for Courtney. Marie couldn't handle the schedule, so I began taking Courtney full time. I got her ready in the morning, took her to daycare, and picked her up after work. We'd grocery shop on the way home I frequently made dinner and got her ready for bed.

Terri was our daycare provider. It wasn't convenient, but Marie insisted Terri was the only person she could trust. Terri couldn't accommodate my overtime. She teased me often about being an inept parent. It was the familiar dissonance of feeling accepted, at the same time feeling minimized or ridiculed.

For eight weeks my fever stayed above 100 degrees. Many nights, I sat up watching my fever hover around 104 or 105 wondering if I should go to the hospital. By the end of my workday, I was too tired to drive home. I took a nap at Terri's house and another nap at home whenever Jamie could help with Courtney. I was grateful for Jamie.

Marie wanted to go to Las Vegas for my birthday. I'm not sure why I agreed, except perhaps, because I never said no to Marie. I also had a sense I was never going to be well again and needed to go on living as well as I could. Marie encouraged me to seek a second opinion: advice I should have taken. I still had the fever when we arrived in Las Vegas. I don't remember any of it except for the first night, sitting in our hotel restaurant. I cried, for the first time admitting my vulnerability.

On my next doctor appointment, he suggested we wait another two weeks. I demanded to see a specialist. A week later, when I walked into the specialist's office, there was reassuring news. He diagnosed my condition from the initial blood tests as endocarditis: a condition in which bacteria lodges itself in the heart where the high blood flows make it difficult for the body to fight the infection. I was vulnerable to it because of a defective heart valve I'd had since birth.

I was admitted to the hospital for what I thought would be an overnight stay. By the second day it was becoming evident there was something seriously wrong, but I still hadn't seen a doctor. The infection had grown into a large mass of cells creating a risk of stroke.

Reflecting on that moment, facing my own mortality invokes memories of a long series of family funerals. I was in Nashua for Dad's seventieth birthday in January of 1995. Dad had an appointment at the heart hospital in Boston while I was there. I heard the prognosis. It should have been obvious to me that Dad was in very poor health, but it hadn't registered, and I didn't want to believe it.

I was soon to lose five family members. The first was my summer mom, Auntie Pat. Her death was unexpected, apparently resulting from a bacterial infection that had gained some notoriety as the flesh-eating bacteria. Not long afterward, my aunt Evelyn's husband passed away. Dad came to Minneapolis to help his sister with the estate, and then I rode back to New Hampshire with him.

During that same trip Mom, Dad, Mark's daughter Staci, and I drove to Toronto to visit Mark. Dad was the only one allowed into their home to see him because he and his wife felt he was afflicted with environmental poisoning. He was dying of lymphoma cancer, very treatable, but he never sought medical attention. It was impossible for me to understand how he could refuse to see his own daughter.

On Easter weekend I drove from Minneapolis to Toronto again to meet up with Dad. I was able to visit with Mark for a half an hour, arriving back in Minneapolis early Easter morning. That afternoon I got the call Mark had passed away. I felt a horrible emptiness in response. That emptiness overflowed at the funeral when I wrapped my arms around the pastor and started crying. Then I felt the awkwardness of it, suddenly feeling embarrassed and exposed.

Mom once informed me that Mark had once said he wished his parents were dead so he could go live with Grandpa. The thought abrades my memories of Mark. It portends the complexity of family relationships and the distance between us even during the brief moments when we seemed close to one another. We had never been brothers in any true sense of the word. I will always feel like I abandoned him when he needed me most.

In late May, Dad was scheduled for heart surgery. He knew the prognosis was poor, but true to his nature, he'd recover his health or die trying. The muscles of his heart were severely atrophied, he needed a heart valve, and there were other problems with normal arterial disease of advancing age.

On the phone with him the night before surgery I asked if I should come. The last thing he said to me was, "Stay and take care of your family." It was the one thing to which he had dedicated most of his life: taking care of his family. It is an admonition, I wish I had disregarded.

The next night my sister Lori phoned to explain Dad was in a coma. She wanted me to get on a plane and come right away. I'd not have gotten a flight out that evening, and true to my father's expectations I couldn't leave my family behind. We packed the van and left within the hour. The next night we were at the hospital in Manchester, New Hampshire.

I had twenty-four hours during the drive from Minneapolis to Manchester in which to contemplate. From the urgency of Lori's request, it was my assessment that I'd become, as the sole surviving male, the head of the family. My senses were immobilized by that ever-jarring problem of how I should behave. Drawing on the patriarchal traditions of my ancestry I searched for the memories that would guide me through what was expected of me. How could I act like a man, be the man when all I wanted was to share this experience, our shared loss, as one of them, another sister, a daughter, and too now, a mother to my two daughters? My mother was the matriarch of those three generations. There was little comfort in analyzing those family traditions. I had a strong model of a family matriarch but my mother would not expect to become head of the family, not under these circumstances; she had a son. I had not managed my emotions at all well during Mark's funeral. I'd do better this time. It's a situation where a man could cry.

The mental exercises did not prepare me for the life and death decision that immediately confronted me upon my arrival at the hospital. The moment I walked into my father's hospital room, and he heard my voice; the monitors lit up. All of his vital signs improved. It was obvious to everyone that Dad knew I was there. I was certain that if I stayed with him and talked with him and connected with him throughout the night, he would awaken from his coma.

Sitting by his bedside, my focus turned inward as I contemplated his choices and the events of the last several months. I reviewed the seriousness of what we had been told at the heart hospital in Boston. I considered the evidence of his failing health, stripping away my veil of denial. Complete recovery was unlikely; he'd become a burden to his family: the thing he feared most. I thought about my responsibility to my mom and my sisters. Certainly, their distress, their sense of loss could be no less intense than my own.

I left the decision to my father. He never recovered. By morning, he was gone. For years I'd agonize over the cowardice of my decision and a sense of betrayal toward Mom, Lori, and Sharon. Alluding to Jesus Christ on the day of his crucifixion, Dad often told me, "A man has to carry his own cross." The only thing I remember about Dad's funeral was discussing arrangements with the funeral director. I joked about his hometown of Cherry Grove sounding like *Little House on the Prairie*. This created some much-needed levity. I tried to be strong, though I hated funerals because of the intense dissonance between how I felt and how I presumed I was supposed to feel.

The last funeral that year was Uncle Freddy's: perhaps, the most beloved of all of my aunts and uncles. Freddy always had time for the nieces and nephews, and he was our principal adversary when my cousin Dianne and I teamed up against the adults in a game of croquet.

It was years later that I finally realized all of those funerals took place within eighteen months. It was a profound realization. At Freddie's funeral, I finally broke down sobbing. You hear it said that it's okay for a man to cry, but it is mostly a face-saving measure. I felt horribly exposed, embarrassed, and vulnerable with all of my masculine training chastising me for acting like a girl.

That experience was still years away from my hospital bed back in 1989, but it's an association that helps me understand how I was feeling about my own illness. Lying in the hospital bed I thought about my mortality. Worse than mortality, I was terrified by the serious risk of stroke and the ensuing disability. Worst of all, was my inability to move beyond my fear of leaving Marie with our two children. Certainly, Marie's distress could be no less than what Mom, my sisters, and I experienced in my father's hospital room.

It occurs to me now, I had already become my father. It occurs to me now, how desperately Marie and I needed each other and how enormous the distance was between us.

It took a long time to recover confidence in my health. I remained on intravenous antibiotics for another two months. I wore a pump on my belt that injected antibiotics directly into my heart. The pump was innocuous, but the regime was grueling. Every eight hours I had to reload the pump and perform injections and sterilizations.

Marie's confidence never recovered. One day when we were at the park we saw an old man take out a syringe from a tiny red cooler to give himself an injection. Marie teased me about the day I'd be carrying around my little cooler. These words cut me deep. Marie could be cruel sometimes.

Chapter Twenty-five: Parenting Styles

Mom called it divine intervention, a miraculous recovery, further evidence that God had a plan for me. "Sure, Mom, God has a plan for me," was my response. During the course of my illness, something did happen that I had once thought to be completely impossible. I became a mother.

Courtney and I continued our daily routine. Mornings had their moments. While I got ready for work and Courtney ready for daycare, Jamie got ready for school. I suppose it's the most conversation I had with Jamie at the time, though it probably wasn't always the most productive conversation. We only had one bathroom.

Courtney was an easy child to care for. She slept well, ate well, never threw up, and never cried. Well, almost never, unless she was missing her pacifier. We bought them in twelve packs.

She gave up her pacifier when her parents got tired of searching for one. Courtney loved her swing and loved riding in the car. Every morning I got myself up with a promise that I'd take a nap when I got home. Courtney slept in the car while returning from daycare. There was never a nap for me. Eventually, I started singing to her to keep her awake. It didn't get me any naps, but it was more fun. "American Pie" was making a come back in 1991. That along with a rendition of "Ants go Marching" was all I needed for the whole trip.

Courtney came with only two speeds, fast and off. She went full speed until she passed out. Then I picked her up and carried her to bed. One night as I carried her to her crib, I accidentally bumped her head against the wall, and she responded with the cutest words I have ever heard together, "Careful, Daddy."

Her loquacious charm rivaled her sister's. Her first word was Play-Doh when she was less than a year old. The cutest single word I have ever heard. Courtney never used personal pronouns. She'd say, "Courtney wants juice." She always wanted dolls, but I always directed her to something more craft-oriented. We had a large collection of naked, headless Barbies, which to me meant she didn't really like dolls.

I loved being a mom. In the beginning, all the mundane things like grocery shopping were an adventure. Courtney loved to help. If I didn't keep her in the middle of the aisle, I never knew what I'd end up with at the checkout. You rarely saw a man in a grocery store, much less a man with a baby.

There were challenges too. Three months of administering bubblegum flavored antibiotics created a collection of pink t-shirts. She also suffered from high fever seizures. She never slowed down for a fever until she lapsed into convulsions. The first time, while taking a bath with Jamie, we heard a thud. When I got to her she was convulsing. I thought she had sustained a concussion.

Marie confessed to postpartum depression and the pain in her neck and shoulders from the car accident continued. She asked me to get a vasectomy. I didn't like the thought of it. I didn't agree with making that choice in the midst of so much emotional and physical stress. We had raised Jamie as an only child, and I felt reticent about doing the same for Courtney. My true objection was more personal. I really loved being a mom.

Just as Jamie declared us a family, Courtney renewed those bonds for a while. She slept in our bed until she was five. She was a nighttime gymnast who always ended up at the head of the bed. I'm not certain I ever got any sleep. I'd often exclaim, "We don't need a bigger house, we just need a bigger bed.

Here is an illustration of how siblings in the same household can have vastly different experiences. Father was the role I played in Jamie's life. Marie was the Mom. Under the circumstances, I felt no authority or opportunity to be her mom. Jamie had a "real dad" though he was, for all intents and purposes, totally absent from her life.

Mother was the role I played in Courtney's life. Some will still correct me. There is a subtle insinuation that any father could be a mom if they chose to. It's unproven speculation, probably as rare as transgender women. I wondered myself at times why men couldn't make the same investment I did, until I started accepting this wasn't a valid comparison. I did use the title and played the father role, as much as any single mom tries to provide male role behavior or male role models, especially for male children.

Jamie was reaching adolescence when Courtney arrived. Along with that came the normal power struggles all families inevitably experience. It emphasized issues in the marriage, primarily our different parenting styles. I had a mentoring approach. Marie believed in tough love, as did her sister Terri.

Marie's friend Terri was the antagonist driving actions that I felt bordered on abusive. I saw no need to humiliate a child for any reason and physical confrontation heightened my anxiety. It left me feeling conflicted about not being more protective of her. Engagement of therapists, social workers, adolescent shelters, and the Job Corps did nothing to address the complex family dynamics underlying the conflict. Child protection, child rights, and data privacy are increasing the difficulty of addressing complex family dynamics.

There was so much I never knew about Marie. She once shared with me that seeing Jamie turning ten was triggering memories. Jamie was ten when we bought the house which certainly explained some mysteries, and while I don't know what happened to her when she was ten, I always imagined it wasn't good.

Not being allowed in mommy spaces was the most difficult thing about being a transgender mom. It was a solitary existence. There were no changing stations in men's rooms. I changed my baby in the car or some secluded floor space. As Courtney got a little older, I didn't want to bring her into a men's room. There were no family restrooms. I'd ask another mom to escort her.

The biggest challenge of being a transgender mom was everyone thinking I was the dad. I didn't have other moms to consult when child-rearing put me at my wit's end. I needed someone to talk to. Unfortunately, that someone wouldn't be Marie.

Random rules of engagement played out in my favor. The conflict with Teri continued to escalate over my work hours. She also had conflicts with Marie, that I felt were constantly overflowing onto me. I was elated when Teri explained she wouldn't watch Courtney anymore.

At the same time, I ran into Dianne. Her family lived next door to us in the mobile home park before their home was destroyed in a fire. Not having seen her for a few years the meet-up was timely. Dianne became the other mom in my life helping to raise Courtney.

Barney the dinosaur was the big hit of the day. I once made a full-size costume of Barney for Diane's daughter Karen who also was great with children. Courtney's first song favorite was "Achy Breaky Heart" by Billy Ray Cyrus. She was three. By age four she denied it but for a time it totally outranked "American Pie."

Courtney called her Dinny. She became my best friend and confidant. She sustained me. She smoothed out the anxiety on mornings Courtney cried, begging me not to leave. Her parenting style was similar to my own. I had coffee with her in the morning, and she listened to my day when I returned in the evening. She enabled me to do the overtime I needed to sustain my career. I remain deeply indebted to her.

My relationship to Dianne did little to reduce the uncomfortable distance developing between Marie and me. It became the catalyst for a traumatic shift in the intimacy of our relationship.

It started out innocently enough. Terri and Marie encouraged me to participate in a male "hot bodies" contest at City Limits in Rosemount. I should have known better. Terri brought the Jose Cuervo. That too was peculiar. She loved her Jose Cuervo but was critical of Marie's drinking and never drank with Marie. She and I did a couple of shots before we left.

I joined a group of young men in a backroom to prepare for the show. I've said that acting like a man around other men was easy. This night would be a clear exception. Undressing and standing around half-naked with a group of handsome young men was definitely not the same sense of camaraderie I felt on the stage with a group of women in front of a mostly male audience.

My uneasiness probably passed as inexperience. They shared their baby oil with me to make my skin glisten and bring out the highlights of my musculature. Having a man caressing my body with baby oil was stimulating and confusing. There was no graceful exit strategy.

It may be difficult for people to realize the intensity of this situation, stimulating fantasies of my summer lover, a mysterious evening in the Ozarks or a careless romp across America. I think about all of the men in my life who never were. These were experiences that were safely contained within the realm of my own fantasies and desire.

This connection with men was intimate, and I felt exposed. My shroud of denial was stripped away. Who in the world am I? Ah, that's the great puzzle. I had plenty of therapists wanting to expose my denial without ever recognizing that what was in denial was my femininity. All of that was exposed in that backroom at City Limits. This was a contest I needed to win, but I wouldn't win. I'd leave the stage wondering how to restore my masculine self-image.

Afterward, Terri confronted me about how I was treating Marie. I had given away too much information about Dinny. Apparently, Marie was convinced I was having an affair with her. It was true in a sense. I was sharing personal feelings with Dinny that I couldn't share with Marie. Sex isn't necessary for an affair. I'll never know Marie's interpretation. It often seemed like any discussion with Marie went through Terri.

That evening in bed with Marie I felt reassured by the sexual intimacy, but I was also wounded and desperate to please her and desperate to prove myself. As always, we didn't talk about sex, and there was no adequate preparation. I gave her what she asked for. Another perspective might be that I accepted what she was offering. It may seem like a meaningless distinction but the emphasis lies in the lack of communication. There was no exchange of expectations and it was painful. When she said out loud, "You're hurting me," I knew immediately I'd made a bad choice. That brief moment became Marie's apex for all the issues expanding the separation between us.

We saw Marie's therapist several times, but it didn't move us toward any resolution. There was no discussion about what actually happened or ways to improve our communication.

The therapist insisted I accept responsibility, which I did. I felt responsible, but this also made Marie the victim, erasing her responsibility for what happened and denying her power in the relationship. The therapist wanted me to explain why. Any explanation I put forward was proof I was denying responsibility. The discussion was circular. I should have expected Marie to take equal responsibility but accepting blame was an inherent part of my vulnerability. Perhaps if I had explained I was a woman struggling with male presentation anxiety the conversation might have gone differently. I can only guess how that may have turned out.

Marie and I dealt with difficult issues. We were together twenty-eight years and raised three amazing children. It's a strong testament to our love and commitment, and I see both of us reflected in our children, most of it good but some of it reflecting those issues Marie and I never resolved.

The therapeutic community was completely incapable of helping us. Social services and the therapeutic community aren't structured around resolving complex family dynamics. Theirs is a binary model of intervention that's evolved around the fundamental gender model of victim and abuser. In other words, one receives treatment, the other is punished, and the children get caught in the middle. The type of resources needed for early intervention and prevention are completely inadequate. More accurately, as I'd soon discover, they're completely non-existent.

Marie and I dealt with that incident, like all issues in our relationship, by simply trying to forget it. Within a few months, we were talking about having another child.

Chapter Twenty-six: One Girl, One Boy

"No meaning in it," said the King, "that saves a world of trouble, you know, as we needn't try to find any."

–Lewis Carroll, Alice in Wonderland

I was excited about having another child. Courtney was two when we started trying to conceive another child. A year later there was still no sign of a baby so we went to see our family doctor. There were no tests. We had a short conversation in which our doctor asked how often we were having intercourse. Marie explained it was every day. Our doctor, as casually as I can imagine said, "Marie, you have to leave him alone once in awhile." I thought it was precious. I must have broken a bit of a smile because Marie made it clear to me we weren't there to talk about our sex life. What would the therapist say, who once told me I was lucky to be getting any sex at all.

Our doctor explained that a day of abstinence was necessary to maintain viable sperm counts. Within two months of switching to alternate days, our third child was on the way.

This time I was excited to hear we were pregnant but also hurt to discover, once again, I was the last to know. It punctuated her fears. I routinely practiced maintaining my voice at low, constant levels because I knew it frightened her if I ever raised my voice. Even at that, there was always "the look." How does one create a look with no meaning in it?

Tyler wasn't at all like Courtney. He hated pacifiers. He hated the swing. He spit up on you all the time. He was positively adorable. That's how babies survive. He was my little darling but he was a handful.

I don't know why we use baby talk, except perhaps it's cuter than trying to explain theories of advanced calculus. I discovered one of Tyler's unique talents when I held him close to my face talking baby talk, and BANG, he slammed his forehead into the bridge of my nose. I saw stars as he nearly knocked me out. Tyler loved to butt heads. Is it anecdotal evidence of something little boys do, or not?

He had another talent for what little boys do. You had to be careful what you set next to him. If he could reach it, he'd pick it up and throw it, which means he broke stuff: stuff he threw and stuff that got knocked over. We wondered if he'd grow up to be a major league pitcher. Maybe if he'd had a sports dad, but like many mothers, I wasn't radical about sports. I enrolled him in dance class.

Both the girls had been in dance class. Jamie basically refused to participate. She was engaging in private family settings but timid in public. I'd bribe her with money encouraging her to buy treats at the store, but she never did. I let her withdraw from dance which I later regretted. When Courtney wanted to quit dance class I refused to allow it. It's an example of birth order effect on parenting. It was a struggle for a while, but she continued on through high school.

Tyler never rejected dance class. Perhaps the extra attention as one of two boys had some impact. Tyler's first dance recital subsumes my maternal instincts. The memory invokes both my emotional engagement as a mother and my emotional isolation from other mothers.

When the four and five-year-old performers get on stage for their first performance in front of an auditorium of people, there is always one who cries. Of course, it's my son. The other mothers would be waiting in the wings, but my son wouldn't get to be with his mom. Fathers weren't allowed backstage. My heart sank, unable to comfort him, unable to encourage him.

Tyler remembers it differently, in a way that overwhelms me with maternal pride. He remembers the nervousness he experienced before going backstage. He remembers my encouragement. He remembers me wanting to race him to the stage door creating an excitement for what was waiting for him behind that door. At the door, he'd go on alone, already a man at the tender age of five.

By the time Courtney was five or six, she had beautiful long black curly hair. Perhaps I was a little envious. It's one of those small ways parents sometimes vicariously live out their dreams through their children. Marie once had a painting done of Courtney with those beautiful curls. It characterizes the subtleties of our family dynamics. Marie knew I loved Courtney's long hair, but I certainly never insisted on. Years later I'd learn from Courtney that she hated the long hair, but Marie wouldn't let her cut it. Marie did that for me. I never knew.

By the time Tyler was five or six, he too had long beautiful curly hair I could certainly be jealous of. Hairstyle remains a powerful symbol of gender differentiation. Even on women hair length relates to professionalism and assertiveness.

I never decided how he should wear his hair either, but I had different concerns for Tyler. It was impossible for me to ignore the impact of gender norms. I knew kids on the bus teased him. I frequently asked him about it, but he assured me it wasn't a problem. Then one day shortly before he started second grade he decided to cut his hair. It was an event. Both Marie and I were at the hair salon. The change was dramatic, giving him a whole new persona, but he was still the same Tyler, was he not?

When parents express concerns to me about their child's gender, I assure them gender variant behavior is extremely common in children and that transgender individuals are rather rare. Those concerns wouldn't exist if not for the transgender myth.

When Tyler was four or five he wanted to be a hunter. It seemed a rather masculine pursuit for such a young boy coming from a family that really had no hunters. I remember my first hunt. I was twelve when dad took me to the woods of Northern Wisconsin to hunt deer. My first time out I leveled my sights on a deer less than fifteen yards away. When I pulled the trigger all I heard was a click, and the deer bolted. The firing pin had fallen out of my shotgun. I'm glad the gun didn't go off. I can fillet a fish or skin a deer, but I don't want to kill it. I figured Dad would be proud of his grandson, but I smiled broadly when he revealed he was going to hunt Easter eggs.

To this day we still hold our annual Easter egg hunt with unbelievable good humor, perhaps momentarily recapturing the free expression of childhood. He also loved to hide things. Items disappeared, only to turn up months later in some totally unexpected location. After the movie *The Borrowers* we started blaming them, for mysterious disappearances of household items.

His passion for hide-and-seek created the most terrifying experience of my entire life. We were at Valley Fair amusement park in Shakopee with my company outing. In a crowded place like Valley Fair, you keep a close eye on your children. One quick check suddenly came up empty. Tyler was gone. A scan of the immediate area quickly turned into a horrible sense of panic. There was no response to calling his name. Then just before the event turned into a full-scale manhunt, Tyler emerged with a major smile on his face. He was playing hide and seek: one of his favorite games. He overlooked the part where we count to ten.

Raising my own children was different than my childhood. My kids' friends loved coming to our house because we let our kids play with scissors. My Cub Scout den mother was my mom. As a den mother myself, I was working with fathers. It was great having the fathers present because it made me feel less vulnerable. I had projects with knives and power tools, things the boys had never experienced, things that were normal to me as a child. I also took them on shopping trips with a little bit of home economics which was something we did not do in my youth.

I spent some time as a Girl Scout leader too. I'm still not certain what made me feel more vulnerable, working with young girls or working with young boys. At least Girl Scouts never required an overnight camping trip.

These organizations reinforce the Transgender myth. Even with the acceptance of transgender kids, without true gender crossover, these organizations continue to reinforce separate gender roles. There has been little evolution of these programs. In fairness, given the current evolution of gender roles in the US, it is difficult to find leadership that can effectively address both sides of the binary gender model. Courtney had little interest in Girl Scouts. She wanted to join the Boy Scouts because they did all the "cool stuff."

Chapter Twenty-seven: Mommy Play Day

"She generally gave herself very good advice, (though she very seldom followed it.)"

–Lewis Carroll, Alice in Wonderland

As a woman with a desire to have children at a young age, it's easy for me to buy into the idea of a maternal instinct. I also knew from a young age that I was never going to be pregnant. It complicates the whole concept of "instincts" as a pejorative of choice. Gillian Ragsdale, PhD. described the situation appropriately, "The press is awash with warnings about delaying motherhood and the short-sighted selfishness of career-hungry women who suddenly realize that 'Motherhood' is in its final week of release and it's now or never."[1] Ragsdale disavows a maternal instinct but a study published in the Harvard Gazette[2] suggests that the choice between family and career continues to weight far more heavily on women.

Sex produces babies, not maternal instincts. Who benefits from this perception? Women who could not or would not succumb to their instincts might experience isolation, harassment, guilt, and depression. This is the traditional feminist conundrum, woman as mother vs. women in careers. Men don't have to make that choice.

Alternatively, men aren't allowed to make that choice. It begs the usual social discourse about the impact of nature vs. nurture as to gender identity and gender roles. It raises the unusual question of whether or not the debate of nature vs. nurture actually applies to men. "Boys will be boys."

Transgender people understand the influence of hormones both physically and emotionally. Ask any transgender woman, and she will likely tell you that testosterone is a poison. I am familiar with the effects of this toxin coursing through my body for a significant part of my life. I have also experienced it with friends transitioning in the opposite direction from female spaces to male spaces. "Why would you do it?" I ask, knowing full well being transgender isn't a choice. It legitimizes transgender identities. For many of us transition occurs following the loss of social determinants that enable us to cope with the extreme dissonance of a pretentious gender presentation. As one transgender woman expressed it, "If you're not ready to kill yourself don't transition."

Experts enforce the cultural model of the dominant class. I have certainly had the pleasure of many experts throughout my life telling me my perceptions were totally off base. I generally gave myself very good advice, (though I very seldom followed it). I grew suspicious of anyone wanting to "help me," because it generally involved some approach to help me shape my behavior to his or her expectations. The dominant class is a white male class. Everyone else is a subservient class ranked according to various indicators of gender, race, and ethnicity. It's easy to view that ranking according to economic stratification though there is also a social class status that determines access to social privileges. There is a limited opportunity to change economic status which may influence one's social status. It creates the illusion of social equity.

Women who conform to the expectations of the dominant male class will generally enjoy a much higher level of socioeconomic status than those who don't, creating a special protected class status. The establishment of protected classes is problematic in any discussion about equality. Transgender women are familiar with the gatekeeper model of transition. Julia Serano illustrates it in her book *Whipping Girl*. This model of transition required extensive therapy and assessment intended to ensure proper conformance to appropriate standards of feminine behavior and appearance. Some transgender women valued this approach. I've also witnessed tragic consequences for women who transitioned without that support but there remains a persistent undertone of protecting this class separation and male expectations of women.

Marie and I dealt with complex issues that most experts, at the time, couldn't comprehend much less provide meaningful action plans. Marie and I resigned ourselves to this and focused on our children, hoping to provide them with a normal life. Something each of us could only imagine for ourselves.

Even at that, my model of individual empowerment conflicted with her model of parental control. Her model was more consistent with our social justice model of retribution. Unresolved conflicts started to overwhelm our mutual commitment to providing stability for our children.

Having children complicated my relationships, both with men and women. Like many women, I wasn't comfortable with the masculine value system dominating the work environment. It wasn't clear to me why other men couldn't make the same maternal investments I did. It wasn't until I stopped pretending to be a man that I fully realized it wasn't a valid comparison.

I was a mother raising three children. I worked full time to provide for them. I didn't have the same career mobility that men had. My children were my priority. I made sacrifices in my career so I could care for them. I had doctor appointments and sudden illnesses that interrupted my work schedule. There were school recitals and field trips. It was difficult for me to work overtime and take on business travel, which was essential to career advancement. I used my vacation time judiciously but I still received negative reviews for missed time. I was fortunate in not having to worry about equal pay. I was always near the top of my pay grade earning more than many of my peers. I was also fortunate in having reliable, affordable home daycare with someone who shared my value system and fulfilled the maternal companionship that compensated for my separation from other mothers. What I wanted is what many women had: more time with my children, more time with my family, time to volunteer at their school and attend field trips and school events, more mommy play days. I wanted to be valued as a woman.

Just as women are minimized in career spaces dominated by men, men too are minimized in a woman's domain. That sometimes made my credibility suspect with other women. There is little acceptance or understanding of the fact that this works both ways. Betty Friedan addresses it quite eloquently in *The Feminine*

Mystique, emphasizing her intention that feminism should not lend artillery to the battle of the sexes.

Women still provide most of the childcare, most of the volunteer hours, most of the family organizing, and care for family members, yet women are taking on an ever-increasing financial burden. Far more women are working full-time today but the low wage scale hardly makes up for the loss of time women invested in caring for family and community organizing. Women are now the primary wage earners in 40 percent of our families. That number jumps to 60 percent for women of indigenous ancestry and African American women. What is society really offering women? More accurately, what are women demanding of our society?

There is an enormous social cost in the presumption that promoting women to high-paying jobs can achieve gender equity. It assumes an assimilation of women into a male-dominated value system. One popular recommendation emphasizes an educational system focused on promoting STEM, Science, Technology, Engineering, and Math. There are reasons why a majority of women aren't attracted to many of these careers.

That model of achieving pay equity presumes women will have affordable childcare or simply not have children. The availability and cost of childcare are becoming a matter of major national concern. Any suggestion that men would fill the gap has not materialized. Childcare also becomes another service level position, generally populated by women, which creates a negative offset to higher pay scales.

If women's work doesn't pay a living wage, how can they ever hope for economic independence? It is exactly this inequality of wealth that sustains the exploitation and abuse of women. The enormous inequality of wealth hurts women and children the most. Women should have the same economic opportunities as men, but defining women by their economic worth doesn't respect women's social values.

Globally, research has shown that ethnically diverse and divided nations that elect women rather than men to key national leadership offices end up with better economic performance.

America now ranks ninety-eighth in the world for percentage of women in its national legislature, down from fifty-ninth in 1998[3]. That's embarrassing: just behind Kenya and Indonesia, and barely ahead of the United Arab Emirates.

No one is proposing a new economic model that encourages more autonomy in family structure and restores the fundamental value of the basic family unit. There are no economic proposals that might allow families to have family time: something that even holidays rarely afford anymore. True social benefits are realized in understanding and rewarding the value of what women do. That isn't a realistic possibility in a society increasingly driven exclusively by profit motives.

Those years with my children are without a doubt the best years of my life. I cherish fond memories and miss those days. I had the financial means to provide for my children and the maternal instinct to care for them.

I have often heard that you cannot be on both sides of the fence, but the reality, for me, is that I have lived my entire life on both sides of the fence, as both my mother and my father, the caretaker and the provider. This has given me knowledge as to how men are deprived of female privileges. I also see how much women are devalued as individuals by their roles and relationships. We cannot possibly realize the full potential of feminism until we embrace the idea that masculinity and femininity are both valuable and contribute equally to the strength and value of our culture. They are not opposites. They are complements. We must also realize that masculinity and femininity can be fully embraced by either sex.[4] At this time in my life, I have experienced the best and the worst of a womans world. I have experienced the best of a man's world, and soon enough, I would experience the worst.

1 Ragsdale, Gillian, "The Maternal Myth," *Psychology Today*, December 18, 2013.

2 Pazzanese, Christina, "The Internal Marriage Tax of Women MBAs," *Harvard Gazette*, April 7, 2017.

3 "Why Does the US Still Have So Few Women in Office?" *The Nation*, March 7, 2014.

4 Overby, Paula, A Season of Pride, Men Talk, Twin Cities Men's Center August/September 2012

Chapter Twenty-eight: Missing Messages

If there was a family gathering with children, that's where you found Marie. She was always prepared with coloring books and other activities. In spite of it, there was a reason Courtney and Tyler were in daycare until they started school. Courtney should have started kindergarten at Pinewood Elementary School in Eagan just a mile from our home. Instead, she started kindergarten in Burnsville, so she could take the bus from the home of her daycare provider. That's why the photo of her first day getting on the bus wasn't taken in front of our home.

Near the end of the fall kindergarten schedule, just before Christmas, Marie said to me, "Wouldn't it be cheaper if I watched the kids at home?"

Obviously, I thought, but I was skeptical. It seemed like an incredibly odd statement, which is, in part, what made it so memorable. Courtney had been in daycare for six years already. Within two months, Marie had Tyler enrolled in Montessori school. Placing an additional strain on our finances.

At the same time, Jamie was feeling her independence which added a whole new dimension to the co-parenting issue. In 1993, she turned sixteen which meant she could quit school, and that's what she did. It was an enormous sense of failure for me. I was unfamiliar with the new teaching techniques, so helping Jamie with homework was difficult. She explained the situation quite well actually. She said, "I don't get it."

I'd ask, "What don't you get?"

She answered, "I don't get what I don't get." I should have made other arrangements to help her.

Marie's parental control model created serious conflict. Jamie spent several periods in youth shelters which I didn't support. In an effort to give her more independence and ease the tension we set up the basement as her "apartment." This didn't last long. Apparently, an employer noticed she was losing weight. Jamie told them her parents weren't feeding her. Next thing, there was a child protection worker at our door. One quick tour of the "apartment" demonstrated she had plenty to eat, but Marie and I still ended up with several months of home counseling sessions. Marie was furious.

Jamie finally entered a residential work development program. I dropped her off on Sundays, and picked her up on Fridays. She wasn't thrilled with it I'm sure, but I imagine it was a welcome relief from the conflict she experienced at home. I'm happy to say Jamie found her own path. She owns a successful business now, but she, unnecessarily, struggled through some difficult years.

By 1997, it was evident that Comten's parent company, NCR, was moving the operation to South Carolina. Marie wouldn't go with me which left me with my first inkling of how vulnerable I was to losing my children. It's an uneasiness that grew with time. I felt trapped without any meaningful options.

I decided to take a position as software development manager with a laboratory instrument manufacturer. It allowed me to work from home and I could generally take the kids to work with me when I had to be at the office. The long hours spent at home added stress to my relationship with Marie. A lawsuit filed by our major competitor inhibited sales and the CEO was draining company resources for personal benefits. I eventually took over as CEO in an attempt to obtain new funding, but it was the height of the dot.com era and funding for businesses outside the Internet realm was hard to come by. My final action as CEO was the orderly shut down of the company.

I joined the dot.com revolution at a company that provided file delivery services. It was an advanced introduction to test automation. I also managed the quality assurance process design. Then came the dot.com crash, and the entire QA staff was laid off. I was at a job fair the day the twin towers in New York were hit on

9/11. I'd be without regular full-time employment for nearly two years.

QA contracting firms proliferated but managing a business did not accommodate my parenting obligations. I focused on new skill development and worked on some private ventures including a couple of school Linux projects.

Marie and I were already living separate lives. Jamie was out on her own, and the family, for all intents and purposes, was split in two. Courtney was entering her teen years, creating conflict with Marie. There's hardly enough of me left to make ONE respectable person! I spent my time helping Courtney. Marie spent her time with Tyler. The conflict between Courtney and Marie became so intense I finally decided to move her out of the house for a while. I wasn't going to follow the same route we did with Jamie.

Marie attended support groups at a women's center. They recommended I attend the Domestic Abuse Project (DAP). It was a clear foreshadowing of where things were going. I did attend an intake session at DAP, but sitting in a room with thirty men, court-ordered to be there for battering their wives was overwhelming.

I searched for a support group. Every call I made eventually lead me to the Twin Cities Men's Center. I decided to try the Sexual Boundaries group at the Twin Cities Men's Center since Marie was frequently telling me I had no sexual boundaries. To the contrary, I had strict boundaries following the night at City Limits. Those boundaries obviously didn't match her expectations. The lack of personal privacy also meant a lack of personal gratification. I was beginning to understand the significance of hypervigilance.

I garnered frequent criticism for not supporting her. In time, I realized I was reinforcing that perception myself in my own desire to please her. I could never meet all of her expectations, so I focused on the highest priority. That contributed to her oft-stated criticism that I never got anything done unless she was screaming at me. When I stopped responding, this conflict escalated, but it wasn't about the tasks. Something more fundamental was taking place.

Shared adversity might normally bring a couple closer together, especially when the outcomes are good. It is a bonding experience, but for us the intimacy was unbearable. That point was illustrated when Marie had ankle surgery. Scheduled for 1:00 PM, we waited there until 8:00 PM before the surgeon was prepared to operate. Marie was anxious about the doctor's performance following a long schedule. I persuaded her to continue with the operation, which did go well.

In the following weeks, I cared for her, attended to her needs, and took her to the follow-up appointments. Communication was sparse and contentious. None of the friends and family she was so loyal to came to the hospital or to visit her at home. I was happy to do it: a simple act of love and kindness, but I also realized she perceived it differently. Marie had a childhood different from mine, perhaps like the one I imagined for my friend LeeAnn. I never understood how to love someone who never experienced the kind of love I knew as a child. It is hard to love someone who never knew love as a child.

Marie and I saw plenty of experts. The first therapist we saw said to me, "You have to stop having sex with her. She thinks you're raping her." That made perfect sense to me and I stopped having sex with her, but it escalated the conflict. I began to understand it as her control mechanism.

Therapy was hopelessly ineffective in addressing our communication or the foundations of our relationship. Therapists fell into two basic categories, those who wanted to work with Marie, and those who wanted to teach me to be a better husband. They were generally split according to gender with females in the former group and males in the latter. In fairness, both Marie and I were presenting seriously false representations of ourselves, fearful of the social stigmas surrounding those experiences. Then again, isn't a therapist supposed to figure that out? Certainly, we gave them ample clues.

I'd learn to give up the pretense. I'd overcome the fear. For Marie, the transference[1] left me responsible for all of the pain in her life. Society would agree with her. The end was predictable and inevitable but I remained steadfast to the end, believing the love in our relationship would overcome the incompatibilities. That is my understanding of what it means to love someone. Truthfully, I could see no other option.

1 A reproduction of emotions relating to repressed experiences, especially of childhood, and the substitution of another person … for the original object of the repressed impulses

Part VIII: Gender Rebellion: Sex, sexuality, gender, and gender roles

The increasing conflict with Marie combined with the growing financial stress and parental challenges pressed heavily against my emotional well-being. I had no interest in abandoning Marie, and I definitely didn't want to lose my children. My solution to that was both extraordinary and effective, evolving from the nature of prior experiences wearing dresses in public. I needed relationships with other women, but I didn't want the potential burden of extramarital affairs. Wearing dresses allowed me to socialize as a woman while maintaining my roles as husband, father, and employee. It was pretentious, but I could justify it through my commitment as the provider.

Interviewers will invariably ask me how old I was when I first realized I was a girl. I never considered the question until I was entering my teens because I never experienced gender conflict in my childhood. I existed comfortably in both genders. Even if I hated butch haircuts, I never considered dresses or long hair as an intrinsic part of being a girl, yet, during the ensuing years, I relied on dresses alone to indicate my female identity.

The gender queer movement, as it presents itself today, is an ideological position based on challenging social norms. The various identities must exist within the gender spectrum but they are not presented in that context. There is a plethora of labels, illiterate pronouns, and a vocabulary with no lexical order, no etymology. In the extreme, there are those who abandon gender entirely, plunging transgender into a cauldron of nothingness, a panorama of frivolous play, impersonation, and imaginary constructions: a community defined by the very inability to define it. Even famed sociologist Margret Mead would be hard-pressed to present a culture where males and females have the exact same social context from birth.

I make no attempt to conceal my personal bias. I expended enormous energy creating a gender presentation that felt completely unnatural to me. I have a huge investment in transitioning to the woman I am today. I'm with the majority. Gender has little context outside of biological determinants. Third wave feminism uses the exceptional case as proof that without social structuring there would be no gender differentiation. To most of us that is an intuitive absurdity. The gender queer movement has confounded its credibility by asserting these physical realities aren't really relevant.

Presenting socially as a man wearing dresses, I spent those tumultuous years examining these intersections of sex, sexuality, gender, and gender roles.

Chapter Twenty-nine: Man in a Dress

In 2003, I finally found full-time employment as a systems administrator for a media distribution company. At the same time, I started wearing dresses most of the time when I was not at work or at home. It was an unusual and interesting period of self-discovery, I generally refer to as a "Man in a Dress Period."

The day I accepted the offer, I stopped at Kohl's department store where I spent the next couple of hours browsing women's fashions. There is elation in contemplating the possibilities. Experts might define it as sexual gratification, but it isn't. That is the definition of a transvestite, a man who derives sexual pleasure from wearing women's clothing, especially lingerie. The image is popularized by the 1975 musical cult classic *Rocky Horror Picture Show*, which is still playing in theaters and on stages.

Socially, I wore skirts or dresses and high heels but no makeup, no wigs. I kept my mustache, just a man in a dress. After leaving work, I put on a dress, changing in my car. I changed in the car again before I got home. Over the course of several years, I must have changed in my car several thousand times. I feared the possibility of being discovered by the police and charged with indecent exposure so I practiced technique for maintaining full coverage and never changed in the same location. As I write that, I might be the first to admit that it seems like rather bizarre behavior, and yet, it was so valuable to my emotional health and well-being.

I wore the same outfit for a long time simply going to different places during each trip home. Over time, however, there were places I'd visit on a regular basis, like the bank and the grocery store. I didn't want to be seen in the same outfit, so I expanded my wardrobe. Shopping for clothes was now an activity I could enjoy. It was something I always hated when faced with picking out men's clothes.

During one of my early trips, I needed to stop for gas. There were cars at the pump and several people inside. I was overcome with fear, and I had to go and change my clothes before I could get my gas. It was a strange response. I had worn dresses in public many times before. People had called the police who had questioned me about my attire. There was nothing at the gas station unfamiliar to me. How could I be afraid?

This was a totally new experience. I wasn't fearful of being seen in a dress. I wasn't fearful of the consequences. This was an internal fear. No longer was I playing dress-up. For the first time in my life, I was presenting my inner self as my true self. I was suddenly taken by the significance of that, and I was afraid.

I confronted the fear as I had been taught to do, by engaging with people in spite of it. I experienced my own hypervigilance. During those first few months, I heard people laughing, and I heard horns honking. I assumed it was directed at me. I had never paid attention to these things before because I had never felt so conspicuous. These things are happening all the time. In reality, most people seemed totally inattentive to my presence or how I was dressed. Overt harassment was extremely rare and always hurled at a distance from some passing car.

What I needed were girlfriends who I could relate to as a woman. Dinny fulfilled that role while the kids were in daycare. It was evident how important she was to me. It was further evidence of how isolated I really was. The emotional distance in my marriage was continuously growing wider. Marie felt it too as she complained about the long hours I was away from home. We tried family dinners for a while, but Marie soon tired of the routine.

To the very end, I remained loyal to Marie. In some respects, I remain so even to this day. Marie was always extremely jealous of other women. She grew more resentful of an expanding awareness that I wasn't the man she thought I was. There was never a way for me to demonstrate how much I loved her. It represents the complex issue of why and when transgender persons choose to transition. It creates the unfortunate perception that a man is choosing to become a woman. Men don't want to become women. The man Marie imagined, however, became a threat to her. There is a remarkable irony in that. She became increasingly disenfranchised by me as a woman and increasingly threatened by me as a man.

In many ways, it was an exciting time of my life because people asked some amazing questions. It allowed me to experience the complex issues of gender within the general population. That is something I didn't get in online chats or support groups and definitely not in a therapist's office. It was introspective, but it also taught me about how people perceive gender. Gender is clearly more about perception than it is about presentation. Why else would people relate to me as a woman when clearly by my appearance I was a man wearing a dress? It is a fascinating idea to consider.

Before 2003, when I wore a dress there was always some excuse. It was Halloween or I was practicing a part in a play or I had lost a bet. It was a common question from men, "Did you lose a bet?" Many men are curious about wearing women's clothes. Lot's of men have worn women's clothing. How many is a lot of men? Nobody knows. There is no data on the subject. In my estimation, the numbers are much lower than many of the guesstimates you might find on the Internet. In eight years of dressing, I never saw more than three or four men dressed as women. In my personal experience as a group facilitator, I also found it could be distressing for a man who dresses up as a woman when he discovers that women's fashions can be sensuous. If men understood that maybe they'd understand why we don't always want to be "dressed up." It's not all that relaxing.

Tri-Ess, the Society of the Second Self is a national support organization for cross-dressers and their families. Cross-dresser is how I identified for a while as a way of legitimizing my masculine role presentation. They have twenty chapters throughout the US, but they don't publish any data about their membership for obvious reasons. Social stigma against men wearing dresses remains high. I attended several Tri-Ess meetings, but it wasn't effective for me. They are men. It didn't fulfill my social need to be with other women. Their rules agreed. It is only for heterosexual men, which I wasn't. It contradicts the popular perception that men who wear dresses are gay.

What was the most common question by far? "Are you gay?" I am not gay. If they asked that more than once I knew they weren't listening.

I had to say I was attracted to women, and I did find women attractive. I was attracted to what they had: what I wanted. I might want to know where she got her outfit. She might ask the same of me. The intimacy I enjoyed in my relationship with Marie didn't correlate with my feelings around sexuality. After the transition, people wanted to know if I was a lesbian. I evaded the question initially by suggesting I didn't really know any lesbians.

For a time, I believed men would wear dresses if they could. I actually tried to frame it as a men's rights issues. It was absurd. Men don't want to become women. Men don't want to wear dresses.

I can't really confirm why people believe a man wearing a dress must be gay. Maybe it's the link between effeminate and gay. Possibly, it's awareness of drag queens who are always portrayed as gay men. Some trans women are drag queens, but most drag queens I met were men. Drag is performance. Frequently it's exaggerated gender stereotyping. As a man in a dress, I wasn't well received among drag queens. They were horrified when I revealed that I did not have a girl name. It was mandatory if I was going to perform "Confessions of a Cross-dresser," during their show.

For a time I became Misty Chimera, a name that would later haunt me. I also received admonitions about hair and makeup and even shaving my legs: a curious dilemma perhaps, since I never had any hair on my legs. Nearly all of the criticism I received came from the LGBT community. Essme Rodriguez, a drag show manager in the twin cities, was the only one who ever stood up for me.

The gay and lesbian community, in general, wasn't accepting of my presentation. They also had strict ideas about gender. Many of them still do, particularly gay men. Many still prefer to think of us as the showgirls but then that representation of women has dominated male perceptions for centuries.

It is certain there was always risk surrounding me, but I never paid attention. My only moment of high anxiety I experienced riding the city bus. A guy chased the bus for several yards yelling and pointing. I was glad I couldn't hear him.

Well-intentioned people were always saying to me "…those people over there are talking about you." But for the constant reminders, I was indifferent to it except for one unusual occasion I simply couldn't ignore. I was meeting some friends at the Bakers Square in Rosemount. I was a little late, and they were all seated way in the back of the restaurant. Walking towards them, I happened to notice the people in front of me staring. I stopped and looked around the room. Everyone in the room was staring at me. It was as if time had stopped. I don't know how long I stood there with some sense of disbelief. Finally, I did a curtsy, and everyone looked away.

Women often surrounded me. I've taken part in a dozen bachelorette parties, bridesmaid walks and even a bride's walk fundraising event for breast cancer. Regrettably, I could not find a wedding dress for the event. Guys were constantly asking me how to connect with the women. I gave them suggestions they probably wouldn't get from most women, but they could never understand why my friendship relationship with them was different than what they were looking for.

What fascinated me most of all was the number of men who offered to protect me. One evening I was at a Minnesota Vikings and Green Bay Packer game at Bogart's in Apple Valley. I was wearing my Vikings cheerleader outfit. A long sleeve micro mini dress with a deep neckline, a Vikings emblem and white go-go boots. As I returned to the bar area from the patio, a tall black man approached me. He was a good six inches taller than me and built like a lineman. My heart was pounding. He was drop-dead gorgeous. He said to me, "I think you're in the wrong place."

I could still feel my heart pounding, but excitement turned to apprehension. I replied as calmly as I could, "Are you threatening me?"

He broke into half a smile and said, "No. There are some Green Bay Packer fans inside, and they're getting pretty rowdy." He continued with, "If they give you any trouble just come and get me." I am thinking I should have gotten in a little trouble that night so he could rescue me.

Another event occurred on University Avenue in St. Paul when my car overheated. I was forced to pull into a mall parking lot. Car problems always left me feeling vulnerable. Assessing the situation, I figured with some tape and some antifreeze, I'd be able to make it home. As I was coming out of the store, I had to walk past three young black men having a conversation in the parking lot. One of them called out rather loudly, "Look! That guy's dressed like a bitch." I could feel my heart pounding, and I paused for a moment. Why, they're only cards, after all. I needn't be afraid of them!

Then I turned around, walked over to them, and said, "I've lost all of the antifreeze in my car. Would you gentleman like to help me?" And they did.

Experiencing men from a woman's perspective was entirely different than what I learned about them presenting as another man. It was beginning to shape a rather profound realization that the majority of men and women are only able to perceive each other and themselves from one gender perspective. How could I possibly explain that to them?

The joy of womanhood belies a continuing sense of dismay over the strict segregation of gender. Today, my relationship to men is inextricably altered with an uneasiness of nostalgic reflection. There are unfamiliar boundaries around male spaces. I recall a men's breakfast I attended at my church seeking to continue a conversation I had begun with one of the pastors. While I was allowed to remain for breakfast, come Sunday I felt like the whole town knew about it. I was informed that my attendance was inappropriate, dramatizing the fact that I really am a woman now. There is no going back. There is no true reality to go back too.

Chapter Thirty: A Common Question

I recall when I was first asked about my husband. For most people, it's a simple question, but I had to stop and think. After an inordinately long pause, I simply offered, "I'm single." Sometimes you're just not in the mood for long explanations.

The most curious question ever asked of me was a conundrum: "How do you know you're a woman if you have never been a man?" The question itself seems to require some knowledge of the fact that transgender women frequently state they have been female since birth. I've never made that claim, even though I am certain I was never a boy.

I've been asked that same question several times. My short answer: "I'm not good at math! Girls aren't good at math you know!" I use the same answer when I can't remember today's date. The rest of the conversation depended on their response.

I'd love to have a clear answer to affirm my female identity to society. People also ask, "Why do you want to be a woman?" I wish my answer: "It best defines me," was totally unambiguous: but it's not. Most trans women will say. "I am a woman" or "I've always been a woman, I didn't choose it."

Few people ever question their gender. Most people seem intuitively satisfied with the belief they're either a man or they're a woman. Transgender individuals perceive the world differently. As a child, I was totally comfortable with the female environment that surrounded me. At puberty, I was totally out of place in the male environment where I was forced to exist. Placed together with boys, it was obvious I wasn't a boy, despite appearances.

Comparing myself to girls was more complicated in a way that girls are simply more complicated.

The more challenging question becomes: If I am not a male, does that mean I am a female? It is a puzzling hypothesis derived from false assumptions. Sex has been defined by reproductive potential, gender has been defined by sex, and behavior has been defined by gender. Pick any subject, and it will be impossible to ignore the differentiation of abilities and behaviors based on gender. Any blog discussion about biological determinants of gender differences invariably includes some reference to the cave man theory of gender differentiation. The polarity of gender is deeply entrenched in our society, and we all internalize the values of our culture. It's by far the most confusing thing I ever heard. When your entire existence is saying you're one thing, it is difficult to conclude you're something else.

When asked how I identify, I say, "I'm a transgender woman," because I believe the distinction is meaningful and quite valuable.

Advanced technologies for examining the brain are providing new insights about the perceived differences in the abilities and behavior of men and women. Most people can intuitively accept that the brain is a larger determinant of our abilities and behavior than our sex organs despite stereotypical assertions about which organ controls a man's behavior.

A comprehensive study by a group of researchers led by Daphna Joel, a behavioral neuroscientist at Tel Aviv University in Israel, found a few structural differences between men and women. They also found there was significant overlap between males and females. To accommodate this overlap, the researchers created a continuum of "femaleness" to "maleness," for the entire brain. The majority of the brains were a mosaic of male and female structures. Very few of the brains—between 0 percent and 8 percent—contained all male or all female structures. "There is no one type of male brain or female brain," Joel says. The overlap between female and male characteristics is intuitively obvious to most people.

Ragini Verma, PhD, associate professor at the University of Pennsylvania in Philadelphia and her team of researchers examined neural pathways, which examines how the brain processes information. They conclude that differences in their "brain roadmaps" (scientifically known as "the connectome") can explain why males and females perform differently on certain tests of mental skills.

Attempts to establish a definitive biological or environmental determinant of gender is fundamentally flawed. The brain is extremely adaptive evidenced by how people recover from a stroke or brain injury. The study by Ragini Verna's team also concludes that even if male and female brains start out similar, they may become different over time as boys and girls are treated differently with different expectations.

The picture is still incomplete because there are many things that affect human ability and behavior such as neurotransmitters, hormones, and even basic proteins. Many transgender people have experienced both male and female hormones to a substantial degree and can assure you the difference is significant. That seems intuitively obvious to most people as well. When women are talking about too much testosterone, we aren't talking about a medical condition.

The transgender community makes a strong assertion that sex and gender aren't the same. More recently that has been expanded to include gender expression, how you dress or behave. What is commonly missing from the discussion is the idea that sex and sexuality aren't the same either. That's the part people find most distressing. Fitbrains website[1] provides a simple comparison regarding the differences in male and female brains. You might find it interesting to see how it compares to your own perceptions of men and women.

My answer to the question of how I know I'm a woman emphasizes my personal observations about my relationship with both men and women, both presenting as a man and a woman. Use of the word presentation is significant because it's more observable and more measurable. I don't subscribe to the emerging concept that I can change my identity by simply changing my clothes, but it can change the way people perceive me and respond to me.

At the same time I started wearing dresses in 2003, I also began attending the sexual boundaries group at the Twin Cities Men's Center. The social incongruity was immediately obvious. I wore a dress when I attended these group support sessions. I was a woman and a rape survivor. Many of the men were registered sex offenders on parole, enrolled in the Pathfinders treatment program. I'd not be there without the male passport provided me at birth and lacking the credentials for entry into the protective safety of a female support group.

That support group also reignited anxieties I experienced during the child abuse witch-hunts in the eighties. Unlike the Domestic Abuse Project, however, I could be anonymous outside the group making it less threatening. I have no doubt that the group facilitators, Bobby and Tommy, made it work. They called it the beast, an uncomfortable physical attraction to minors. At times they injected their own personal experiences and how they resolved these uncomfortable feelings. There is little funding available to help these men. Funding goes to empower the criminal justice system to prosecute them.

Initially, I struggled with these responses. Over time there evolved a deep respect for their commitment to the group and their ability to maintain emotional stability and dignity in the midst of extreme social persecution for circumstances not inherently of their own making. It became obvious that most, if not all, of these men were themselves victims of violent or incestuous childhoods. Their lack of boundaries seems self-evident. They did not grow up with any insight into the dysfunctional or damaging nature of these behaviors. This escape clause doesn't work for men.

My relationship to the group was one of victim to perpetrator. It became apparent to me why that model is counter-productive. It is the victim-perpetrator antithesis of oppositional sexism that frames masculinity as superior to femininity. It empowers exploitation through gender differentiation and segregation. It is a reactionary model based on treating the victim and punishing the perpetrator. It empowers the criminal justice system. It defies standards of evaluation, early assessment, and intervention focused on prevention. As my own experience with the Domestic

Abuse Project affirmed, there is no pretense of restoring functional family dynamics or healing a relationship.

With rare exception, I was at the sexual boundaries group every Saturday morning from ten until noon for eight years. These men never challenged my gender presentation. These men respected me. These men protected me. In return, I came to believe in them. Over the years I'd experience the depth of their emotions and observe an amazing transformation. I'd also come to understand that these men would never be allowed to experience the full social benefits of that transformation.

It seemed like many of the men at TCMC were gay. I couldn't say the percentage. That type of data disrupts the inclusiveness that existed at the men's center. TCMC was among the first to provide a gay men's support group. TCMC was open to all men, and it was also evident to me that many of them were not gay. Sure, some men are gay and some men are not. Today most people consider that a trivial observation. For me, that dynamic was part of a pathway to a broader understanding of sexuality and gender, neither of which is perfectly linked to a person's sex assignment at birth.

In the mid-00s, people assuming I was gay told me, "You should go [downtown] and be with your own kind." I did sometimes. For a while, I went down to the Eagles Club, a gay men's nightclub in Minneapolis for happy hour. The downstairs had great dance music and a vacant dance floor. I could wear a bikini and dance; the whole floor available to my own choreography. After a while, an audience started to develop, and I eventually stopped going, but for a time it was a great workout.

To me they were men. Fay Weldon author of *The Life and Loves of a She-Devil* says it's because they have a penis. We might readily assume which organ she believes men use to do their thinking. This demonic representation of men remains deeply rooted in the American myth about gender and sexuality. Then again Fay Weldon is in her eighties, and old people are set in their ways. Such is the language of social stereotyping.

Understanding gay relationships was an important step in understanding broader issues of sexuality and gender. It advanced my understanding of why my attraction to men was different from theirs, and it began to unravel the relationship between sex and gender. I volunteered for training as a facilitator in the Among Men Project. Among Men was a weekend course about man-to-man relationships and sexuality intended to promote healthy relationships and safe sex. The program was developed to protect men from the AIDS epidemic. I was one of the facilitators the first time the course was offered at the Men's Center.

In my TV view of the world, I realized that I had internalized certain perceptions of a "gay lifestyle" which emphasized a social prejudice of promiscuous sex. While sharing their experiences, listening to their stories, and reviewing the course materials with them a different image emerged of highly monogamous relationships, not unlike heterosexual relationships. Certainly, some had open relationships, but it was based on a mutual acceptance and understanding unlike the extramarital affairs common to heterosexual relationships.

Traversing the network of social services centered on issues of sexual violence, child abuse, sex trafficking, and domestic abuse would parallel my own transition and facilitate the evolution of my gender presentation from male to female.

The Men's Center would continue to be a valuable resource. It's where I explored the male side of issues I had long been conditioned to believe were women's issues; issues like sexual violence, intimate partner violence, child abuse, domestic abuse, and divorce. These issues structure a social model where women are victims and men are perpetrators. Those insights guided me and sustained me when charges of abuse were falsely leveled against me. It was their support that shaped my emotional and legal defense.

1 Niu, Ariel, Gender & the Brain: Differences between Women & Men, Fitbrains, February 18, 2014, Web. May 20.,2017. http://www.fitbrains.com/blog/women-men-brains/

Chapter Thirty-one: Unraveling

"You ought to be ashamed of yourself for asking such a simple question." added the Gryphon

–Lewis Carroll, Alice in Wonderland

Wearing dresses worked well for me, but it magnified Marie's anxiety about social harassment which was often projected on the children. Protecting children is a common projection of adult anxieties. The fear was exaggerated. Many of their friends did know.

A year later in 2004, Marie and I separated. It was a painful experience. I remember vividly the day we told our children about the arrangement. They would get the house and Marie or I would stay with them on alternating weeks. Marie stayed with Terri, and I stayed with my friend Jim. It was an awkward situation at best. I missed her. She missed me too. We had long conversations on the phone and by the end of the third week, the separation was over. I had taken the first week and the last week. It was a foretelling footnote when Tyler said to me, "That's not fair, you had to go for two weeks and she only had to go for one."

As parents, heavily invested in our children, it's easy to overlook the fact that they are also heavily invested in us. According to the old adage, "do as I say, not as I do," we sometimes fail to realize what we are teaching our children as they closely watch what we do. The plan may have been more successful if we had a separate apartment for the away weeks. I knew I couldn't afford it. Relying on friends proved uncomfortable for both of us.

When the company in Chaska restructured two years later, I took classes in database administration and started doing contract work in quality assurance. Marie never did find meaningful employment after she left bartending. She experimented with different options form airline pilot to stockbroker. We invested a tremendous amount of money in her education but with no return on investment, it added to our accumulating monthly payments. We were living with negative cash flow, but Marie viewed budgeting, or any discussion at all about money, as abusive for trying to control her spending. She loved to reference studies she heard on Oprah proving her services were worth $50,000 annually as if I ought to be ashamed of myself for asking such a simple question. I never disputed her equal contribution to the marriage, but I also didn't discuss the value of my domestic services either: car repair, home repair, remodeling, and yard work; not to mention I was still paying for daycare,

I spent a lot of time with Courtney, regretting that I hadn't done the same for Jamie. Instant Messaging was at its height, and I received many IMs from Courtney over the disagreements she was having with Marie. I still have copies of some of those dialogues. It is interesting to review from an external perspective, how seriously dysfunctional the family's communication was. I made a lot of visits to the school, trying to identify options. Finally, I agreed to a school transfer from Eagan High School to Rosemount. Courtney is a graduate of Rosemount, though she never spent a day there. She was accepted to the School of Environmental Studies, popularly referred to as the Zoo School for its close proximity and connection to the Minnesota Zoo in Apple Valley. It was perfect for her, providing the challenge and independence she needed.

I understood my relationship with Marie wasn't going to end well. I started reading books on divorce and attending divorce workshops. I even found an attorney whom I wanted to represent me. I also knew that if I left Marie I'd lose my children. I felt trapped.

I encouraged Courtney to move on with her life, graduate high school, and go to college. Sometimes it was subtle in terms of assisting her with career goals, but sometimes it directly engaged her conflicts with Marie. I assumed that once Courtney moved on, I'd have time to focus on Tyler. He was, after all, four years younger than Courtney. It didn't work out that way. Besides the money and teen/parent conflict, there was another conflict buried in secrecy.

My Linux training brought technology into our home. Everyone had their own computer, a rare thing just ten years ago. Ours was the only home where Tyler and his friends could play multiplayer computer games as Internet gaming was just starting to evolve. There were unintended consequences that went along with it. Linux is open source. It belongs in the public domain. It's free to use, modify, and copy.

Linux came with a default screensaver that created an ever-changing collage on the computer by drawing images randomly downloaded from the web. One afternoon the screensaver started drawing a rather large photo, in a prominent position on the screen, of an erect penis. I have already explained that these images were taken randomly from sites on the Internet, but Marie was convinced it was pornography I had stored on my computer.

That one image was enough to convince a therapist with a PhD in clinical psychology, but it wasn't enough for Marie. During this time frame, I was working on the Among Men Project focused on male sexuality. The training introduced me to a wide range of sexual expression and behaviors I had never experienced or even heard of. I realized how completely naive I was. I didn't really feel like I could facilitate discussions among men about male sexuality if I didn't even recognize the terms. I did my research on the web. That too had unexpected consequences.

I believed in Marie. I trusted her. I had faith in her. She didn't feel the same about me. She searched my personal effects, read my text messages, and reviewed my email.

My browser history was a different problem. Beyond the sites I viewed, she followed browser links to sites I'd never visited. Starting with sexually-oriented content, I don't need to speculate that she found some disturbing imagery. I'd not know about it, and I'd not know the impact it had on our relationship.

Open Source Software also gave me GIMP, a graphic art program with capabilities similar to Photoshop. I was fascinated by the way our mind interprets images. I enjoyed working with flesh tones and the complexity of color variation and shading. Mostly I worked with photos of nude females, constructing images of things I might imagine for myself; many depicted bondage. Creating these scenes allowed me to escape from the emotional stress of my life. For a time I was relieved of the overwhelming responsibilities; my destiny, my pleasure, at the mercy of a dominant lover. I wanted time to feel helpless and vulnerable, to feel sheltered and protected. This wasn't possible in my lived reality. Any sign of vulnerability always met with increased demands upon me or an assault upon my "manliness." For a time those personal moments devoted to graphic arts helped relieve some of the sexual anxiety surrounding the complete lack of any physical or emotional intimacy in my marriage. The activity is, perhaps, antithetical to classic feminism but also reflecting a fundamental weakness of placing gender equity so deep within the confines of male sexuality. Marie understood it as a threat. To her, it was hardcore pornography.

I wanted to share with Marie. I was open to compromise. I read the books she suggested. One, in particular, we read at the same time, discussing it, chapter-by-chapter. The book was *Miss America by Day*. I saw many parallels between her marriage and ours, but what Marie saw was how her husband didn't measure up to the compassionate husband she saw represented in the book. Marie was determined to trust her intuition but never willing to assess the basis of it. No matter how steady my voice, how calm my demeanor, be it genuine or rehearsed, there was always "the look." Marie was always deciphering my inner thoughts and motives according to an internal matrix, which I'm certain she herself did not understand.

Chapter Thirty-two: Last Showdown

"It sounded an excellent plan, no doubt, and very simply and neatly arranged; the only difficulty was, that she had not the smallest idea how to set about it."

–Lewis Carroll, Alice in Wonderland

Metaphorically, I was attempting to keep myself centered in the eye of the storm, hoping beyond hope that the storm would eventually wear itself out. I called it "my plan:" keep my earnings ahead of the expenses, and help Courtney and Tyler to find their own path. It sounded an excellent plan, no doubt, and very simply and neatly arranged; the only difficulty was that she had not the smallest idea how to set about it.

My goal was to keep Tyler in his home until he graduated from high school. Anything after that was a black hole. I wasn't convinced I'd even survive that long. It wasn't really a plan. It was more of a commitment involving sacrifices I couldn't imagine.

My career rebounded in process design and data analysis. I thrived on the challenges and the opportunities, and the money was good. For about a month, it seemed like my plan might succeed.

The issue of survival came suddenly in the fall of 2006. I'd known it was inevitable since my early twenties when I first learned about a defective heart value I had when I was born.

The timing was bad, very bad, just a month after starting on one of the most challenging projects of my career. I was in the backyard with Tyler wrapping up the pool for the winter. It was heavy exertion, and when I stood up, I suddenly fell short of breath and had to lie down. I remember telling Tyler, "I just need to rest for a few minutes." He says I was unresponsive. Tyler went for Marie. I was talking to her when the paramedics arrived. She told me I'd passed out. I didn't believe her. She told me I wet my pants. I still didn't believe her. I was clearly disoriented.

The ambulance took me to the hospital for observation. Marie arrived later. She came to me in the emergency room, but when they released me she was nowhere to be found. I felt abandoned. Looking for her at the hospital is when I first realized that in fact, my pants were soaking wet. Then I was upset that Marie hadn't brought me dry clothes. I didn't mention any of it. In the car on the way home, I was upset about the cost of the ambulance. I regret that, at the same time realizing the immense level of stress I was under.

I was advised to see a cardiologist immediately. They wanted to schedule me for surgery right away. The thought of listening to a mechanical valve clicking for the rest of my life wasn't convincing. I just wanted to see Tyler graduate from high school. I only needed five more years for that. I thought about the little cooler of needles in the park, what Marie had said to me, and I didn't want to be on blood thinners either.

I know for certain Marie was terrified, because she often told me I was scaring the children. I spent nearly four months researching options and attempting to find a surgeon in my insurance network. I continued working the entire time, afraid that any indication of the problem at work might end my contract. I used my lunch hours for medical tests and doctor appointments. Sometimes Marie went with me, but it was sporadic. I arranged a PTO day for an examination at Mayo Clinic. Each day I walked nearly a mile from my car to the office. Most days I'd take rest stops along the way fearful of passing out. At times my heart palpitated, beating rapidly while I tried to breathe deeply and relax. It happened one night after going to bed. When the palpitation stopped I heard dead silence and then this thought, *I'm dead … it's over,* then momentarily, *I'm still breathing … I'm not dead.* I spent that four months wondering every day if it might be my last.

When I asked for a leave of absence my boss was immediately suspicious, so I acknowledged I was having heart surgery. She was very supportive. My mom and my sister Lori came to support me. I was extremely grateful, but Marie felt preempted. Failing to survive the surgery weighed heavily on me, feeling like I'd never wake up, just like my father. I thought about giving power of attorney to my sister because I wasn't certain Marie would be emotionally up to the task. In the end, I decided to maintain what little faith I had left.

I was in the hospital on my birthday. Marie gave me clothes but took them back home the night before I was released. She wasn't there to pick me up, so I left the hospital wearing my mother's robe and slippers. I felt totally undignified. I had a beautiful dress and high heel boots at the hospital, another gift for my birthday from friends at the men's center. Marie had not taken them and I can't imagine her thinking. Lori didn't think Mom could handle the dress.

I had one of the best heart surgeons in the world. His team called him Yoda after the old sage in *Star Wars*. Except for the valve I was in good health, and the replacement gave me a new lease on life. I was in the hospital four days and ready to go back to work in a week. In our final appointment, the surgeon said natural heart value was a good choice. He said if I was in California, that's what most people would choose. It made me cognizant of the fact that I was living in a medical device state.

In spite of the renewed vitality, there was a subsequent period of depression. It may have been a common side effect of the anesthesia. If I'd known, I may have handled it better. One month later Jamie delivered our second granddaughter. Marie went down to the hospital late one evening. She was upset I didn't go with, but I was already sleeping and had to work in the morning. "Memories," she called it. She was right. Again I felt left out, isolated from my family by the demands of my family. I was down at the hospital the next day with our other two children: Courtney and Tyler. It was another dimension to the divisions within the family.

Shortly after the delivery in 2007, during the Minneapolis Pride celebration, I joined, with Courtney and her friend Mateo, in the first transgender march. It's the first time I met Essme Rodriguez. Essme was a professor of gender and women's studies at Macalester College. She was also a drag performance artist.

As a definite sign of the times, we weren't allowed to March anywhere near Loring Park, the location of the pride festival. It was, in essence, a protest march with protest organizers giving us instructions on what to do if confronted by police or harassed by spectators. We wrote phone numbers on our wrists. The march was rather uneventful. There were a lot of people in the area so there was a lot of visibility but no news coverage.

The after-party was at Pi bar in Minneapolis, and Courtney was the master of ceremonies. Ellen Krug, the author of *Getting to Ellen*, was also at the after-party that day though I didn't know it. It would be five more years before I actually meet her. She describes it in her book as the first time she presented in public as a woman. She talks about meeting Tempest who was performing that day with Harsh Reality, a heavy metal band. It is the first time I met Tempest and Jendeen, formerly with the band All the Pretty Horses. Coincidentally, one of their lead singers, Odie, was a person I frequently sang karaoke with at Casper's in Eagan. I did follow their band for a while and during the time period performed as a march girl for a few performances. That was interesting. It was fun too but definitely not my ambition. I have a photo of me with Tempest in which I am wearing my pink Pride dress. It must be the first time I ever wore it because I hadn't previously attended the Pride festival.

A manager from my department at work was in the crowd that day and recognized me participating in the march. When I returned to work on Monday morning, it seemed like everyone in the company knew about it.

Chapter Thirty-three: Family Therapy

"How do you know I'm mad?" said Alice. "You must be," said the Cat, "or you wouldn't have come..."

–Lewis Carroll, Alice in Wonderland

From the date on the impound receipt, it must have been January 23, 2008, probably around 9 PM, because I left the karaoke show early that night. I normally sang karaoke two nights a week during that lonely period of my life. Singing is good for the soul. It provided a sense of community around people with whom I at least had one thing in common. On the seat next to me sat the to-go box for the meal I'd barely touched. I was in the acceleration lane on Interstate 494 entering from Concord Street in South St. Paul when flashing blue lights appeared in the rearview mirror. I didn't feel any cause for concern. I never finished my third glass of beer so I figured approximately four twelve-ounce beers, more than usual but still under the limit.

According to the weather map, it was five below zero. All I had on when the officer made me get out of the car was a short halter dress and a light leather coat. As I am reciting the alphabet backward, I wondered about the potential for frostbite. According to the Breathalyzer, I was over the limit, and he put me in the back of his car.

The back of the police car was warm, and I felt safe. Here was a man taking control. It's a strange way to feel about an arrest and was a clear indicator of my emotional distress. I was certain Marie wouldn't be sober enough to accept responsibility for me, so I asked Courtney for a ride home. A month later, the test came back right at the legal limit of .08. To this day I maintain that the test was wrong, and I decided to retain an attorney. There were already legal challenges to the accuracy of the testing method.

Minnesota was using urine testing at the time because of the major software issues and legal challenges around the Breathalyzer testing devices. Minnesota was one of only three states still using urine testing because of its inaccuracy.

Justice in America is expensive. There were nine of us challenging the test. All of us contributing to the cost of expert witnesses and presenting the case. I spent nearly $7000 myself. I gained new insights on American justice. Education is expensive.

The case was never about science. The judge concluded that the test was "close enough." The remaining eight went on to appeal. I decided I could no longer afford the cost or the stress of it and plead to a petty misdemeanor charge. I don't know what happened to the other eight, but the Minnesota Supreme Court eventually ruled that a warrant is required to issue the test.

I spent a month with my cousin in Saint Paul, so I could ride the bus to work. After that, a sixty-day work permit forced me to be at home. It was stressful. I didn't drink during that period but Marie did. I spent a lot of time in the basement, pacing back and forth like a caged lion.

At the end of that ordeal, Marie agreed to attend family counseling as one last resort. It was an exercise in futility. I scheduled an appointment for family counseling with Eagan Counseling Clinic. Mr. R was the first therapist we saw. According to the clinic, he is a qualified family therapist. I can say with certainty, he never worked with a family like ours.

The conversation degenerated quickly, as the therapist focused on the overbearing husband. It's a classic gender scenario we got from all of the male therapists we saw. It is exactly what I didn't want to happen. He informed me, with an obvious sense of pride, that he had published an important paper on how to offer a sincere apology, and he was eager to teach me those skills. Obviously, he thought he was talking to a man. What a woman needs is to stop apologizing.

Before I suggested I was a woman, Mr. R concluded I was a cross-dresser. He said to me, "I understand cross-dressing. I have a friend who is a cross-dresser. He knows I don't like it, so he doesn't dress around me. You could do the cross-dressing in your room." S*ome friend*, I thought. *You want me to play dress-up in the closet? That's your solution?* I wanted to say this but didn't.

What I said was worse, ending any possibility of a therapeutic relationship. I said, "I have a black friend too. I just don't invite him to white parties." I'd already said too much, but I went on to explain I had two gender presentations, living socially as female and presenting as male in my roles as father, husband, and employee. I said, "I'll demonstrate."

I began to debate the meaning of "I'm sorry," according to his proclaimed expertise with apologies. I took the position that "I'm sorry" expressed empathy, as in "I'm sorry your dog died," but it's really not my fault. Women are constantly apologizing, and I was no exception.

From my perspective, it was a typically masculine attempt to apply logic and reason to properties of female emotion. How often I recall men saying, "Why can't women just be reasonable?" to which women might reply, "Why can't men just learn to express their true feelings?" I'm caught in the middle.

The debate continued until he finally said, "I find you overbearing, and I am offended by you." I was expecting it but still amazed the therapist injected his feelings into my therapy session. That was the point of the exercise.

I switched to a more female presentation. "I'm sorry I offended you;" we apologize. "I'd love to read your paper;" we accomdate. "I should respect your expertise;" we minimize our opinions. "I was wrong;" we discount ourselves. Mr. R told me I was being passive-aggressive. What a classical therapy expression. It took me back thirty years to my own experience in counseling when pop psychology books were all the rage, and we were all studying transactional analysis. I told him exactly what I was going to do, and he missed it completely. Marie got up in disgust and stormed out of the room.

Mr. R looked at me with an obvious sense of shock and said, "I can help you if you will let me."

I politely declined, "I don't believe we will be returning."

Mr. R indicated in his assessment I was paranoid, a poor communicator, and incapable of understanding the position of others.

He concluded, "Seems to have a severe personality disorder."
"How do you know I'm mad?" "You must be," said the therapist,
"or you wouldn't have come here." Apparently, Mr. R thought
gender dysphoria is a personality disorder.

Passive-aggressive is a behavior from women trapped between
the innocence of feminine purity and raw female emotion, which
remains so mysterious and incomprehensible to men. It is an
attempt to gain power in a relationship where there is none. It is
another name for the bewitching, beguiling power of women.
There is a lot more to being a woman than putting on a dress and
getting your hair styled. Still, it's where many transgender women
begin.

I didn't spell it out for him: GID, gender identity disorder. Now
it's called gender dysphoria, the condition of feeling one's emotional and psychological identity as male or female to be opposite
to one's sex assignment at birth.

The kids saw no reason why they should attend family therapy
sessions to sit in the waiting room for forty-five minutes. While
they were waiting, Courtney, being her usual gregarious self, had
engaged Dr. G. In retrospect it made little sense to select another
therapist from the same clinic.

Dr. G exaggerated the conundrum of therapy, the trust issues,
and the often-overlooked polarity between restorative therapies
and developmental therapies. I was seeking a communication
channel with my partner, even if the goal was unrealistic. Dr. G
had his own agenda. Dr. G's previous experience was with
Pathfinders. Remember the sexual boundaries group at the Men's
Center? Remember the sex offender model of male sexuality?
Remember that many of the men in the sexual boundaries group
were in the pathfinders program?

He never had any intent to save the marriage. I should have
realized his agenda. I understood how personally offensive he
was. He is the first professional I ever told about the rape in college. His reply reinforced the reasons I never reported it. He said,
"You were experimenting, that's what boys do." It's the classic
"boys will be boys" model of male sexuality.

In one session, I talked about the lack of privacy in my relationship and my use of self-care to manage the sexual anxiety. Self-care is an extremely important concept in Pathfinders therapy that overcomes an overt dependence on someone else to fulfill those needs. I described the warm baths and the candlelight. Dr. G joked about the "good jerk," a comic routine by Chris Rock. Consider a male therapist telling a woman a joke about jacking off. Forgive me if the language is offensive, but that's how I felt: sexually assaulted. I'd given Dr. G something to work with right out of his own playbook, but he disregarded it. Aside from his sexually exploitative behavior, I'd later discover he was making personal assessments that proved more damaging later on.

What I disdain is the arrogance of expert opinion. Perhaps prior to GID, the DSM-5[1] should contain an entry for EID, Expert Identity Disorder, the perception that one's own knowledge base is inherently superior to a dissimilar knowledge base of another individual. Dr. G made no attempt to assess the problem he was presented with.

I'd contrast Dr. G's behavior with that of my medical doctor, whom I trust completely. I respect his medical knowledge and insights, but my absolute trust depends on his willingness to emphasize what he doesn't know. Because of that trust, my medical doctor would in time, with a single statement, completely turn my life around.

I started doing my own research. When I first started exploring my own gender dysphoria I read books like *My Husband Betty* by Helen Boyd and *My Husband Wears My Clothes* by Peggy J. Rudd. I explored the Internet, which generally led to cross-dressing sites. It all felt like men who enjoyed dressing as a woman. There were suggestions of the "second self," the idea that a person could be both masculine and feminine, but the personification of the second self always reflected male attitudes toward women. None of it came close to describing what I was experiencing.

Looking for more concrete explanations, I read books like *As Nature Made Him: The Boy Who Was Raised as a Girl by John Colapinto* that chronicled a gender reassignment experiment[2] conducted by John Money at Hopkins University. It presented me with credibility for what I already knew to be true. *Transgender*

Warriors by Leslie Feinberg provided the context I needed. Her book explores the history and cultural diversity of the transgender experience. Finally, *Whipping Girl by Julia Serano* emphasized the social context of transgender women in a sexist society. Her book linked together so many of the emotional connections I've had with other women throughout my life. *Whipping Girl* was the last book in my literary exploration before I started actively engaging in the transgender community.

1 https://www.psychiatry.org/psychiatrists/practice/dsm

2 "Who was David Reimer?", Intersex Society of North America, Accessed May 20, 2017, http://www.isna.org/faq/reimer.

Chapter Thirty-four: Revolution

What do you know about this business? The family model of Mr. R and Dr. G was so simplistic and rigid, one could hardly expect them to have any meaningful interaction with the Overby family. Overly possessed of their own Expert Identity, they overlooked the opportunity to learn about some complex family relationships. In truth, our family was already well connected to the transgender movement through another of our family members.

His chosen name was Mateo and I respectfully choose to omit his given name. My first recollection of him was a poetry presentation he made at the Caponi Art Park in Eagan. He and my daughter met at the School of Environmental Studies.

For a parent to relate to a child's partner is itself a challenge, but the fact I was a transgender woman and he was a transgender man invoked an additional range of gender conflicts that are fully manifested within the transgender community. These complications included the fact that I did not fully represent myself as transgender though we walked together in the first Minneapolis transgender march.

Mateo was adopted from Colombia by a fairly wealthy white middle-class family. Mateo rejected the privilege of his adopted family in opposition to the systemic repression of people of color. It was clear he also experienced cultural isolation from his native heritage: something that is a highly under-reported consequence for children of foreign-born adoptions. Because of his transgender identity, he was deeply engaged with a transgender community in the twin cities that was heavily invested in the intersectionality of race and gender identity.

He was, by my account, a revolutionary. As the daughter of a freedom fighter myself, I could not disrespect that, having sought to tear down the establishment in my own youthfulness. That did not mitigate my distress in the disrespectful ways that he communicated with my daughter. I often found his behavior to be abusive and highly disruptive given to his extreme interpretations of white privilege that he assigned to anyone not a person of color.

Decisiveness around the issues of race and ethnicity spotlights the challenges of a community attempting to unify around gender identity but divided by the full range of social issues. The oppressiveness of sexism and male privilege do not seem any less intense within the transgender community than they do within the cisgender[1] community. As a trans woman myself, it is easy for me to postulate that trans men and women would experience a more cooperative narrative, each having a lived experience in both genders. However, this postulation does not generally hold true. What it does suggest is how readily we internalize the cultural values of our trans identity even when raised in the opposite gender. Ironically, that internalization becomes a powerful affirmation of transgender identity.

Conflict over social diversity portends a harsh reality for the transgender movement toward advancing the notion of gender diversity. There is strong resistance to the concept of gender diversity. Public reaction to the gay rights movement focused predominately on men. Public reaction to the transgender movement focuses predominately on trans women. That alone underscores the impact of sexuality in masculine dominance over women through the protected class status of women.

1 denoting or relating to a person whose sense of personal identity and gender corresponds with their birth sex

Chapter Thirty-five: One Last Detail

"Then it doesn't matter which way you go," said the Cat.

–Lewis Carroll, Alice in Wonderland

When I first thought about writing a book, I began writing about some of my personal experiences. Singing was good for the soul, but writing preserved my emotional sanity. In those writings, themes of my life began to emerge. My story wasn't about me. There were the obvious issues of gender and the women's movement, but throughout my life, there has always been a cast of survivors. It has influenced the path of my life. I thought about the blackboard in my friend's home back in Grafton. I wanted to talk to LeeAnn, to know if I could write about those experiences.

There were times when we were in close proximity, as when we were both in Grafton for her brother's funeral. I had updates about her life, her marriage, and her children. I knew she had become a prison guard. I was curious about that. I even had a chance encounter with people from Grafton who knew LeeAnn. In spite of this, I hadn't seen her for nearly forty-five years.

I located her in the Wisconsin Dells and made arrangements to visit her in the middle of June. Just before my visit, the embankment between Lake Delton and the Wisconsin River failed. The county highway was washed out, and the entire lake drained into the Wisconsin River. Twelve inches of rain fell that same night, and there was major flooding in the area. I postponed. Two weeks later, when I arrived, there was still significant flooding in the area, and the lake was nothing but a sea of mud, eerily reminiscent of the sea of mud that first welcomed us upon our arrival in Grafton.

She called herself Lee now, and I was finally hearing about the reckless male abandon she grew up with: stock car racing, handguns, fireworks, and county fairs. We had both struggled against the cultural shackles of a feminine identity. It was a curious juxtaposition.

Old friends have to talk about the old days. Lee remembered the Blue Eagles Club and our trips to the covered bridge. It was validating to know we both shared similar memories of it. Those were some good memories. I did have to ask about the blackboard. I knew what I expected to hear. I'd already explained it to my Mom. "How come you never told us," she asked. What would I have told her? I couldn't verbalize it myself. I only sensed the fear my friend was experiencing. Societies unwillingness to deal with abuse in constructive ways helps sustain the secrecy that perpetuates dysfunctional family dynamics.

Lee seemed relieved to know I remembered the blackboard. It's clearly the first time her memory of it had been validated by anyone. This is a significant issue with survivors of childhood abuse. You're trained to deny reality. Your perceptions are constantly being denied or contradicted. I experienced it repeatedly in my own marriage. Marie was frequently enraged if I expressed any doubt about how she remembered something. The problem was exacerbated by her associative memory.

Lee remembered times when her sister's name was removed from the blackboard. It was consistent with my own memory that she was the one most impacted by it. She was the principal subject, but it also could have been that she was older and responding to a helpless inability to protect her sister. That is one of the horrible dynamics that exist among siblings between fear and guilt.

I was glad that she was able to share her experience with me. I know it was helpful to her. Her first husband was abusive, as was her sister's first husband. I'd seen other indications around her brother's suicide. It had all pointed to an obvious conclusion.

Lee told me about her experience as a guard. Physical threats and emotional harassment were so severe her career ended with an emotional breakdown. She prevailed in a lawsuit against the Wisconsin Department of Corrections, but it didn't re-write the experience or do much to correct the problem.

We spent a peaceful weekend together. I taught her how to bake an apple pie. We went into the Amish country and browsed their markets and purchased some groceries. We shopped for furniture and spent time talking while enjoying one of their patio swings. Visualizing it now I can easily forget that I wasn't presenting as a woman that weekend. Then again, she wasn't LeeAnn either. Perhaps it didn't really matter at all. Two best friends sharing quiet moments on a patio swing.[1]

She seemed happy, and I was happy for that. She had a wonderful partner, a beautiful garden, and time with her grandchildren. She clearly had found peace in her life, something I might never see, but I wasn't envious. Mother had assured me, I have a calling.

That's how I chose to interpret a sequence of events that began one afternoon at Boulevard Bar in South St. Paul. It was unusual for me to be at the bar on a Saturday morning. A Native American friend was also there. I have forgotten his name and wonder if I ever knew his name. He was Cherokee, having arrived from Oklahoma, but his metaphors seemed more upper Midwest, so maybe he was Ojibwa or Sioux. He always seemed to be there when I was distressed, and I referred to him as my spirit guide. If you don't know where you are going t*hen it doesn't matter which way you go*. That day was the last time I ever saw him, and I remember clearly his last words to me. "The spirit is like an eagle. It cannot show you your destination. It can only stay near you and guide you down the path that you must follow."

That night I was at LaFonda's Cantina in Eagan where a woman asked about my experiences. She was devote in her religious beliefs and invited me to attend her church in the morning.

I answered the call. Sunday morning I picked out the only dress I had that felt appropriate for Sunday service and went to Chapel Hill Baptist Church. The congregation was welcoming and engaging. I felt comfortable with the pretense. I attended services there for about eight weeks and volunteered for multiple charitable events they sponsored in the community.

The woman from LaFonda's was Kathy, who I soon discovered, was the pastor's wife. Upon my inquiry, she indicated she'd never been to LaFonda's. People who don't believe in metaphysical events, miracles, or divine guidance would dismiss it as a case of mistaken identity on my part. I could accept that myself. What's more curious, however, is that people who do claim to believe in divine guidance will call me a liar. I have no purpose in trying to persuade people one way or the other.

In the seventh or eight week, I attended a women's breakfast to hear about one woman's experiences parenting children with Down's syndrome. That was more than the church leadership could accept. The next Sunday, they asked me to leave. They described it as a distraction, like a woman coming to church in a bikini. I couldn't help but note the sexist imagery.

I have been invited back by parishioners on a couple of occasions, even asked to bring my son. The church leadership told me I could return if I dressed as a man. My response to them was simple enough, "I'm not a man!" I know I change the world every day simply by going out into it. But I surmised that I had misunderstood God's calling.

1 After Lee read the first draft of this manuscript I went to see her again as Paula. She was ecstatic about the fighting lady because she had inherited one herself from a cousin. She thought it was a very cool toy. What could I expect from a girl that grew up around stock cars and 38s? I felt a little sadness as she described all of the things that were not the same after my family left Grafton. It leaves me to wonder how it would have been if we had grown up with each other's support rather than fighting the gender wars on our own. It is clear that she was my best friend and always will be.

Chapter Thirty-six: Shattered Dreams

Alice felt so desperate that she was ready to ask help of any one.

–Lewis Carroll, Alice in Wonderland

Courtney graduated from high school in 2008. I was very proud of her, but it also engaged the disconnect within the family. I brought Courtney to New Hampshire for a graduation party with my side of the family.

Courtney had been accepted to the engineering program at North Dakota State University (NDSU). Of the colleges Courtney and I had toured, she wanted to attend Michigan Tech in Michigan's Upper Peninsula. She was excited about the great snowboard trails which should have given me some insight into her academic commitment.

Courtney was good at math and loved science, but she wasn't well adapted to the authoritarian structure of spaces dominated by men. Courtney's experience emphasized my own assertion that there is an inherent contradiction in models of gender equity based entirely on economic achievement. Efforts to assimilate females into a male value system continue to reinforce the premise of oppositional sexism: that masculine is simply better than feminine; that what men do is more important than what women do; that perhaps we should simply eliminate feminine altogether.

Hanna Rosin in her book *The End of Men* depicts a new social context where women are the dominant gender. It certainly contradicts the preeminent political narrative. It continues to emphasize feminism as a conflict among women over conflicting ideologies. Success in a masculine social model contradicts a nurturing feminine identity. The missing component continues to be a conspicuous absence of men in the traditional women's roles of nurturing and social organizing.

It portends the inherent conflict in women supporting each other. Hillary Clinton emphasizes the dilemma in one simple statement when she said, "I suppose I could have stayed home and baked cookies." Men don't have to make that choice. It remains cliché: a successful man has a faithful wife. The reverse of that never works for women. It was visibly apparent with America's couple. Hillary gained respect for being the faithful wife but it didn't play out the same when she needed a faithful husband.

I trusted that Courtney was moving on to a great opportunity and things would settle down at home. This was little more than contrived optimism mixed with a dose of denial. Marie became disagreeable when we brought Courtney to NDSU for orientation. What should have been an exciting weekend was a serious disappointment. I left Courtney with some encouragement about engaging in campus life, but I could sense that she wasn't ready for this.

Mateo followed Courtney to NDSU. She moved off campus with him. Their relationship was not entirely clear to me, seemingly compatriots in a war against social injustice. It further damped my hopes, knowing she'd be separated from campus life. That wasn't the worst of it. Courtney was advised she was missing one-third of an English credit. She wouldn't be able to continue past fall quarter and she wouldn't be eligible for her financial aid. I paid most of her tuition and a dorm room she wasn't using, nearly $7000. I couldn't believe the bureaucratic dysfunction of an educational system that at once did not know it was missing and then couldn't create some accommodation for one-third of a credit. Courtney would have to go back to high school.

The expense compelled me to make a realistic assessment of our financial situation. It wasn't sustainable. I set up a budget and asked Marie to try to limit her personal expenses to $120 per week. She was outraged by my lack of concern for her needs, becoming more fuel for the fire.

Courtney was back home by mid-December. At the same time, Marie received a $60,000 settlement for a personal injury case. It didn't take long to realize it wasn't going to benefit the family's finances. Mateo also came to live with us. Instead of one less we now had one more.

His presence was highly disruptive. He criticized Courtney harshly, in ways I considered abusive. Loud verbal arguments accentuated Marie's anxiety. I wanted him out of the house, but Marie wasn't going to agree to anything I wanted. To Marie, he was an ally.

It would be technically accurate to say the situation was volatile, but it was more like watching the fuse burn down on a stick of dynamite, waiting to see if it would really explode. I felt so desperate that I was ready to ask help of anyone.

I searched for another therapist, for myself this time. Marie refused to meet any therapist, and it was becoming evident she was arranging a divorce.

Courtney was drawn into the hysteria. Marie claimed the upstairs as her space, and Courtney decided to trash my room because I took a nap on the couch. Courtney attended two therapy sessions exploring a child-parent reconciliation. It was constructive but insufficient.

Marie was fond of calling the police. In one incident, she had awakened me multiple times during the night. She was angry when early morning came, and I decided to stay up. She called the police. They came and ordered me to go to bed. Police really have no tools for assessment or intervention. To make an arrest is really the only option they have. The police have infinite discretion in that regard since no complaint is required. They are trained to protect the female. I'd see the inadequacy of that approach working with same-sex couples where the choice cannot be made by gender. The response escalated with frequency. On their last visit, they insisted I go to a hotel threatening charges of domestic abuse. Guilty or not the charge alone is damaging. There was absolutely no basis for it. Marie consistently reported that she wasn't afraid of me. Without any evidence of abuse, their assessment is entirely gender-based.

The men at the sexual boundaries group understood all too well what was happening and they advised me to keep a log. They recommended that I install cameras as well. I did start keeping a log but never installed cameras. I doubt that I'd have used the evidence anyway. It's also unlikely the cameras would have captured a meaningful sequence. The evidence would be ambiguous. If a female is abusive, it is easily interpreted as reactionary or self-defense.

The abuse escalated quickly to a physical assault on March 21, 2009, when Marie hit me with a mirror while I was still in bed. She proceeded to break all of the mirrors in my room, throwing them into the backyard. She scattered things from around the room. She grabbed a space heater from my room and tossed that into the backyard. She challenged me to call the police. I was afraid to call the police. I already knew what they would do. What frightened me, even more, was not knowing what she might do if I did call the police.

Attacking the mirrors and the space heater were not random choices. These items had significance to her. There was one special mirror that was once a part of Jamie's bedroom set. That mirror survived the attack. Marie instructed Courtney to hide it.

Marie and her friend Terri had placed the mirrors several years earlier. They redecorated my bedroom including the installation of four full-length mirrors at the end of my bed. It was hard to discern the significance of it. Marie had said, "Now you can look at yourself in the mirror." I can't think of any way to interpret that in a positive manner. That's how it was with Teri and Marie. It seemed like a nice gesture; it also felt like teasing or ridicule. It represents the enigmatic nature of abuse. Just as it was in my childhood, lying in bed waiting for my father to go to work. Terrified as I was, his behavior wouldn't be considered child abuse.

The space heater was a slightly different problem. The basement was cold during the winter. It was comforting to sit in front of the space heater until the room warmed up. It was more efficient than trying to heat the whole basement. Marie gave it some sexual connotation, which goes back to the broader issue of sex as a control issue or perhaps just a symptom of her hypervigilance.

I went to the sexual boundaries group that morning. While I was gone Marie enlisted Courtney to clean up and get rid of the mirrors. I retrieved them and stored them for a long time, but like the video, there would never by a meaningful purpose in presenting this evidence. Ten days later I'd provide Marie with the opportunity she was waiting for.

Part IX: Uncommon Origins: A two-family divide

Statistically, divorce was an absolute certainty for our marriage. I can invent scenarios that would defy the odds, but the social travesty is less about the dissolution of our marriage and more about the manner in which it was dissolved.

It is a tragic irony that our divorce began with the marriage of our daughter. It emphasized the differences in our family origins. The strength of our commitment to each other was dependent on separation from divergent family backgrounds. Just like our first Christmas, Marie and I needed to establish our own traditions. The best times in our relationship coincided with times when it was just the two of us, and, of course, our children.

Chapter Thirty-seven: Wedding Day Blues

Either the locks were too large, or the key was too small.

– Lewis Carroll, Alice in Wonderland

When Jamie was little she often reminded me, "You can't tell me what to do! You're not my real dad!" As she got older, she started realizing the influences I had in her life; she started offering more assurances that she viewed me as her real dad: when she got married I'd be the one to walk her down the aisle. I looked forward to that day, not only because of my relationship with my daughter, but because I believed it would mean greater joy and happiness in her life. That day came on April 1, 2009, but it wasn't the way I imagined it.

I had two job interviews that morning. When I returned home from the second interview, Marie, Courtney, and Tyler were all dressed up, preparing to go out. I inquired as to why Tyler wasn't in school.

The answers were evasive, but I didn't press the issue. I was accustomed to being excluded from anything Marie was planning, but they were all lying to me.

The family also acquired a purebred Yorkie when Courtney came back from college. Dogs love me. I've learned to accept it. They just need more attention than I could afford.

The need for attention was evident that evening of April Fool's Day, 2009. I needed a nap, but as I'd lay down the little Yorkie started barking, and then our other dog, Riley, started barking. I tried multiple times to calm them. Finally, I called Courtney to come and get the dogs, but Mateo answered the phone. He was abrupt. He said, "It's not my fault that they didn't want you at the wedding." *Wedding? What wedding?* I thought. That's how I found out about Jamie's wedding. I was equally abrupt. I told him to come and get his dog or I was calling animal control.

I didn't walk Jamie down the aisle. I wasn't even there. I was excluded. Adding insult to injury, Jamie's "real dad" was there. That bit of information, as was the way it was delivered, hurt me deeply.

I was emotionally distraught. I went over to Cooper's, our neighborhood bar, to share the story with my girlfriends. One of them was Debra Vance. It's the oldest memory I have of our friendship. I can't recall how long I've known her, but her support was pivotal to a number of upcoming decisions.

I was compelled to take some affirmative action. I did not want Mateo in our home any longer. I changed the lock on the basement door and barred the back door. For Marie, locking herself in a room was symbolic of a need for safe space. It was rather interesting how that gesture played out in the criminal justice system, but, at the moment, it was meant as an advanced warning. I drank another glass of wine and lay down on the living room couch, another invasion of Marie's space.

The next day the kids came home first. Children are not locked out if there is a parent home to let them in. I'm going to make a point of that. Whether the locks were too large, or the key was too small, they knew I was home. They could have knocked on the door. They could have called me. They could have used the front door. They came up with a far more sensible idea, and I awoke to the crashing sound of glass breaking as a rock came sailing through the kitchen window. The cracked tile where the rock hit the floor is still there.

I met them at the kitchen window to ask what they wanted. Courtney said she needed her work shirt. I asked them to go around to the back door, and I let them in. She got what she needed, and they left. As they were leaving, I reminded Tyler he was supposed to be in school and told him he could stay if he wanted to.

When Marie came home she knocked. When I opened the door, she was there with two police officers standing behind her like armed bodyguards. One police officer went upstairs with Marie, and one stayed downstairs with me. He was pragmatic. He said, "There's nothing illegal about changing the locks on your house." He said, "You need to file an Order for Protection (OFP). That's what she's going to do."

I understood completely. There was nothing he could do. Despite all of the powers granted to the legal system by the Violence Against Women Act the police still have no meaningful options for intervention. Inherently, it isn't a legal problem. It is a social problem.

I went to the Northern Dakota Services Center that afternoon and filled out the OFP using the information from the log I'd been keeping which described the abuse I'd been subjected to over the past three months. I didn't file it. I couldn't do it. I couldn't put my partner out on the street. I couldn't pursue a path of recovery based on escalating the conflict through legal harassment.

I knew where Marie had been when she came back to the house on Friday morning. If there were a real threat of intimate partner violence, what she had done would have been very dangerous. Marie knew perfectly well that there was no threat of violence. It's a strategic maneuver in divorce to take possession of the home and custody of the children. It's not legal, but the courts encourage it. It was a quiet weekend, as I watched the fuse slowly burn.

Monday morning around seven AM, I'm awakened by a Dakota County Sheriff standing beside my bed. I wasn't happy to see him, but I wasn't surprised. The room was still disheveled from the chaos ten days earlier. On the end table were a full ashtray and half a glass of wine. They were all obvious signs of depression, but also obvious signs of an abusive drunk depending on your perspective. He handed me the extradition order and explained the provisions about having no contact with my son. He didn't want to leave the room, but I was naked, and he agreed to let me get dressed.

It was all pretty casual in a strange way except that he kept asking me to hurry. It's my first time being tossed out on the street, so I'm not certain what to take with me. I ask the deputy if he has a list. He did not. He asked me if I had a gun. I said, "No." I should have let him impound the guns, and I might still have them today. It's odd that he didn't ask Marie. I didn't want to deal with it. I didn't really feel like packing either so I overlooked a lot of things. When I was about to leave, I did remember one thing that proved invaluable, my computer.

I was getting in my car at the same time Courtney was leaving the house. She gave me a hug. It felt a little like a kiss from Judas, but I know she was facing her own internal struggle.

From the house I went back to the Northern Dakota Services Center to file the OFP I had previously completed, with one addition: I asked for protective custody of my son. The OFP is a first-come, first-served process. Putting the primary care parent out on the street placed the child at greater risk, but the court has no way of assessing that. The court made its decision based entirely on the vague allegations of an angry parent reporting on the claims of a rebellious teenager. Marie described the scene this way in the OFP.

"4-2-09 Kids denied access to home. Changed lock so key work. Came in throught window and was Emotionaly and physicaly threaten. He physicaly pushed Tyler and was stopping Court-ney [boyfriend] and Tyler from leaving, causing extreme fear for all of Them. He was physicaly threatening by standing over them, blocking them from leaving and verbal abuse of yelling at them.

** verbal threats to stay jobless saying I'm losing everything anyway"*

** 1 other are records at Eagan Police Dept."*

My OFP was also signed by the court, except that custody was already granted to Marie. The process is extremely vulnerable to abuse. So much so that it is actually becoming a mechanism of the abuse.

After that, I went back to Cooper's bar to withdraw from the situation. It was a sunny afternoon and sharing a few beers out on the patio was perfect for that. By relieving me of my parental rights, the court also relieved me of my parental responsibility. That was a discomforting position for me. It left Tyler with no one to represent his interests. This would be the central issue.

Men know about couch surfing. I had more connections to that network than I realized, but I didn't make any that first day. I spent a sleepless night in my car, shivering from the cold and avoiding the police.

The law requires that I be allowed to retrieve personal possessions from the house, but the police refused to enforce it because Marie refused to allow it. That's one of the major strategic advantages of using the OFP process to initiate a divorce. Not only did Marie get possession of the house and custody of our son, she got control of all of our records. That was problematic for many reasons. It emphasizes why my computer was a critically important after thought. The most immediate problem was the need to contact my attorney. I couldn't remember her name and couldn't return to the house to retrieve her contact information. That left me seven days to find a replacement and prepare for the OFP hearing. The only attorney I knew was a criminal defense attorney, which seemed like a reasonable choice.

The Twin Cities Men's Center helped me to locate a couple of members able to share a room for a couple of weeks. There I acquired a temporary level of stability. I finally gained access to my email to discover that a job offer from one of the interviews two weeks earlier had already gone to an alternate during the time I spent adjusting to homelessness.

Chapter Thirty-eight: Expert Identity Disorder

"No, no!" said the Queen. "Sentence first, verdict afterwards."

–Lewis Carroll, Alice in Wonderland

The first OFP hearing was April 13, 2009, in Apple Valley. Marie and her attorney were in a conference room with Courtney and Mateo discussing their strategy. As the accused, I'd have no voice in the family's future. Courtney was coached by Marie's attorney. This concerned me, not because I thought their story would be believable, but because Courtney would have to face cross-examination.

I waited by myself for my own lawyer, who was running late. Tyler wasn't there. He was too young to have a voice in the family's future. His fate would be decided by the experts. Exiting the conference room, Marie's attorney handed me a divorce petition. That left me thirty days to find another attorney and file a response.

The two attorneys went in to address the judge before the preceding. When my attorney informed me the case was being continued until May, I said, "That's another five weeks without my son." His response was clear enough. "You can proceed," he said, "but you'll lose." Sentence first – verdict afterward. I believed him, given the frivolous nature of the OFP complaint in the first place. It would be the first of many delays. That's strategy: use the OFP to get possession of the house and custody of the child, then draw out the proceeding until it becomes status quo. I didn't understand it then.

I talked to many attorneys, friends, and, even total strangers. The overwhelming consensus was the same. "No judge is going to give you custody of your son," they said. "Just wait until your son is nineteen," they told me, "you'll get him back."

I said, "That's four years in the life of an adolescent boy. That's forever."

Marie was asking for full legal and physical custody of our son Tyler, claiming I was unfit to parent because of my lifestyle. She was also asking for permanent spousal maintenance and fees for her attorney.

Health insurance also became a complicated issue. Both the divorce petition and the response state that she was on Minnesota Care. It's a curious inaccuracy because neither of us ever qualified for Minnesota Care. It was the first of many inaccuracies that would complicate the proceedings.

I requested that neither party pay spousal maintenance. That would turn out to be a subtle mistake as well. I requested that each party pay their own attorney's fees. After all, Marie had $60,000 and I was unemployed. I agreed to pay child support but expected joint legal and physical custody. I wasn't going to abandon my son. That was my line in the sand.

I also withdrew my order for protection, as an act of good faith. I hadn't learned the fallacy of acting in good faith. A custody battle is totally adversarial. An act of good faith is fundamentally an admission of guilt.

My attorney assured me I'd feel better once the response was filed. From my recollection that didn't help at all. I knew Tyler would wonder what was happening. Any attempt to contact him or even send a message to him could result in a felony charge. There was a risk just in talking to his siblings.

The waiting was unbearable, so I went to visit my family in New Hampshire. Tyler loves lobster. Lobster is cheap in New Hampshire. I felt I'd be seeing my son soon so I brought lobster when I returned. It's funny I don't remember where I stored it.

My only other link to sanity was my weekly therapy appointment. I recall sitting in the office scanning the magazines on the end table next to me. I'm the only one there, but I'm still conflicted about how I'm dressed. My skirt suddenly seems much shorter than when I got dressed this morning, and I feel conspicuous when I cross my legs. I'm still possessed of the idea that I need to act more normal, but there is no incentive, no standard of normal I can rely on.

After several weeks of couch surfing, I've finally found a little travel trailer out in the country, where I can stay at no cost. There's no bathroom, but the small heater keeps me warm during cold nights. Spring is late in arriving. It feels safe like a cocoon, but the last thing I need is to swaddle myself in layers of self-pity and remorse.

Right now I need to feel real and the dress helps with that in a way I still don't fully understand. I've waited all week for this appointment, anxiously counting the days since last week's appointment. It's the only thing I have to look forward to, and I can't help thinking about what's become of me and how pitiful I am. Luckily gas prices are down because I've driven seventy miles to get here.

I finally decide on the *National Geographic*. There is an article about the negative effects of light pollution, showing incredible nighttime satellite photos of the earth displaying the unnatural lighting that illuminates the planet. The author is asserting how difficult it is to find true darkness and I can't help noting a metaphor alluding to the darkness in my own life.

Dr. H knows about the OFP, the lawyers, the police, the loss of my son, and the conflict in my marriage. He knows I'm homeless. As dark as it seems, this isn't the low point.

I have an old car, a cell phone, and the library computers to try and convince employers that I'm stable enough to take on a $90,000 a year job. The issue of employment seems to be the only issue where I remain clearly cognitive. I'm apprehensive about finding employment as a woman.

Dr. H is the first therapist I have been to who isn't attempting to pattern me according to the delusions of their personal success stories. I respect him. He is helping me to work on my side of the conflict while learning to let go of her side.

I'm finally weighing the consequences of being a woman but still fearful of accepting them. I confide to Dr. H during this particular session, "I think I need to stop drinking and stop wearing dresses, but I don't think I can do both at the same time."

Now I'm the one grasping at delusions of normalcy. Dr. H didn't respond to it.

"Perhaps it is time to clean out the sock drawer," he said.

I didn't get it.

He revealed the metaphor, "Sometimes simple tasks can help to sustain us when faced with overwhelming stress.

He recommended a book about an experiment in managing chronic pain entitled *Full Catastrophe Living*. He said, "What you're experiencing seems like full catastrophe living." I can't help wondering if it has always been that way.

Late in the evening, the night before the hearing on May 14, I had a message on my phone indicating we had received a great offer from Marie's attorney. My attorney would meet me at the courthouse early to discuss it. The timing is strategic. I was constantly pressured to make decisions without time to consider the options, weigh the alternatives, or discuss it with anyone. Never did I have more than a few minutes or a few hours to consider major, life-changing decisions. I never had more than a few days to prepare important court documents.

That morning my attorney was late in arriving, just to add to any level of anxiety I might already be experiencing. According to the offer, Marie would get possession of the house and custody of Tyler. I'd get visitation every other weekend and one evening on alternate weeks, which could be an overnight if Marie agreed to it. Anything that was up to Marie's discretion wouldn't be happening. These types of clauses create the impression that parents are cooperating "for the best interest of the child."

The offer also agreed to defer any financial considerations until Marie and I could consult with a bankruptcy attorney. Think about the court ordering a woman to cooperate with an abusive spouse. Does anything seem irregular here?

I do believe my response was pretty clear. "That's a horrible offer," I said, "It's absurd. It's degrading," I said. "You can't parent a teenage boy in two weekends a month." If I accepted the offer they would drop the OFP: "…and that's extortion." I didn't say it. Again the attorney reminded me what would happen if I lost in the OFP. They also emphasized that it was only a temporary agreement.

I took the offer. I had a pretty good idea what the outcome would be. The court would award Marie custody of our son and harass me for child support. For the moment I'm going to call it harassment. After all, it was Marie obstructing my job search. I was willing to assume full custody of my son as the primary care parent. I wasn't demanding child support or alimony. For me, there was a larger consideration around the hope that the family might recover from this family conflict which I believed was externally motivated by social prejudice. I didn't want to put Courtney on the witness stand to testify against a parent. She was being manipulated. She would be no match for a criminal defense attorney.

I did not want to drag the family through a courtroom indictment of our complex family dynamic. Initially, I thought it would be most expedient if I presented myself as a responsible father emphasizing my commitment as the provider. There was also the likely reality that the court would have it's own prejudice against a transgender parent since It was quite unheard of at the time. I presented myself to the court as a man. For a time, I struggled against dressing as a woman socially. It was not an emotionally sound decision.

At each step in the process, I chose the option that allowed me the most time with Tyler. It's risk mitigation. The risk was moderate, but the consequences were enormous. If the court sustained the order I might not see my son at all for an entire year. They might do it "just to be on the safe side" or because that was their normal routine. That would be the worst case. I chose the only option that guaranteed me time with my son.

I hadn't had any contact with my son for six weeks. The lobster smoothed things over. I called him as soon as I left the courthouse and made arrangements to go to the park because I didn't have anyplace where I could cook. I purchased picnic supplies, including a couple of T-bones. We grilled the lobster and steaks on the park's grill over hot charcoal. To this day Tyler swears it was the best lobster he ever had. I totally agree, but I like to think it was better because I was with my son. Courtney was there too. I hate thinking this, but at the time she was, in part, acting as a spy. I'd learn Marie was claiming I was trying to bribe Tyler. The idea that I was trying to turn Tyler against her was part of her anxiety, but it would also be part of a broader legal strategy. I had a lot to learn about family court.

It was a pleasant day in the park. The weather was cooperative, offering us a warm sunny afternoon. It was a casual meeting. I explained the arrangement as I understood it and assured him I'd be there. He wouldn't have to move or leave his school. I didn't know it would be another six weeks before I'd see him again. I was still presenting as his father but it would soon enough become clear that it wasn't really an issue for him.

Chapter Thirty-nine: Only Temporary

"Unimportant, of course, I meant," the King hastily said, and went on to himself in an undertone, "important—unimportant—important—"

-Lewis Carroll, Alice in Wonderland

It was only temporary they told me; it's only temporary until it becomes permanent. My attorney must have understood that. To her it was just routine: "Unimportant, of course, I meant." Maybe she thought it was a great deal, because I wasn't going to jail, at least not right away.

I was also told it would be better to address the issues in family court. What they didn't tell me is that there really is no family court in Dakota County. It's a collection of criminal law judges who circulate through family court cases. Sixteen different judges and a magistrate would eventually have some part in the custody dispute. It was obvious none of them had ever reviewed the case prior to a hearing. Some actually stated as much.

Marie's attorney was charged with drafting the temporary order, which wasn't completed until a month later. That was typical. Documents were rarely submitted in a timely fashion according to rules of civil procedure or even by order of the court. The attorney was never censured by the court. I was starting to gain some perspective.

Marie wouldn't allow Tyler's weekend visits with me because she hadn't received any order from the court. She informed me that joint custody wasn't an option because I did not have suitable space for Tyler. I know the routine. I've seen *Mrs. Doubtfire.*

The temporary order came with standard verbiage:

(A.) The parties shall confer and consult …

(B.) The parties shall keep one another informed …

(C.) Each party shall keep the other advised …

(D.) Both parties shall have the right to receive their child's medical records …

(E.) Both parties shall have the right to consult with school officials …

(F.) Both parties shall have the right to receive … school report …

(G.) In an emergency … the parent with the child at the time shall have the authority to act …

Imagine two parents engaged in physical violence being ordered to cooperate in such a manner for the "best interest of the child." Our communication strategies were completely dysfunctional, something no therapist seemed capable of recognizing or addressing. The court certainly couldn't address it with standard legal verbiage. Parenting was unilateral. Worse than that, if I tried to communicate with Marie they reported it as harassment.

In early June, I decided to sublease a room near the University of Minnesota. The house was unoccupied at the time, but there were two couples and three other people living in the house most of the summer. Marie came to the house to deliver the visitation schedule she had decided on.

It was a small room with a single bed, a desk, and a loveseat. More importantly, I could connect to the Internet and I was finally able to begin a more aggressive job search. Separation from my son created a lot of anxiety for me. Teenagers struggle for independence from parents. With the separation, I worried he would drift away and eventually stop coming for visits. Maybe the attorney was counting on that. I didn't have to worry. He was always glad to see me and I was always glad to see him. Overall, it was a bonding experience. Adversity and common purpose strengthened our relationship. In a peculiar sort of way, for the first time in my memory, Marie had the responsibility and I was having all the fun. That's not to suggest Marie was actually executing those responsibilities, but there was nothing I could do about it.

I know it was hard on him. I gave him the bed. I slept on the floor. I was never able to retrieve anything from the house, despite an additional order from the court, so I had just a few things my cousin Rolf had given me. Tyler wanted to bring his video console so we could play games, but I didn't have a TV. I asked him to bring a small TV/DVD player we used in the van on vacations. I know he was scared to take it out of the house and planned to bring it back. I said he could leave it, which pretty much summarizes my parental authority. Later we bought a twenty-four-inch monitor, a major upgrade to our gaming experience, which typically involved obliterating zombies. I hadn't played video games since the days of Quake when Tyler was seven or eight. He was so terrified of the zombies; he couldn't play that level unless I was playing with him.

One weekend I was going to help him upgrade his computer. Marie wouldn't let us take the monitors, because she thought I was going to steal them. I try to imagine myself stealing my son's computer monitor. It worked out fine. We upgraded to a flat screen monitor.

We had use of the kitchen, which inspired us to new heights of creative cooking. I'd never made toast in a frying pan before. I have so many fond memories of that house, which is pretty amazing considering we only spent four weekends there. It seemed so much longer than that.

What to do with the weeknight was a bigger challenge, because the time was pretty short. I didn't want to be a restaurant dad. It's not a bad thing, except that I'm not the dad, even as I continued to play that role. That's how I felt about behaviors typed as male. Mini-golf was the answer. We played every mini-golf course in the Twin Cities. Pretty cool, actually. We also played the arcade at Mall of America, trying to win enough points to purchase a radio-controlled helicopter. Just as we were reaching the required count someone else purchased it. It was the only one. We never cashed in.

In early August I was hired for a new automated-testing development. It was a great project that kept me engaged and allowed me to cope with the escalating stress of the divorce proceeding. I vividly remember standing on the corner of 7th and Marquette in Minneapolis talking to my attorney about child support. She was working with Marie's attorney to make the temporary arrangement permanent. I told her, "I want my son. I want my house back." She said, "That's going to cost a lot of money." She was right about that. You can take a child for free. To get him back you have to pay an attorney a lot of money. I dismissed my attorney. I didn't need to pay her $125 to open a letter and send me a copy.

Clearly, I wouldn't be going home soon, so I leased an apartment. Debra Vance talked me into renting an apartment in her complex. It was within walking distance of Tyler's school. I felt it would help assure him of some ongoing stability at his school, whatever else might happen. I will never be able to thank her enough for all of her support during a desperate time.

Debra was one of those single moms dealing with a disengaged father, who spent little time with his sons and failed to make regular child support payments. The court really has no authority over these situations. If a delinquent parent doesn't have the income, all they can do is invoke penalties which simply exacerbates the situation. In my experience, the court's only function was to distribute income and collect money for their legal colleagues. They seemed to have no idea of how much income there was or how best to distribute it.

Debra furnished my whole apartment with items left behind by other tenants. My daughter Courtney was there to help us move, reflecting the dissonance of strong family commitments within the context of extreme family conflict. My relationship with Courtney has continued to grow in a slow and irregular fashion. My own anxieties were part of the problem. I saw her as so much like me I worried she would make all of the same mistakes.

Debra was also the first person to confirm I was a woman. She wasn't at all persuaded by any of my male pretenses and encouraged me to express my self appropriately. She did so much for me in the short time I lived at Lexington Apartments.

With my new income, I started sending Marie $200 a week, far more than required by standard child support calculations. That too was a mistake. It was another of those good faith gestures. By order of the court, I wasn't obligated to pay Marie anything. The only responsibility I had for my son was every other weekend.

My values as a provider came from my father. It was substanti-ated in his final words, "you stay and take care of your family."

I thought about my father a lot that summer during all of the lonely time. My father was a Cold War veteran. I thought about the Russians, twice overrun by two of the most powerful armies in the history of humankind: Napoleon and Hitler. Twice they pre-vailed against these foes by withdrawing, sacrificing everything but their own determination until the enemy had exhausted itself. That's how I viewed my options. They had all the power, the money, the police, the judges. I had nothing but the love of my son. That would be my resolve: keep withdrawing until the enemy exhausted themselves. I didn't have the means to take an offen-sive position.

Marie's attorney scheduled a child support hearing for Septem-ber. In my opinion, it violated the order because we hadn't yet reviewed the bankruptcy option. The court had already scheduled a pretrial hearing for October. A child support hearing fourteen days prior to a pre-trial hearing is excessive litigation. They with-drew the child support motion in lieu of the payments I was mak-ing.

After I notified Marie's attorney that I'd dismissed my own attorney, she invited me to a settlement conference. I submitted my pretrial statement the same day of the meeting. It was cordial enough since there really was nothing to talk about. Health insur-ance remained a big issue. As long as we were married, Marie would be covered under my employer's health plan. The bank-ruptcy issue was still pending.

They'd had three months to affirm a position on bankruptcy, so I had some idea they were using it as a delay tactic, but I was still focused on damage control. My biggest concern was the family dynamic and trying to preserve family assets. I didn't know it yet, but Marie had already exhausted her $60,000 settlement. I did know the path was obscure. I'd lost sight of my spirit guide.

Chapter Forty: Faith

"Somebody said," Alice whispered, *"that it's done by everybody minding their own business!"*

–Lewis Carroll, Alice in Wonderland

If I'd know then what I know now would I have made the same decisions? It's an unanswerable paradox. It's the nature of faith. A different choice creates a new path and most likely a different outcome. It's really a test of one's own values. Are you confident you remained true to your own values regardless of the outcome? That is the definition of integrity.

My feminine responses were attractive to Marie in the beginning. In the end, having never found a career path, she wanted security. Yet she was unable to give up the control I needed to provide that security. I saw it in her sister Randi's relationship to her husband Greg. They lived in Hawaii for years. During that time Marie spent long hours on the phone with Greg counseling him about his relationship with Randi. If I'd had that kind of support, my relationship to Marie may have been more clear.

Randi's husband Greg was authoritarian. Yes, he could also be kind, patient, and generous, but that's secondary. Marie wanted a man like Greg, though she never made me feel it directly. I had similar feelings myself. He was a stabilizing energy amidst the frequent chaos of female drama.

It was affirmed in the final moments of his life. He lost a hard fought battle with cancer. Marie spent a lot of time supporting her sister and helping with Greg's care. It was appropriate but also isolated me, leaving me with all of the responsibility for our own children.

I was at their home the night he died, and I said to him, "How am I going to cope with these women after you're gone?"

Even in his final hour, he assured me, "You'll be okay," and I cried.

The foundation of our tenuous relationships had passed into eternity. I knew it well, but Marie and Randi wouldn't discover this for a long time to come. That side of the story will never be told.

Forced to leave my home and my family, I realized what men must experience when their existence is reduced to a cold calculation of how much money they can provide. I learned that father's plan their big family events on Father's Day because it is the only time when all the fathers can be certain they will have their children.

I could hardly disregard their enthusiasm, as they planned one such event. It also left me with a profound sense that gender equity isn't about quantity: it's a whole series of factors that fail to match up. Adding to one side meant taking from the other, but it didn't balance the equation.

"Temporary" is a legal fallacy. Life isn't frozen in time. It's done by everyone minding their own business. A fallen tree leaves a gaping hole in the leafy canopy, but new growth quickly fills the vacant space. My vacancy was filled when Courtney and Mateo inherited my space downstairs. Perhaps it was a fair trade for their cooperation in the OFP. They were pernicious about removing my possessions. Marie made changes too. Once the temporary order from the court was in place, Courtney was forced to leave as well, Marie having no further need for them in the OFP. In one of the few brief exchanges I had with Marie, she said it wasn't worth it for the rent they were paying.

Temporary could have lasted forever except for the economic pressures pushing us toward some harsh realities. Marie wasn't paying the mortgage on the house. There were credit card bills that were going unpaid and collection agencies calling.

Guidance came to me in early November as a result of the sub-prime mortgage crisis in 2008 and the subsequent Troubled Asset Recovery Act. A small portion of those funds had been targeted to help with refinancing home mortgages. I was able to obtain a loan modification on our home. Part of the qualification process was making three on-time mortgage payments. Far from receiving any benefit from the government, it was costly.

It would have been impossible if not for the fact that I was the only signer on the mortgage. They planned on sacrificing the house. Marie could continue to live in the house rent-free for a year or more before the bankruptcy and foreclosure would be complete.

I wanted to keep Tyler in his home. If I had the house, I'd have custody of my son. Marie had said it herself, "You can't share custody until you have appropriate living arrangements." Getting the house meant getting custody of my son.

I notified Marie I was reducing support payments by $60 per week in order to pay the mortgage. Marie wasn't paying Tyler's living expenses. They never responded, but the waiting game was over.

I'd made a generous offer. Tyler and I'd have the house and she would get $1000 a month spousal maintenance. I knew some level of parity with Marie was important for the kids, even as Marie was attempting to exclude me entirely.

A trial was inevitable, so I found another attorney through legal services who agreed to represent me, in part because she empathized with my situation.

I sometimes referred to the two attorneys as the pit bull and the poodle. I had learned through various attorneys that Marie's lawyer was considered a pit bull. I'll just refer to her as Ms. Pit-bull. Poodles are the feminine counterpart. We see them with fluffy French cuts and a pink bow in their hair, but they are ranked second most intelligent dog breed right behind border collies. Ms. Poodle did good work but wasn't a match for the pit bull and a court system that turned a deaf ear to flagrant abuse of the process. As far as I know, she retired from divorce law after I dismissed her from this case.

My pretrial statement represented my parenting relationship. Marie's pretrial statement attacked my parenting relationship. It goes back to different parenting styles. I sent multiple letters to them requesting conferences to establish parenting contracts that would allow me to coordinate with her. I only had Tyler five days a month. One thing, preempted by allegations of abuse, is mandatory parenting classes. It's what Marie and I needed.

They invoked the prejudice of the court. I offer a perfect example of associative context: "He discusses his being a role model for the parties' son yet shows up at the parties' church and other public places near the parties' home dressed in women's clothing. (The clothing includes fishnet stockings, short mini-skirts, and other inappropriate outfits, which are embarrassing to a sixteen-year-old boy.)"

I've worn sexy costumes, but so has Marie. The only one seen by Tyler was the one I wore for the play I performed at Patrick's Cabaret. Marie was with us. The only person who attended church with me was Tyler. It was the church elders who objected to what I was wearing.

Marie and I made several attempts to connect with each other on some level but we were no match for the adversarial pressures of the family court system. One night I experienced a brief muscle spasm in my chest, while she was at my apartment for dinner. Marie feared I was having heart problems and wanted me to come to the house. During the night she came and laid down with me. For a short while, it was like the pillow talk time from the early days of our relationship.

Ms. Pitbull and the poodle argued about who was exploiting who. Ultimately, the poodle was right. Ms. Pitbull presented it as exploitation. Marie trusted her attorney. I often wondered if Marie even read the documents she was entering into the court record.

The pretrial conference in January 2010 produced nothing. They wouldn't drop their demand for sole custody. The trial was scheduled for May 2010. Refusing to submit, invoked a full-on attack from Ms. Pitbull. On January 15, 2010, we received a demand for a deposition allowing just three days' notice. This was unprofessional. The only thing they could have learned was they had no case, but depositions can easily be used to create false representations by presenting things out of context.

Ms. Pitbull filed a motion for temporary support, scheduling a hearing for February 16th, again showing her disrespect for a colleague by failing to consult her about possible schedule conflicts.

In addition to $775 per month child support. They wanted payment back to August and $1559.42 per month spousal maintenance and $10,000 in attorney's fees. The back payments were based on a claim that there was an agreement to pay child support made August 18, 2009. There was no such agreement, illustrating the problem with acting in good faith.

Ms. Poodle said the response was aggressive, unlike anything she had experienced. We denied back payments and denied spousal maintenance because I'd be paying the mortgage. We agreed to attorney's fees, which the court deemed reasonable and fair, but not to exceed $10,000. Ms. Poodle anticipated the fees could run into the tens of thousands, and I'd be ordered to pay it. She was hoping to put a cap on that.

I didn't have the money to file another motion for child custody, so Ms. Poodle suggested we ensure a temporary agreement by requesting the order terminate on May 31 and emphasize our intent to seek custody of Tyler. We included an affidavit from Tyler that expressed his feelings about custody. I had no part in it. His sister Courtney helped him write it. I've included it in Appendix B because I find it to be one of the few heart-warming segments of the whole ordeal. I liked Ms. Poodle's approach.

It didn't stop Ms. Pitbull from filing a responsive motion and a memorandum of law claiming we were violating court rules by raising new issues. She was asking for additional attorney's fees to cover the additional delay and expenses wrought by these new issues. Ms. Pitbull was always demanding attorney's fees and asserting rule violations.

More chaos followed the hearing. Ms. Pitbull drafted the order, making false claims about the child support agreement in August and misrepresenting the amount and number of payments made to Marie. It misrepresented my income, alleged that Marie couldn't work and asserted that Marie was paying the mortgages. No documentation supported any of these claims.

Ms. Poodle submitted a revised copy which corrected the errors consistent with the actual documentation we submitted. It further included a termination date of May 31, 2010.

The judge wrote her own order. It noted the agreed upon child support exceeded state guidelines. My gross monthly earnings were calculated by my hourly rate: $34 an hour at a forty-hour workweek, at 4.33 weeks in a month, or $5888. Subtracting my monthly expenses of $4469 leaves $1419. From that, the judge concluded I could pay Marie $1000 per month in spousal maintenance. That's family court math. The judge knew I had to pay taxes, as she referenced my tax bracket in the order.

According to actual pay stubs, my total monthly take-home pay was $3599. The judge ordered me to pay to Marie $3420 per month; $775 for child support, $1645 housing expenses, and $1000 spousal maintenance.

Take home pay	$3,599
Total payments ordered by the judge	-$3,420
Remainder for my living expenses	$179 per month

The judge was a female. Maybe girls really aren't good at math. I was given sixty days to pay $10,000 to Ms. Pitbull. No termination date demonstrates it really wasn't temporary. It would stand for another ten months.

I was delinquent before I even left the courthouse.

Chapter Forty-one: Bankrupt

"You mean you can't take less," said the Hatter: "it's very easy to take more than nothing."

–Lewis Carroll, Alice in Wonderland

At the pretrial conference in January, I first learned Marie had filed for bankruptcy. Ms. Pitbull had used it as a delay tactic and would present it as an example of my unwillingness to cooperate. I had no choice but to file my own bankruptcy. I had to find another attorney and devote time to preparation. It was precarious but turned out favorably. Had I waited just two more weeks, my income would have forced me into Chapter 13, making me responsible for all of our mutual debt, as well as individual accounts. Ms. Pitbull tried using it again to delay the trial. She claimed Marie's bankruptcy was pending. I thought this odd since she filed long before I did. When Ms. Poodle checked it, she found it had been discharged in May.

I was upset when Ms. Poodle advised me about the results of the support motion, and I criticized her unfairly. She had done well. She was in no way responsible for the outcome. I absolutely couldn't pay what the court had ordered. The bankruptcy hearing was pending. I was preparing interrogatories. The discovery motions were excessive. They had all of our documentation. There was little else I could provide.

The legal work, the waiting, the economic pressure, the emotional harassment all took their toll. I was isolating myself unable to engage in meaningful activities outside of the legal and financial obligations. I stopped socializing. I stopped singing karaoke. The full authority of the court was focused on me. Marie had no responsibility. Every time I appeared in court I felt threatened by something: loss of my son, felony charges, more attorney's fees, jail time. The orders from the court were arbitrary with no relationship to the facts presented. A sense of hopelessness started to overwhelm me and depression overtook me.

Going to work was my only escape. I remained indifferent to the reality it too would eventually fail me by the path I was on. I drank heavily and was drunk a lot. Outside of work hours I was never sober, except when I was with Tyler. During his visits, we watched all four seasons of *Prison Break* in which the main character masterminds new strategies for every new twist in the plot. It became a metaphor in responding to each twist in Ms. Pitbull's tactics of deception and character assassination.

One night Tyler came over unexpectedly when I was pretty drunk. I apologized. I told him about the risks of alcoholism my father had shared with me. Tyler said, "Mom's a far worse alcoholic than you." I took some perverse comfort in this, but it wasn't enough to shake me free. Mentally and emotionally I was giving up. That was my mental status by the time of the trial in May. I was planning to drink myself to death. I was starting to wake up to a cocktail before going to work.

Oddly enough, there was an upside. Framed by a death wish, I abandoned my fear of the court. If jail was my destiny, then so be it. There was nothing I could do about it.

Three weeks prior to the trial Ms. Pitbull contacted my attorney asking to extend the date of the trial. Ms. Poodle declined straight away without even talking to me. I wasn't giving up custody of my son and I couldn't afford further delays.

Then Ms. Pitbull sent my attorney fifty photos of me wearing dresses. It didn't concern me, but it rattled my attorney. It wasn't evidence. It was blackmail. Ms. Pitbull included our family therapists on their witness list. What Mr. R. and Dr. G. had written in their notes was a shocking indictment of sexual bigotry. I didn't sense that Ms. Poodle felt confident to cross-examine these "experts."

I included Courtney and Tyler on our witness list and sent a request to the court to interview Tyler because you can't call a minor to testify. Ms. Pitbull filed a motion in limine, which was a motion to the court asking that Courtney and Tyler not be allowed to present testimony because I was coercing them. The court never responded to my request or the motion in limine. I couldn't afford any more legal services to provide a responsive motion.

The final twist came when Ms. Pitbull subpoenaed my attorney as a witness at the trial, falsely alleging that she had consulted with Tyler. I vividly remember sitting in my car on Sunday morning, May 2nd, just five days before the trial discussing the situation. Ms. Poodle suggested I dismiss her and represent myself. In light of the subpoena there seemed to be no other option. I'd already considered it. Even without the subpoena, she couldn't possibly gain sufficient background knowledge regarding transgender issues that would be crucial in dealing with the photographs and the therapists. She offered to help with some training in courtroom procedure such as raising and responding to objections, calling and recalling witnesses, and basics of cross-examination. With that, I was on my own.

On the day of the trial, I felt well prepared and confident to proceed, but I wasn't prepared for what happened. Right off, Ms. Pitbull asked the judge to issue a breath test which was so theatrical. Tactically, I should have requested one for Marie, but I wasn't willing to respond to her in-kind.

Poodle and Pitbull met to review items Tyler had given her: a copy of a Father's Day card. I'd have preferred if Ms. Poodle hadn't provided anything because there was absolutely no justification for the subpoena. At least she didn't have to stay for the trial. As an attorney providing testimony at a trial, Ms. Poodle was entitled to payment for her time, but of course, Ms. Pitbull refused to pay her. It was another example of her disrespect, and it angered me. I've struggled with a lot of abuse. I'm accustomed to it, but I cannot tolerate watching other people being abused.

The instructions from the judge weren't encouraging. Trial judges hate divorce cases. The judge rebuked us for failing to reach an agreement about what was best for our son. I couldn't have agreed with him more, but I really had absolutely no choice in the matter. It wasn't about the best interests of our son; it was really about Ms. Pitbull's arrogance and greed.

Ms. Pitbull challenged the witnesses, Courtney and Tyler.

Courtney was there that day for moral support but decided she didn't want to testify. I supported her decision. The judge agreed to talk to Tyler suggesting it would be absurd not to talk to a sixteen-year-old boy about where he wanted to live. I had to decide if I'd get Tyler out of school in Eagan to come to the trial in Hastings: a bit of a logistical problem that I wasn't prepared for. The trial did not commence. We were given time to negotiate a deal. I wasn't prepared for that either. The only real option I had was to ask for a continuance, which I could have easily gotten, but another delay wasn't an option. It was me against Ms. Pitbull, Marie, and their accountant in a small conference room next to the main courtroom.

I said "I had to have the house." They agreed. They offered shared custody with Tyler switching households on a weekly basis. I said, "that's ridiculous," but they insisted, and I agreed. Neither of them showed concern for Tyler's interest. Marie wanted financial security. Ms. Pitbull wanted her ten grand.

I offered $1000 a month for spousal maintenance: an extremely generous offer. They demanded $2500: a totally absurd request. That would be half of my gross income assuming I could even sustain my current income. The next several hours were spent with the accountant creating scenarios to show how much money we would save in taxes by eliminating child support. Ms. Pitbull kept threatening to withdraw from the negotiation and start the trial. She kept referencing the two family therapists. She was posturing.

I understood what they wanted, and I understood it was impossible. I was assessing the risks, wondering if Tyler's testimony would really make any difference, wondering if there was any possibility of a reasonable outcome from this judge. It's risk mitigation. The risk of an unfavorable outcome seemed moderate to high and the consequences would be completely unacceptable. We could lose the house altogether. In the final analysis, I didn't want to question Marie on the stand. The questions I had prepared would be brutal.

When Ms. Pitbull started reading the agreement into the record, she started adding additional items: life insurance, health coverage for Tyler, $10,000 in attorney fees. It's a typical strategy of negotiation: ask for half my income, then ask me to pay all of the expenses out of my half. I simply agreed. The more absurd the better, except for the $10,000. I refused to pay an additional $10,000. It's an illustration of why a motion process is so inadequate in a divorce proceeding. It's a package deal. You really can't settle it one piece at a time, because there are a lot of dependencies.

The judge was impatient as well, noting that the trial had to be finished that day because he had a major criminal trial on his calendar starting the next day. That was also an influence. I didn't want to proceed to a hasty trial, and I couldn't request a continuance. It didn't suggest a positive outcome.

I had what I needed. Ms. Pitbull indicated on the record that we had agreed to include child support in the spousal maintenance. She also indicated that the agreement would be reviewed in two years. When we left the courthouse that day nothing was really settled. My mental status was still engaged with simply drinking myself to death as my only out.

Tyler was really upset when I told him about the agreement. He didn't want to switch houses every other week. He felt he had been denied the opportunity to speak on his own behalf. I felt like I had betrayed him.

Ms. Pitbull would draft the final decree, and we were given until June 2, 2010, to file it with the court or appear again on June 25, 2010, to show cause. On June 8, 2010, already six days past the deadline, I received an email from Ms. Pitbull's paralegal asking me to come to their office to sign the agreement. They were required to send me a copy of the decree and a transcript of the trial, which I hadn't received. I requested copies. Other things added to the decree weren't specified at the hearing. The lawyers called it standard boilerplate.

I did ask for a couple of adjustments which was pointless. I agreed to sign if she would withdraw the $10,000 for her legal fees. It's very easy to take more than nothing. She wasn't really concerned about the interests of her client. She wanted her fees. I just wanted to confirm that. She was in violation of the court order, and I was still contemplating my options.

Then, by the grace of God, just a few days before the deadline I was rear-ended in a four-car collision. The pain compelled me to see my doctor. He knew the problem instantly, and I waited in the appointment room for the results of a blood test. When he returned, he said matter-of-factly, "You can quit drinking, or you can die. Those are your choices." I started crying. I was emotionally bankrupt. He had been my doctor for twenty-five years. I trusted him completely. I'd been telling myself I was fighting for my son, and it was suddenly crystal clear that I'd not be much good to him if I was dead.

I already had one foot in the grave. My legs were black and blue from internal bleeding. Had I suffered any internal injury in the car accident, I'd have bled to death before I ever got to the hospital. I received a referral for counseling and a prescription for vitamin K. I went home to my last drink: a full bottle of wine.

Chapter Forty-two: Step One

At any rate, there's no harm in trying.

–Lewis Carroll, Alice in Wonderland

That evening, I was at an Alcoholics Anonymous meeting in Rosemount. AA is a twelve-step program, and the first step is to admit that you're powerless over alcohol. That wasn't hard. I was a mess. They took care of me. They gave me a twelve-step book and told me to read it. They assigned me a sponsor, a person who acts as a mentor: a guide. To have a man caring for me was a unique experience.

My sponsor met me for coffee before each weekly meeting. I told him, "I'm not really an alcoholic, I just have issues."

He would say, "Your problem is alcohol." He was right, of course. Alcohol had masked a lot of problems in our marriage. We never resolved anything. If you've ever wondered if you might have a drinking problem, find an AA meeting, go for awhile, listen to their stories. You'll know.

When I finally abandoned all pretenses of being a man, it was understandably awkward for him and I moved to a different group. I have not seen him in over six years, but I will never forget what he did for me.

Ms. Pitbull was noticeably perturbed at the courthouse on June 24th. She complained about coming all the way from St. Louis Park. She demanded travel expenses.

I couldn't sign the divorce decree. In legal terms, it represented an agreement which was improvidently made: *A decree rendered without adequate consideration by the court, or without proper information as to all the circumstances affecting it, or based upon a mistaken assumption or misleading information or advice.*

I wasn't aware of that legal terminology at the time. I understood they were demanding money in exchange for custody of a child. I had a name for that. "Adequate consideration of the court" would take on increasing significance, as my knowledge of the law progressed.

The judge gave me seven days to file a motion to vacate or sign the order. A motion to vacate is a request to disregard the entire trial proceeding. If successful we would be starting over.

Debora Vance helped me to draft the motion. I didn't know if I'd survive another month. My Doctor said I should be okay if I lasted thirty days. Debra understood what I was feeling and helped me to verbalize those feelings, so I could better focus on the legal details of a motion to the court.

The motion was simple enough: vacate the terms of the agreement that were read into the record on May 7, 2017. I submitted an affidavit claiming diminished capacity to justify the request. An affidavit is just sworn testimony submitted to the court as a notarized document. It isn't a good way to create a legal argument, but it was the only tool I had. I was emulating the conduct of my opponent, which I later found to be highly improper, as her case relied heavily on the bias of the court.

The agreement gave me possession of the house on September 1, 2010. The hearing date was July 27th. Ms. Pitbull asked for a continuance, a date beyond August 16th. The court granted every single continuation request made by Ms. Pitbull. There was never any justification: a violation of court rules.

This was prejudicial because delays were costly for me. The hearing was rescheduled for September 17th, and later to September 14th. My lease expired in August. A month-to-month lease cost me an additional $50 per month or 28 percent of my $179 monthly allocation

The delay actually seemed provident when the kids came to me with a business proposal. Courtney was the one bold enough to confront me. She presented me with a family business idea she'd been working on with Jamie. I appreciated their optimism for the future of our family. It was heartwarming, the way they cast the organizational structure according to the titles of a royal family.

Jamie wanted to open a piercing shop in a shopping mall. It

would be the first of its kind. Her business plan was well developed, and she certainly had the experience. I felt some obligation to her. Failing to establish financial boundaries with Marie had, in essence, failed my children as well. I didn't make a real commitment to the plan. It was more like Jamie jumped into the deep end of the pool and I didn't want to watch her drown. I invested almost $20,000 and a month or more of my time helping to remodel the space for the grand opening in August of 2010. There were major obstacles, and she worked diligently to overcome them.

Fraidy Cats opened for business on August 1, 2010, in Maplewood Mall, Maplewood, Minnesota. It was the first of its kind. It was an impressive establishment, and I was proud of my daughter. Continuing the hearing had given me time with Jamie.

It was never really a family business even though Courtney, Tyler, and Marie all worked there. It was worth the investment. For a while, it provided a renewed sense of belonging to my family.

Fraidy Cats was just one part of a busy summer. Late one evening Marie called noticeably distressed and wanted me to come over. Tyler had been mugged. In addition to an array of cuts and bruises, he had two teeth that were barely attached. I brought him to the University of Minnesota, which was the only emergency dental services I could find.

Courtney came to the hospital and stayed for awhile until we knew that his condition was stable. There was no dental resident, so we waited several hours for the on-call person. They were able to set the teeth, uncertain if they would attach properly. The sun was up by the time we finally left the hospital. I brought Tyler to a half a dozen follow-up appointments. I was still responsible for my son. I'm happy to report we did save the teeth.

The restoration took another $2000 out of my $179 monthly allowance. That would be bad enough, but as it was, the three teenage assailants were black, and Mateo made it a racial issue, attacking everyone in the family for being racist. That reiterated his disruptive behavior and had a negative impact on Fraidy Cats' becoming a family business.

I was still discovering significant problems with the divorce decree . Ms. Pitbull filed a responsive motion which included affidavits from our two favorite family therapists Dr. G and Mr. R. I filed a response to her response making corrections and submitting supporting documents. She filed a response to my response followed by her own motion to dismiss which included a demand for $24,000. She included five months of invoices totaling $46,000. It was clear that Marie wasn't paying these fees which to me was contingency billing: something that is both unethical and unlawful. If that's hard to follow you're starting to recognize the chaos.

As my emotional status improved I felt compelled to address the threats and the allegations of abuse. Filing a false claim of child abuse in order to influence the outcome of a custody case is a misdemeanor in the state of Minnesota. That is exactly what Marie had done. I went to three different police departments: Eagan, Apple Valley, and West Saint Paul, and the Dakota County Sheriff's department. None of them were willing to accept the complaint. I made multiple contacts and wrote multiple letters. I needn't be surprised by it. The police didn't even allow me to retrieve personal property from the house.

Finally, the Apple Valley Police chief agreed to accept the complaint. There was no investigation. The officer who heard the complaint concluded that a new lock on the house was proof of child neglect, so it wasn't a false report. As previously noted, a child is not locked out if a parent is at home to let them in. They weren't going to get involved in a child custody case. The more I learned about child support services and our county attorney, the better I understood that position. It isn't an issue with the law. If there is no one to enforce the law, there is no law.

Later, an Eagan detective came to my apartment and explained to me that the statute didn't apply because the false report was made to a judge who approved it by signing the OFP. It reinforced a growing suspicion that the whole process had nothing to do with the interests of the child and everything to do with collecting child support.

Minnesota statutes are clear about the responsibility of the court in child custody cases when there are allegations of abuse. The court has an expressed responsibility to represent the interests of the minor child. The law recognizes that a vulnerable parent could be coerced into an untenable agreement. I believed the court had an obligation to conduct its own discovery in that regard, through the appointment of a guardian ad litem or, at a minimum, interviewing the child since the reasonable preference of the child is one of fourteen factors the court must consider in deciding child custody cases. That was the position I took at the hearing. I also provided evidence that I was now seventeen weeks sober and could provide our son with an alcohol-free environment, something Marie was unable and unwilling to do. I emphasized the interests of my son and the fact that his rights and interests had been violated by the agreement.

Ms. Pitbull argued that the agreement should stand because it met the Tomscak factors:[1] (1) the party was represented by competent counsel; (2) negotiations were extensive and detailed; (3) the party agreed to the stipulation in open court; and (4) when questioned by the judge, the party acknowledged understanding the terms and considering them fair and equitable.

From my perspective, it didn't matter if I understood the agreement. The real question was whether the agreement was improvident. The answer would later become evident to the court when it came time to untangle the tangled mess.

Ms. Pitbull also ran through the usual laundry list of what an irresponsible, uncooperative, abusive person I was. She claimed my two attorneys had withdrawn. She kept referring to her two hired experts as my psychologists and my treating physicians. Mr. R was just a social worker. Dr. G said I raped my wife. Mr. R, who concluded that I was paranoid, incapable of understanding others, and a poor communicator with a severe personality disorder, suddenly realized what a calm, collected, and communicative individual I really was. I couldn't find a better example of expert identity disorder. He claimed he knew me well, following multiple sessions when he had only seen me once.

I'd later file complaints with the board of psychology and the board of social work, but that's another whole story. I have recently discovered that Mr. R was sanctioned by the board of social work, a small consolation, I suppose.

At any rate, there's no harm in trying. I wanted to stay focused on my son's rights, so I kept my rebuttal simple. I responded to a couple of the most obvious lies. I noted the family had only seen Mr. R one time and questioned the reliability of any of his paid testimony. My final statement to the court: "Finally, again, I think the law is very clear about the rights and interests of the child in this matter, and I feel that he had the right to be represented. He wants to assert that right. And he wants to present his own interests to the court. Thank you, Your Honor."

A friend of mine, who is also an attorney, once told me that the facts of a case are irrelevant. The only thing that matters is what the judge believes.

The judge exempted the court from any obligation to adequate consideration for the best interests of my son. He did consider the issue of depression and alcoholism but denied having sufficient evidence to know if those conditions existed at the time of the trial on May 7th. Ms. Pitbull was to draft a new decree according to his attached memorandum. Three months were added to the dates. Transfer of the house was revised from August 31, 2010, to November 30, 2010. The effective date of the agreement was revised from September 1, 2010, to December 1, 2010. The $1400 IRS debt would be split between the parties. If I failed to sign it, I'd face contempt proceedings. He denied any new attorney fees: a significant victory. Contempt proceedings certainly seemed like another threat.

1 *Tomscak v. Tomscak*, 352 N.W.2d 464, 466 (Minn. 1984).

Chapter Forty-three: Returning Home

The divorce was an agreement between Ms. Pitbull and the court. Neither Marie nor I ever signed it. Ms. Pitbull sent a letter to the judge requesting permission to file a motion to amend the order. The letter also stated that a motion wasn't necessary because my rebuttal was proof I'd not sign the order. With the letter, was a copy of the decree that included a six-month extension instead of the three months ordered by the court.

She convinced the judge to agree to her motion in a letter without a hearing which is a serious rule violation. I sent a letter to the judge challenging the order. My letter was rejected as an ex parte communication.

I'm not certain why, but she subsequently submitted a second decree which did comply with the court order. The judge revised his own order due to "administrative delay" caused by Ms. Pitbull's deception. Giving Marie another month in the house and leaving me with an expired lease.

Marie invited me to stay at the house for the month of December. It was awkward, but it was nice to be home again. I stayed downstairs, same as it had been for many years. Except for a couple text messages, there was no interaction. I was sober now, and she wasn't. It reinforced the reality that the separation was complete, crushed by the brutal indifference of our family court. No matter what I could do for her, it would never be enough. I couldn't allow myself to dwell on it.

It was a memorable Christmas, perchance for the simple joy of returning home. A little blue Christmas tree the kids helped picked out the year before stood as a subtle reminder of my time away. It was the last time we all spent Christmas together. Marie had Christmas upstairs, and I had Christmas downstairs.

Memories of my time at the apartment felt surreal. What I remembered best were all the nights I spent at FedEx Kinko's printing and copying court documents. It was my portal to the outside world, my one remaining connection to society at large. One of the women working there gave me the first purse I ever owned. Even in the worst of times, one finds kindness in uncommon places. We swapped stories, often many nights in a single week and sometimes several times in one night. I gave them the ongoing saga of my divorce and heard about their own personal struggles, personal drama consuming the late night hours. I sometimes mused that these conversations would be a scene in a movie someday, with the whole story unfolding in the background of printers and packing boxes.

Tyler and I did have some good times at the apartment. I remember the night Tyler bought an alarm clock that accepted voice commands. The clock wasn't cooperating, and Tyler's commands kept getting louder and louder until I started laughing hysterically. There was our quest to create the perfect deep-dish pizza, and the night we tried to make hot fudge volcano cakes.

Jamie had her own Christmas party that year for her employees. We rode in a limo viewing Christmas lights, followed by dinner and a show at the Comedy Gallery. I was happy to see her doing so well.

I don't remember New Year's Eve at all, but at midnight the house became mine. A new beginning causes me to reflect upon all of the experts making harsh assessments of a relationship they couldn't begin to understand, unaware of the challenges they couldn't begin to imagine. I am riled by their arrogance, challenged to keep my temper. Marie hadn't found a place yet, and I agreed to let her remain upstairs until she did.

I have a letter from the judge, which says the divorce was final on November 23, 2010, just two days before Thanksgiving. I was at an annual AA thanksgiving time-to-be-grateful meeting, but I couldn't think of anything. Indubitably, I had plenty of things to be grateful for, but I was emotionally exhausted. Hardly a day went by when I didn't think, *I sure am glad I quit drinking.* The thought of losing Marie was painful. I had invested so much in her. It was difficult watching something that started so beautifully morph into something so ugly.

The last of three versions of the decree weren't issued until January 3, 2011. It still didn't match the order, and it still didn't contain rudimentary requirements like financial statements. That's when I decided fighting with Ms. Pitbull and her colleagues on the bench was a hopeless approach. I started focusing on an appeal.

In drafting my motion to vacate I made an assumption that the judge wouldn't want to invest in generating any findings with respect to the best interests of the child. In a sense, I was right, but the easiest solution for the judge was simply to agree with Ms. Pitbull. The court wanted to be done with it and perhaps prove to me that a deal is a deal is deal no matter how impossible or absurd or improvident. Confirmation of the Tomscak factors is itself arguable but more importantly, Tomscak wasn't a custody case. With respect to the interest of the child, it was totally irrelevant.

When the court chose to sign the decree without the consent of either parent, they assumed responsibility for my son. I believe they failed him.

Any notion that the case was finished was improper since the court had created a lifetime agreement more binding then the marriage it was supposed to dissolve. In so doing, the court obligated itself to a lifetime of responsibility for ensuring the agreement remained fair and equitable as life's circumstances changed over time. Creating an order that was so vague and unrealistic would be problematic. I already knew that. At this point, I was counting on it.

The next step was to file a motion for amended findings to correct blatant inaccuracies. I emphasized the court's responsibility for the ongoing maintenance of the agreement and the importance of correct information.

I went to see my attorney, the one I had chosen long before the divorce began. She was perturbed with me for approaching her after the fact, though she empathized with my circumstances. It was clear to me once more why I had chosen her. It would have been different if she had represented me. She reviewed my motion for amended findings and helped me outline the appeal.

When the judge reviewed the trial transcript he noted it was disjoint with a lot of activity in a short period. Remember my original divorce petition when I said neither party should pay spousal maintenance. According to legal logic, by asking that neither party pay spousal maintenance in the divorce decree, I unilaterally waived my right to any future request. Good thing I had an attorney.

The court called it buyer's remorse, something I found particularly offensive. I paid the ransom for the sake of my son, plain and simple. The court couldn't possibly entertain that notion. The motion to vacate and the motion to amend were necessary steps toward an appeal. My principle objection was the assignment of motive to the agreement that created a factual basis for claims not in evidence. I consistently denied the claim that Marie was disabled and couldn't be self-supporting. The judge notes they intended to present that information at trial. I hate to imagine a precedence that relies on evidence that would have been presented.

The judge concluded that spousal maintenance isn't awarded unless it is necessary, therefore by agreeing to spousal maintenance I was affirming their basis for claiming it. I offered the District Court ample opportunity to examine the improvidence of the agreement but they were fixated on buyer's remorse. I was accused of being disingenuous for suggesting I didn't understand her lack of employment.

His judgment was based on a preponderance of past experiences and, more importantly, the weight of judicial prejudice. If they wanted those "facts" reflected in the record, then they should have gone to trial. There were many things I didn't want in the court record, which I believed injurious to family dynamics. I got what I wanted. I wasn't the one with buyer's remorse. Ms. Pitbull was the first to ask for an amendment to the order. She placed her client in a serious predicament. I anticipated at the time of the trial that the case would eventually go to appeal. There was absolutely no possibility of negotiating anything with Ms. Pitbull and a court willing to sign everything she submitted.

The female attorneys didn't seem to understand my female perspectives. I decided I needed a man, able to accept he was representing a woman, even as I was still playing out a male role in court. I contacted several attorney referrals and even paid an ethics attorney for some advice. He talked familiar legal jargon about boilerplate.

A person representing themselves in a legal matter is acting pro se. In choosing to represent myself, I studied the law, studied court cases, studied the court rules, and studied my opponent. Then I discovered that nobody really follows the rules. I began to understand why my attorney seemed more concerned about what I was wearing than the details of the case. How would it have been different if I'd been wearing a dress?

As a pro se litigant, I wasn't simply representing my case, I was challenging the authority of the institutions of law. I could do things that attorneys wouldn't. Some attorneys have applauded me for it, but it was still risky business. Attorneys were not offering me solutions but understanding how they perceived the court's interpretations helped me to formulate my arguments.

I contacted every LGBT and civil rights organization I could find. No one would help me. Lambda Legal gave me some referrals that led me to Jason. I found Jason to be very attractive, but I insist it had nothing to do with my decision to retain him as my attorney. He had an integrity I found lacking in many attorneys. He did in-depth research and didn't require a huge retainer. He wasn't distressed by a transgender woman. Ms. Pitbull wouldn't have the huge latitude in an appeal that she had in district court.

Regrettably, the appeal was denied because it was filed after the deadline. An appeal must be filed within sixty days of the final order which I thought was January 3, when the final order was issued. The appeals court used the November 23rd date when the first order was issued. The appeals court agreed that my motion for review filed on January 16th was proper and would extend the time to file an appeal but a notice of filing limits that time to thirty days. A notice of filing for the November 23rd order was filed on December 6th. The deadline for my motion was January 11th, not January 23rd. A clever manipulation of the process based on a fraudulent filing. Many attorneys would have missed it. It was disheartening to see all that work and optimism go up in smoke over five days. Still, it was comforting to know the appeals court found my motion to be proper, contrary to the claims of Ms. Pitbull and the district court judge who agreed with her.

Chapter Forty-four: Natural Consequences

– Lewis Carroll, Alice in Wonderland

Recovering from a near-death experience, I could no longer be the victim. By January, Marie owed her attorney $64,000, and the case was nowhere near complete. Marie had already paid her $27,000. The court had ordered me to pay their colleague another $10,000, which was more than double what I had spent on my own behalf. Before it was all said and done, I estimate the total cost at close to a quarter of a million dollars. I wondered who was protecting women from that kind of predatory legal practice.

A good attorney understands their opponent. If Ms. Pitbull had known anything about me, she would have known I'd refuse to drag my family's complex issues into court, and how, as a mother, I wouldn't abandon my child. She never gave an ounce of thought to how the court would react to a female pro se litigant.

Returning to the house with my son was a major contribution to my emotional morale, but the battle was far from over. I was still in retreat. There would be more sacrifices.

I helped Marie with her move. Anything I had of sentimental value with monetary worth had long since disappeared. There were things I wanted to keep, one being a jewelry chest from my father, but I understood why Marie wanted it. She had all of our family photos. It remains an empty space in my life. I have all of the family videos. Perhaps it's a fair trade.

A week after she moved, it was time for Tyler to spend his first week at her home. He didn't go until nine or ten o'clock at night. He was back at our house before he went to school. One night he didn't go at all. On Friday I said to him, "Tyler if you don't want to go over there, you don't have to." That was the end of shared custody. Marie brought over a pot roast for us one afternoon. Like any truce between enemies on the battlefield, it was the illusion of what ought to be but never would be.

Judges favor stipulated agreements. It works to compel an agreement in difficult cases and gives the attorneys and the courts wide latitude to complete the agreement to their own satisfaction.

If you wondered how I was paying all these expenses, I'll tell you I wasn't. On July 15th, I received a notice of default on the mortgage. A couple days later I received notice of the appeals court decision. A couple of days after that I received the contempt motion for failing to execute the terms of the divorce.

The hearing was set for August 23. I already had plane tickets to take Tyler to New Hampshire to visit family that week. Ms. Pitbull refused to reschedule. No surprise there, she was always asking for professional courtesy, never extending it. I filed a request with the court explaining the situation. My one request was denied, underlining the imbalance. Tyler had to go off to New Hampshire by himself. I joined him on Wednesday after the hearing at an additional cost.

In April the Minnesota Department of Revenue levied our bank accounts. They took $953 from my account and $479 from Marie. Ms. Pitbull claimed I was responsible for it, as an undisclosed debt. It was Marie's accountant that filed our tax returns. She knew about the debt and she had equal liability for it. It was a joint tax return and joint debt, which is why they levied both our accounts. She actually owed me $237.

Talking to Jason made it clear to me why I needed a man. After reading my motion he said rather bluntly, "Do you want to win?"

Quickly I responded, "Yes, of course." I'd written an emotional appeal. It's a feminine attribute or perhaps just motherly. Referring back to the research of Ragini Verma, PhD, associate professor at the University of Pennsylvania in Philadelphia, we might ask if the physiology of female judges is functionally different than the average female. Can all women aspire to positions of power and control and abandon any notion of baking cookies? Is it disingenuous for a woman to want to care for a child, a family, and her community?

For me, it contradicts a commonly accepted notion of a male ally. It wasn't important for Jason to understand my feelings or my vulnerabilities. It wouldn't matter to the judge. I needed a clear perspective of how I was perceived. I've often failed to recognize how feminine my responses were.

The judge agreed with Ms. Pitbull. He said I failed to pay the debt according to conclusions of law 9C. This is what conclusions of law 9C says: "In the event there is a debt or obligation that isn't heretofore disclosed, that obligation shall be and hereby is the sole responsibility of the party that incurred it."

The debt was incurred jointly; it was a joint obligation. How could I possibly state that any more clearly?

He ordered me to pay Marie $479. He also ordered another $1,000 for his colleague, Ms. Pitbull. He also ordered me to pay the $1,400 IRS bill. The judge who reviewed the oral stipulation ordered us to split the IRS bill. There was no IRS bill. It was another misrepresentation from Ms. Pitbull.

It was a total loss but all in all still favorable. At any rate, I'll never go THERE again! I wasn't going to jail. Not yet anyway. The judge ordered a jail sentence of thirty days with a stay of three years, as long as I complied with the stipulations in the order, which was impossible.

Soon after the order was issued I got a call from Ms. Pitbull's paralegal asking me to contact the investment company to correct stipulations in the order created at the contempt hearing. I was blunt. I said, "No, it wasn't done correctly, and now it has to be done over." I sent their office a letter, for the first time addressing the issue of harassment.

A contempt proceeding is where the court determines consequences for failing to follow a court order. Their lack of scrutiny exacerbated the problems. Nobody was abiding by court orders. For me, it was impossible. For Ms. Pitbull, she would face no consequences. Quite the opposite, she had the full support and cooperation of the court. The court signed her requests without meaningful review. I see clear illustrations where the court's decision was in total disregard of the presented facts. There was absolutely no possibility of a meaningful negotiating process when there was such a huge imbalance of power. Imbalance of power is the fundamental basis of abuse and the court was fully represented. My principle challenge toward making any meaningful progress in the case was overcoming my fear of the court.

The judge was right. I didn't understand the law. I should have filed a contempt motion for each attorney violation of a court order. The contempt order provided some useful insight into the thought process of a criminal court justice. According to the order, "…the court finds that conditional confinement of Petitioner is reasonably likely to produce compliance with the order." The judge actually believes this: that the threat of confinement could persuade me to do the impossible. Never mind that he meant the respondent, not the petitioner. He is technically correct in referring to her and not him, but he wouldn't have known that. Let me examine that "belief" in more detail.

Think of her [me] being dominated in a male institution regulated by a masculine superiority complex. It wouldn't be pleasant. It would be humiliating and degrading. It is by its very nature not rehabilitative. It is punitive, as emphasized by the judge. That's their job, to punish people for bad behavior. I probably wouldn't be raped or murdered in a Dakota County jail. Compared to a year and a half of legal, emotional, and financial harassment that nearly drove me to suicide, thirty days with no responsibility, being dominated by men, might seem like a vacation. Some women might experience this self-defeating thought process, as rape fantasy. It doesn't mean she wants to be raped. To the contrary, it's a manner of emotionally submitting to overwhelming circumstances without actually giving up.

What else could the judge do but stay the order for confinement? My income was paying everyone's bills. What would he do at the end of thirty days when I was unemployed and possibly facing a much longer period of unemployment? Would he sentence me to another thirty days or perhaps ninety days or maybe a stint in a state prison? That's how courts create criminals.

What happens to the best interest of my son after putting his mom in jail. Isn't that what this whole thing was about, the best interests of the child? The judge can't think about that. They have to be impartial. They can't be personally involved in the emotional and functional dynamics of the family. That represents the inherent contradiction of a trial court judge determining the best interest of a child. The best interests of the child need to be determined before the disposition of any financial considerations.

The reality, at least in Dakota County where I live, is that child custody has little or nothing to do with the best interests of the child. It's about collecting child support and keeping children off county welfare roles.

Part X: Flowering Gardenia: Acceptance and triumph

The custody battle lasted just three months shy of four years. My life stood still. Actually, my life almost ended during the nineteen months I was away from my home and isolated from my son. In the midst of all that drama, I made my physical transition from male to female.

Caitlyn Jenner's story encourages us to believe transition is some instant metamorphosis, completely disconnected from the reality of an extended physical and social experience. Like Clark Kent dashing into a phone booth and exiting as Superman, in one moment we see Bruce Jenner and the next we see Caitlyn as a beautiful cover model on Vanity Fair. It never happens that way. Transition is really a process of bringing other people's perceptions into alignment with one's own identity. From a transgender person's perspective, the change in identity is really something people around them experience because their own identity is already different than how others perceive them.

I had my son and my home, a safe place to establish roots to support a lovely gardenia bush that would stand strong against the surrounding storm. Once again, I had the freedom to express myself in ways that I hadn't had since I left my best girlfriend behind, forty-five years ago. In time, I'd realize the gardenia could flower once again.

Chapter Forty-five: Transition

– Lewis Carroll, Alice in Wonderland

Once Tyler and I were living back in our home, I realized another compelling transition: returning from a "weekend activities" parent to full-time parental responsibilities. I had always considered myself the primary care parent. I was intensely aware of my role as mother, even while acting like the dad. When I was caring for the children, I was the mom. When Marie was present, I was the dad. Marie expected that. She expected me to discipline the children. There is a profound irony in the image of a father, responsible for disciplining the children, being put out on the street for raising his voice to a son. That risk was gone.

Being sober suddenly meant dealing with a whole range of issues: the rape, the suicide, the abuse in my life, the broken relationships, all the men who never were, and the breakdown of my marriage. I'd given up on therapy early in the divorce because I could no longer afford it. Dr. H had been supportive, extending service well beyond my ability to pay. AA provided that support for a minimal donation.

My son would remain my highest priority. It did not take long to determine what had been happening while I was gone. He'd found his own community among many of the less-privileged children of our community, teenagers searching for their identity, exercising their independence, exploring their future. It was a strangely diverse group, so different from my youth. Some had wealthy families. Some had virtually no family. Some were in college. Others were struggling with part-time jobs. They were the social fringe of a conformist society. Generally, they were well-mannered and respectful but undisciplined by the natural rebelliousness of youth. In some ways, through my own teenage years, I could relate. I garnered my own popularity outside the core of the high school elite society of my day, the athletes and the cheerleaders. I was a social rebel myself. After all, I'd campaigned for George McGovern.

Control issues were always a major point of contention in my marriage. When Marie was here, our house was her home. In the final analysis, she forced everyone out. To me, our house existed for the family. It's a principle reason I wanted to keep the home. I wanted our children to always have a place to return to if adversity should befall them. My parents had few years together when one of their children or grandchildren wasn't living with them.

Boundaries, based on strict authoritarian rule, don't internalize well. Tyler had been without active parental involvement for two years. He had established his own boundaries outside the confines of home rule. Marie blamed me for not enforcing her rules in every court document they submitted. I followed his school progress through parent-teacher conferences which always produced good reports, but it was apparent he was becoming socially isolated. Like many teens, Tyler isn't a forthright communicator, and it takes a lot of active involvement to understand what's going on in his life. I couldn't possibly achieve that in two weekends a month.

There were positives. I don't deny that. It was Marie who helped Tyler find Riley and enrolled them in obedience classes. He's a beautiful dog, chocolate brown, half husky and half golden retriever. Riley had a lot to do with Tyler's passion for animals and his career choice. Marie also enrolled Tyler in Taekwondo while he was living with her. I was there when he graduated to black belt. Marie probably did many other things for our children that I never knew about. Never sharing with me what was going on in their lives was part of the problem.

Now I'm going to state it bluntly: That first year together with Tyler was absolute chaos. The place was already suffering from neglect after several years without maintenance. Tyler had absolutely no housekeeping skills, and I didn't have the time or the inclination to clean up after him. I couldn't invite anyone over to my house. Of course, when the neighbors call, the police come uninvited. It felt like they'd all been to my house at one time or another. One night the police were there telling Tyler to get out because he couldn't be there in an abandoned property. Tyler said, "I live here" and produced his driver's license. We still laugh about that. It's a clear indication of where we were starting from.

One day the entire garage door completely disintegrated, just finally gave way to the ravages of time. I told Tyler to check what his friends had done to the garage door. He had to admit I'd gotten him pretty good on that one. Fair trade for some past April fool's jokes.

Tyler knew it was his home and his right to have friends over. I didn't disagree. Mostly, it was small groups and sometimes moderate amounts of alcohol. The music was loud, but I was able to sleep through it. That social interaction was important to him, and I was happy to have them at our house.

I trusted Tyler and, for the most part, his core group of friends, but there were things Tyler didn't understand about underage drinking parties, like friends of friends and professional thieves preying on naive youth. There would be some major incidents before he started to get it. I wasn't happy to come home to a houseful of underage drinking but it didn't seem like a good option to send them out on the roads. There were a few times when I definitely raised my voice but there was no one there to report me to the police.

They did a lot of damage, and there was a lot of stolen property. After each incident I said, "no more parties," but I suppose it was difficult for Tyler to get control of it. Even after the parties stopped, the thefts continued.

We started working together to try and trace the stolen property. One of his solutions was to install video cameras. Regrettably, the system failed the night we could have gotten video of one major theft. One of the laptops was a work computer. I lost my job because of it. A new desktop computer had all of my backup data that I was restoring to a new computer when it was stolen. I lost a lot of information creating a huge hole in my life.

After one party, I received reports of complaints from neighbors about the parking on their street and some damaged property. I went to each of the neighbors and asked if they had any damaged property I needed to replace. They were gracious about it. I was at the police station multiple times to report stolen property. It was embarrassing and I couldn't help believing they were thinking, *she must be a terrible mother.*

I'd console myself with the thought that this wouldn't be happening if the police hadn't put Tyler's mother out on the street. People, who were once telling me to wait until he was nineteen, were now advising me to throw him out. My reply was always the same, "I am not going to throw him out. A parent is exactly what he needs right now."

Tyler's friends knew me as a woman. By this time, according to HIM, I was always presenting as a woman, except at work.

Forty percent of trans-women have attempted suicide. It's widely accepted that the cause is social isolation from discrimination, violence, and harassment. Transition following a suicide attempt is common in the transgender community and is, in a way, a part of my own experience. Following a near-death experience, it was clear that accepting the challenge of being a transgender woman was far better than dying, or worse, abandoning my son.

I wore a dress on Halloween in 2010. I had on a black halter dress, with Halloween stockings and a bat in my hair. My boss emailed a photo of me to the office. A lot of people thought I was a new employee and were asking about her name. This a positive experience for a transgender woman.

Under normal circumstances my contract at the bank would have ended in October because of strict time limits on contract duration. My contract had been extended three months, which was a testament to the importance of the project I was on and the quality of my work. I was happy to be employed during the transfer of the house in December and January.

Financially, 2011 was a strenuous year. I had a short contract during the summer followed by a contract starting in November that ended abruptly in January because of the stolen laptop. At that time, in the beginning of 2012, I started looking for new employ-ment as a woman.

I was unemployed at the time of the contempt hearing at the end of August. It's another case of divine guidance I'd say, because it led naturally to the next option I had which was to file for child support due to the change in circumstances. After reviewing the statutes and some related case law, it seemed pretty straightfor-ward. Ms. Pitbull would turn it in to another legal nightmare.

Chapter Forty-six: The Abyss

"They're putting down they're names," the Gryphon whispered in reply, "for fear they would forget them before the end of the trial."

–Lewis Carroll, Alice in Wonderland

Examining the time before and after the divorce decree, I am entranced by how quickly and dramatically my life was transformed. Despite a dynamic career and my responsibilities to my children, my emotional self had shrunk down to a tiny room in the basement drinking wine and spirits to dull the edges of my disquietude. Escaping the chemical dependency was critical, but the dramatic change came from escaping the emotional prison I had created for myself. Women are grounded in their emotions and allowing myself that freedom was powerful, even a little unmanageable at times.

The transgender community in Minneapolis seemed quite invisible to me in 2011, sequestered in visible form, mainly around several area nightclubs. As an example of how naive I was, I wanted to meet every transgender person in the Twin Cities, unaware of just how many of us there really are and how many of them I already knew.

I may have gotten some notion of that at the Creating Change conference, which was held in Minneapolis in February, 2011. The conference, sponsored by the National Gay and Lesbian Task Force was just a couple of skyway blocks away from where I was working downtown, so I brought clothes with me on Friday and changed on my way to the conference. Even after years of trying on dresses in male dressing rooms, I've never felt comfortable about changing in public spaces. I didn't want to attend the conference as a guy. What would people think?

For me, it was an entirely different world, people of all sexes and genders. I know that will sound strange to people indoctrinated by the transgender myth. I had a sense that I was finally someplace where I belonged. I wondered, *Why can't the whole world be like this?* What's most memorable to me is the amusing stories about past conferences with the Gay and Lesbian Task Force meeting in the same conference centers with groups like the National Organization of Women and the Girl Scouts. It was an affirmation of how much things had changed since the late sixties.

On May 6, 2011, I was at the Demand Change Project organized by Breaking Free and MATTOO, Men Against the Trafficking of Others. Breaking Free is an organization in Saint Paul that helps women evolve from prostituted lives in the sex trade. Abuse against women was always central in my life. Prostitution is something I felt I understood, in part from the violent nature of my own experience with rape but the conference illuminated how brutal and unregulated this underground industry really is. People who will ask me so casually why I didn't go to the police will ask the same question about a woman in the captivity of a brutally violent pimp. They fail to understand that the protections provided by the police do not extend equally to all classes. Working in the servitude of a pimp is itself a crime punishable by harsh penalties. The moral justification for this is extremely biased against women.

I enjoyed meeting the staff and clientele of Breaking Free: amazing women. I attended multiple events with Breaking Free and did some volunteer work on fundraising over the next couple of years.

Saturday the men marched to the town square, where the women were assembled. The march was a show of solidarity with the women against the abuses of sex trafficking. I was presenting as a woman. I spent most of my weekend with the women, but I marched with the men.

I still need a phrase to define my gender: male to female transgender person. Normally, I use the closest match we have in our language, which is woman, her, and she. I present myself as a transgender woman. To most people, this means I was born a boy, and now I'm a woman. I don't mind if people accept me that way.

In support of a natural gender spectrum, it's certainly more precise and more meaningful than insisting I'm just like every other woman.

Gender-typing negatively impacts women. Attending the recent Martin Luther exhibit at the Minneapolis Institute of Arts, I was intrigued by all the references about containing the "bewitching" power of women. In pre-revolutionary America, women were still being tortured and hanged in order to control this illusory threat. Paintings depicting the head of John the Baptist invoked memories of biblical stories about the beguiling power of women over men, as in the familiar story of Sampson and Delilah.

Feminism has drawn women deeper into patriarchal models of power and control while leaving behind any meaningful integration of feminine values. Feminism has failed to engage men in meaningful comprise. We have failed to define any complimentary notion of gender. We are continuing to reinforce the oppositional sexism that we rebel against. Defining domestic abuse according to how a woman feels, has brought us no closer to a solution. In truth, it reinforces the notion that women are too emotional. Why would men, deprived of their children and their livelihood by false allegations of abuse, be inclined to believe we need more protections for women.

My son was deprived of his mother by the simple fact that the court perceived her as a man. They really had no other justification. The judges were enforcing Marie's female privilege, which has so long been defined by a woman's dependence on a man. Marie was asserting that privilege to dominate our household years before the divorce. There was never a place for a dialogue, not in therapy and not in the court. At no time did the court consider that there might be an alternate scenario. My case is not unique in those respects. It's a clear example of how the exploitation of fear transforms itself into an abuse of power. The promise didn't match the reality.

It didn't matter if the judge was female. It's another exhortation of the transgender myth allowing the court to base its decisions entirely on the gender of the participants. It was also emphasized by Marie's attorney and echoed by three of my four attorneys, including one who was a man.

Marching with the men to join the women was symbolic of the complementary notion of gender. I wasn't a man marching in solidarity with the needs of women, but a woman marching in solidarity with the value of men. I am standing on the bridge between masculinity and femininity, and I am inviting others to do the same and to solidify a common purpose. I am impressed by the values presented to us by the leadership of Breaking Free. The demand for sexual gratification comes from men. Sex trafficking is a slave trade forcing girls to meet that demand. Eliminating that demand would certainly relieve the problem but demonizing male sexuality doesn't present a solution. It's underscored by the "bewitching" power of women that's rarely factored into the equation. Women too, rebuke the victims of sexual violence. We face a dichotomy of victims rights and victim shaming. Men become the executioners for female aggression.

Five days later, I am headed to the capital in Saint Paul for the final Senate vote on the marriage amendment. It was a full house, but good fortune provided me a parking spot kitty-corner from the capital. As soon as I crossed the first street and before the light changed, so I could cross the second, two Saint Paul police officers stand before me. I try to keep a positive attitude toward police, but as part of a marginalized community, confrontation can be intimidating. This wasn't my first transgender experience with police. They want to know if I am prostituting. I tell them I'm heading to the capital for a Senate hearing. One of the officers says, "There is a lot of prostitution in this area you know."

I'm thinking, *Of course, we're right next to the capital*, but I contain my sarcasm. Instead, I say, "Yes, I know. Your chief was down at the Demand Change Project last week talking about that."

With that, they said, "Thank you," and got back in their car. I realized increased visibility might actually be safer for me.

All the same, I felt defensive and assaulted. I'm ready to take back anything I may have said about compromising with men. After I calm down, I reconsider my position. They didn't ask to search my purse. I never carried condoms in my purse, because I knew it could be used as evidence of prostitution. It's a complicated situation. Sex work may be a woman's choice but she may also be a victim. In either case, she is still a criminal. She may fear arrest, or she may want to escape an abusive pimp. It occurred to me that many St. Paul police are familiar with Breaking Free, and maybe it was a rescue effort, though their approach didn't suggest it.

The Senate vote was disappointing. We heard so many reasons why a marriage amendment was bad for Minnesota, then we watched the Senate pass it on strictly partisan lines. It was my first introduction to the dysfunction in our two-party system, At the time, I was willing to believe the problem was the Republicans. That final vote initiated the historic Minnesota "Vote No" campaign for the next eighteen months up until the vote in November of 2012. The battle had been fought in thirty states and thirty times been lost. Minnesota was thirty-one.

Alongside the ongoing custody battle, it would be a major part of my life over the next eighteen months, including marching in the 2012 pride parade wearing my first wedding dress. That led to an interesting exchange with Senator Al Franken. I spent many hours phone banking, petitioning, doing faith outreach, and attending events. Faith outreach engaged me in some interesting discussions about the separation of church and state. Much of the debate centered around marriage as a religious sacrament and marriage as a legal entity of the state. I felt a certain amount of trepidation in fighting for marriage equality in the midst of an ugly divorce.

That convergence of marriage and divorce was drawing me into the arena of politics. In that summer of 2011, I asked the city council of Eagan to consider a domestic partner registry. Opponents saw it as a stepping stone to marriage equality but others supported it as an alternative to same-sex marriage. There were many who felt it would be okay to have same-sex partnerships as long as you didn't call it a marriage. The initiative was driven towards same-sex partners, but it had other applications for roommate arrangements. I also addressed the city council in Northfield on behalf of a trans girlfriend who was living there at the time. The measure passed in both communities. The mayor of Eagan was instrumental in passing the ordinance, and I agreed to support him in his election bid for State Senate during 2012.

Chapter Forty-seven: Child Support

Why is a raven like a writing desk? "Have you guessed the riddle yet?" the Hatter said "No, I give it up," Alice replied: "what's the answer? "I haven't the slightest idea,' said the Hatter."

–Lewis Carroll, Alice in Wonderland

It took ten months and dozens of legal exchanges to execute the divorce decree. I filed the first child support motion before I even obtained title to the house. It seemed like one continuous action, but my motion for child support was a separate action. The master of chaos and confusion would do her best to undermine this fact.

I filed the motion, as soon as the law allowed, based on a significant change in circumstances. I was providing full support for my son, my income was substantially reduced, and I no longer had health insurance.

Ms. Pitbull responded with a long list of court appearances as proof of my failure to comply with the court order. She repeated a long list of false allegations she'd been making throughout the proceedings: (a) Problems with custody and child support, (b) no address for service, (c) failure to maintain health insurance, (d) failure to provide documentation for the loan modification, (e) refusing to file joint bankruptcy, (f) failure to pay the state income tax, (g) allowing Tyler to submit his own sworn testimony, (h) failure to comply with temporary orders [okay, that one is true but also true to the heart of the problem], (I) failing to comply with the order pending the appeal [technically, that's correct as well], (j) discharging attorney fees in bankruptcy [that's a completely different case], (k) refusing to sign vehicle title provided by petitioner, (l) Delaying information provided to opposing counsel (rather ambiguous), and, finally, (m) [refer again to item l].

From my perspective, the court was simply abiding by the

word of a trusted colleague. They threatened me and sanctioned me every step of the way. They told me I didn't understand the law. I did understand the law, and I was following it. Naturally, Ms. Pitbull wasn't happy about it, but a good attorney would have acknowledged this in the beginning, instead of leading her client through an ugly court proceeding. I didn't design the process. The motion to vacate, the motion for amended findings were an essential part of filing the appeal. Perhaps I shouldn't have agreed to something I knew to be utterly absurd, but they shouldn't have put me out on the street and taken my son under false pretenses.

I'd been conciliatory in the beginning. I'd withdrawn my OFP order. I paid Marie's rent. I gave her support payments in excess of the state guidelines. At the pretrial conference, we agreed to continue paying her rent, offered her $500/month child support and $10,000 in re-employment assistance.

I didn't want to drag the family through an extended court case over who said what. I resisted Ms. Pitbull's efforts to define the difficult issues our family struggled with as a simple case of domestic abuse, which it clearly wasn't. If anyone could make that claim, it would be me. Trans women can be extremely vulnerable to abuse. Public notice of a trans person's identity can be intimidating, it's called "outing."

Item (k), refusing to sign the title is a typical example. I was driving the Dodge Neon. It was "my" car. I was given use of it in the temporary order, but the title was in Marie's name. She refused to give me the title. Then one night in early December of 2009, I was on my way home from work when a minivan drove through a stop sign and broadsided my little Neon. Lights were flashing when I came to. My first thought was, *My life is over*. It was the first time since I'd quit drinking that I felt compelled to go to the bar. I was saved by a coworker still at the office. He gave me a ride home. The next day I had a replacement vehicle, and I was still sober so my life wasn't over. As I write this, I realize that I was involved in three major car accidents during the divorce. I keep my guardian angel busy.

The Neon went to the impound lot, where it started collecting storage fees. There was nothing I could do about it; I didn't have the title. I also couldn't retrieve any of my personal property still in the car. I'd lose all that, including my favorite pair of high heel boots. When I received the collection notice I sent it to Marie's attorney. Several days later I got a certified letter from Marie containing the title for the Dodge Neon. So, item (k) is incorrect. Nearly all of those accusations could be assigned to Marie and her attorney.

Miss Pitbull wrote a letter to the judge, asking for a sua sponte dismissal of a child support motion. That means the judge denies child support without considering the merits of the request and without any responsive motion or hearing. A rather outrageous request, I thought.

I don't think the court responded. Next day I got an order from the child support magistrate referring the matter to district court for a hearing on November 22, 2011. This process is so exceedingly complex that details are easily overlooked. The court administrator had scheduled the hearing before a child support magistrate because it contained a motion to review child support, but it also contained a request to revise custody, which must be heard before a district court judge.

We had agreed to cash out one of our retirement accounts in the amount of $10,000. At this time I was counting on that money to help with Tyler's medical expenses. The check went to Ms. Pitbull, of course, so I never saw any of it. Some of it went to Marie for past-due spousal maintenance, but the part Ms. Pitbull kept for herself wasn't authorized by the court order. I addressed the health care issue to the judge as well. He advised me to file a motion which was already in progress.

On November 1, 2011, I sent an addendum to my motion asking that Marie be ordered to pay the $1000 she had taken from Tyler's savings. The next day we were assigned our own judge. I knew the judge, not on a personal level, but I had engaged with him in court before on a previous matter. For the moment, though, I wasn't completely sure if that was a good thing or a bad thing.

A couple of weeks later I appeared on my first transgender panel discussion following the presentation of *Genderf*kation*, a new documentary about gender variant identities. Our hostess,

June Remus, asked me to participate the night of the show. I could certainly speak meaningfully to my range of experiences but I really wasn't overly familiar yet with the wide-ranging issues of the broader community. It was the first time I met Ellen Krug, who was also on the panel.

I'd met June at the Townhouse in Saint Paul the past summer during another showing of *Genderf*kation*. She invited me to the showing at MCC, All God's Children's Church in Minneapolis. Metropolitan Community Church is a global denomination founded in Los Angeles in 1968, ministering to the gay-lesbian community. Ironically, it was my involvement in the LGBT movement that returned me to my own faith when I recognized that many of the conferences were being held in churches. I grew up in the Missouri Synod Lutheran Church which continues to maintain one of the strictest anti-LGBT doctrines of any denomination.

I joined All God's Children MCC church because of their strong focus on social justice. I worked with June in the transgender ministries program. In November, we traveled to Berkeley, California for the transgender ministries conference. It was intensely spiritual. The diversity of the participants transcended the physical manifestations of God so prevalent in religious doctrine. At the opening service, there was, as I can recall, a Catholic priest, a Presbyterian minister, a Jewish rabbi, a Native American spirit guide, and a pagan priestess. It emphasized the narrow boundaries of my own religious background and was a prelude to my own spiritual calling.

I also worked in prison ministries at the Minnesota Sexual Offenders Program in Moose Lake, Minnesota. A group of four or five of us performed church services for some forty men at the facility. Listening to their stories and learning about the history of the facility complimented my experiences with the sexual boundaries group. It reinforced my understanding of fear factor politics, even though I hadn't yet formulated my own concept of it.

June was my mentor, promoting my development from a teenage girl into a mature woman, even if perhaps still about twenty years shy of my actual age. It's a curious conundrum that's difficult to understand or acknowledge even for those of us who are experiencing it. I was handling a complex legal battle, maintaining a demanding career and looking after my family, while struggling with the emotions of a teenage girl.

This may explain why I understood I needed a man to represent me. Many feminists would reject that notion straight away. I've often remarked that this whole gender thing was a cruel joke. Men and women are fundamentally incompatible. Sure, it's great to have a man around if you need to move some heavy furniture, but what else are they good for? In an equally crude representation of gendered relationships, we know what men want from us. The analysis extends to same-sex partnerships reinforcing the popular stereotype that one partner is the "man" and one partner is the "woman."

People who don't agree with this stereotype are rejecting the transgender myth in favor of a meaningful spectrum of gender and sexuality. It's not meaningful to apply general norms to individual relationships. When I'm with a group of gay men I know I am with "men." When I am with a group of lesbian women I know I am with "women." An interesting footnote to the macroscopic view of gender is that you rarely find lesbian women in large homogeneous groups.

Successful relationships demand an accommodation of the differences rather than some perceived notion of compatibility. That principle extends to any relationship. It's easy to create fear, anxiety, discontent, and polarization. That's what drives most political and social agendas. It's far more difficult to create accommodating compromises.

Once a judge was assigned, Ms. Pitbull asked for another sua sponte dismissal. Her accusations convinced the judge to issue an order to show cause why he shouldn't dismiss it as frivolous litigation. I was flabbergasted; dismiss a child support motion? It's also a huge threat. It could make me responsible for tens of thousands in legal fees and prevent me from filing subsequent motions.

Reading Marie's affidavits was the most painful part of the whole ordeal. It outlined constant repetition about what a horrible parent I was; how totally irresponsible I was; how I was abusing and neglecting my son. She claimed Tyler was lying in his sworn statements because I was pressuring him. I'll never know how much of it she believed because I know she didn't write them. That's how Ms. Pitbull presented her case, and it was inappropriate.

Marie's affidavits contained many legal opinions that she wouldn't have understood. They were stated in biased or misleading ways to create an appearance of legal precedence, which didn't exist. By this time I knew the judge wasn't reading them anyway, but I still had to respond. I had to draft a response to Marie's affidavit and a response to the order to show cause. It was a time-intensive exercise. Part of Marie's argument suggested they should deny my motion because she couldn't afford her attorney. It wasn't fair I wasn't paying an attorney. Marie always had the option to drop her attorney. I'd done my best to help her understand that.

Fortunately, I was able to retain Jason again. It is difficult for a pro se litigant to obtain legal consulting.

Chapter Forty-eight: Order to Show Cause

This is how I remember it because I don't have an actual transcript of the hearing, but then a true story is only completely true for the person telling it. At the child support hearing, the judge acknowledged he hadn't read the motions. Then he indicated he wasn't going to hear any motions. He was going to go to the order and get this straightened out. The intense frustration I had experienced during this process couldn't begin to compare to what I felt at that very moment.

The judge explained he could put me in jail. Certainly, "Give your evidence, and don't be nervous or I'll have you executed on the spot." Even as I wanted to say, "Go ahead," I knew jail wasn't a good plan.

I wasn't the person he was expecting. He wouldn't remember me, just another nameless face on a court docket. A solution was elusive. Health insurance was a major problem. When I was working I could get affordable rates through my employer, but when I wasn't, I couldn't afford the same coverage through COBRA. Neither of us currently qualified for Minnesota Care for Tyler because of the way the finances had been structured.

Their demand for $50,000 of life insurance was also troublesome. I can't qualify for reasonable rates. For effect, I indicated the hole in my cheek, where an abscessed tooth was draining through the side of my face. The judge ordered me to get two quotes.

I kept asking about my son. Finally, he did engage with me about Tyler's current living arrangements. With respect to child support, he wanted to review the financial statement, but, of course, our decree didn't have one. Ms. Pitbull argued that I was trying to modify the spousal maintenance. I argued it was her income and just because it was her only income didn't exempt her from her obligation to support our son.

Much to my relief, the judge agreed with me. I got custody of Tyler and $375 a month in child support to be deducted from the $2500 a month spousal maintenance payment. That boosted my net income allocation to almost $750 a month for Tyler and me. In three weeks, because of the stolen laptop, I was unemployed again.

In a letter to the court, I asked for several modifications citing them as clerical errors, which the court can correct without additional motions or hearings. I wanted child support to begin with the date of the motion, not the date of the order. The judge advised me to file a motion. On February 2, 2012, I filed a second child support motion. Ms. Pitbull made the same claims about frivolous litigation. This claim was even more baseless than the first. I had full custody of Tyler and an award for child support. I already had permission from the court to file the motion.

Barring that, she wanted the motion heard by a district court judge rather than before a child support magistrate. That would be highly irregular. Her requests were denied and the hearing was scheduled for April 19, 2012.

There were discovery motions on both sides with neither side really willing to cooperate anymore. They weren't going to answer my request and everything they were requesting was already in the record. Ms. Pitbull's final effort was to submit an intent to enter and docket maintenance judgment. I responded with a request for hearing and stay of judgment arguing that Ms. Pitbull was essentially trying to preempt an unfavorable judgment at the April child support hearing.

I invoked the dreaded presumption of potential income, something anyone who is paying child support is probably familiar with. It is essentially what Ms. Pitbull was doing when calculating my income based on some maximum hourly rate I had received during my career. I argued that if Marie was truly disabled than she was eligible for SSI disability and her minimum potential income was at least $2000 a month.

Maybe I was feeling overconfident and comfortable around a courtroom when, in the midst of all this chaos, I filed a motion to change my name and my gender identity.

There was something spiritual about choosing a name. Relatives had suggested the name, Samantha, a long time back, at a family funeral. I certainly was flattered by the comparison to her character on *Sex in the City*, but I didn't want to be called Sam. I wanted to stay close to my original name and finally decided on Paula. I tried out different middle initials and finally decided on M. Then I picked out a bunch of M words until I finally came upon Mirare which I discovered was Romanian for mystery or mysterious. It seemed so romantic, as I'd henceforth become known as Paula Mirare Overby. The hearing was scheduled for March 31st.

On the 7th of February, I was at my precinct caucus. I wish I could remember what I was wearing. I was surprised that people would accept me as a woman simply because I said I was. I know that Paula Mirare Overby first appeared on Facebook Feb 15, 2012, a week after the caucus, but the first picture posting of Paula was on January 31, 2011. It remains hard for me to imagine that so many things were compressed into such a short period of time.

I volunteered to be my precinct co-chair, a humble launch to my political career. I am illuminated by the fact that I was always Paula from the start of my political engagement. Now I pause to contemplate this. Knowing I am transgender isn't the same thing as knowing me before transition and after transition. I'm compelled to recognize that for friends and family who remain in your life, it is for them a transition as well, but for future relationships, it isn't.

As Paula, I searched for a new job contract for several months without a single interview. It frightened me. I withdrew once more from whatever calling I was driven to. I accepted the bank interview as a man. When I took the job at the beginning of March, I knew I'd be changing my name at the end of March.

After three days on the job, I experienced an emotional meltdown.

I'm okay with that. Women are grounded in their emotions. The problem results from a society that defines "too emotional" as a negative issue. Telling women they are "too emotional" is a formula for self-doubt, shame, and emotional negligence. It reiterates the fallacy of defining gender equity through women achieving masculine standards.

For me, I was dropping pretenses. A meltdown is based on fear. Each day I became more fearful that the longer I presented as a man, the more difficult it would be to start presenting as a woman. The fear was irrational as fear often is. Many of the people I was working with, most of them women, were Hindu and had a naturally fluid concept of self.

That evening I emailed my boss and said I was transgender and that I was coming to work the next day as a woman.

It was inappropriate. Who could imagine doing that?

The next day I was there as a woman. Who could imagine doing that?

So I have a male ID, and I'm presenting as a woman. Would anyone think that is strange? Nobody seemed to. Nobody said anything.

I got a call from HR wondering if I was going to remain as a woman. They didn't want me switching back and forth. They said I should use the women's bathroom. After three days, they wanted me to take a week off while they worked out their communication plan. My contract manager stood up for me. She said, "You're going to pay her, aren't you?" I worked from home for a week and after that everything was fine, though I couldn't get a new ID until after the court hearing.

Courtney and Tyler testified for me, and my friend Shannon also agreed to testify on my behalf. Up to now, I haven't mentioned Shannon. She was my most true and loyal friend the entire time I presented as a man in a dress. She was among the first people to whom I shared the thought of writing a book. She wanted to know if she would be in the book, and I wrote for her a paragraph of what I'd say about her. That paragraph has disappeared in the chaos of the divorce, but I am certain the sentiment remains captured in "true and loyal friend." She was with me the first and only time I was ever asked to leave an establishment because I used the women's restroom. Only twice was I ever asked to leave an establishment for presenting as a man wearing a dress: Moose Country in Mendota Heights and the American Legion in Apple Valley, where I'd one day become a member of the Women's Auxiliary. The world has changed so much since that first transgender march just ten years ago.

I had a letter from my medical doctor, which probably contained the most powerful affirmation I could ever hope for. He said, "I believe her." He said other things, but that is what touched me deeply. Courtney had written a beautiful letter. Both Courtney and Tyler referred to me as Mom. That too was heartwarming, and I admired their courage. The judge wouldn't consider a gender change without sexual reassignment surgery, which I didn't have yet. I hadn't even started hormone therapy. The judge wouldn't even look at the letters. She asked me, "Do you still want your name changed?" It felt like sarcasm, but I pleasantly replied, "Yes, of course."

The same day, I went to renew my driver's license and apply for a variance to get female on my license. My picture would be Paula, my name would be Paula Mirare Overby, but next to it would be a big letter M. I didn't want to think about it.

Tyler came with me to the child support hearing. He wanted to be heard and I respected that. As Paula, it was my first court appearance in a dress. There was a long tense waiting period as we were last on the court calendar.

I had missed one detail. The case was IV-D[1] because Marie had received child support through child support services. Because of the way the child support payments to me were structured I was technically not receiving child support, so no IV-D case number was assigned to me. The child support magistrate wasn't authorized to hear the case. Marie's attorney had billed her an enormous amount of money to preempt that hearing, and it wasn't even going to be heard.

It was a costly mistake for me as well. I filed for an IV-D case number, but it would never be used. Time was running out on the issue of child support.

1 County child support offices, subsidized by the federal Social Security program, are called IV-D agencies, referring to Title IV-D of the Social Security Act. Cases in which the county is a party are called IV-D cases.

Chapter Forty-nine: Woman's Prerogative

As a woman, there was a wide range of services available to me that men didn't have access to. I received legal counseling at Chrysalis where Marie attended counseling. I felt that's where she learned her identifiers of abuse that she'd entered in her OFP. I was comfortable there, and I didn't hold any animosity. If there was any trepidation around my presence at Chrysalis, I never felt it. If anything, it reminded me of a need for better ways to assess and address risk in our relationships. Much the same way the "stranger danger" campaign failed to teach children what they could do to feel safe. I'm afraid I can't put it more clearly.

My own experience bears witness to the way anxiety can be exploited by well-intentioned or even unscrupulous therapists and attorneys. I continued to explore the issue in abuse advocacy training and promoting services for same-sex couples, where models of abuse cannot be defined by gender.

I saw my gynecologist on April 17, 2012. She's really an endocrinologist, but I preferred gynecologist for emphasis on my female senses. Of course, I understood going to their gynecologist wasn't a woman's favorite thing to do. Obviously, I never had to deal with a period, which is horribly unfair. I never had to shave my legs or my underarms. That's not fair either. I did have ugly dark facial hair most of my life. That's not fair either. Body issues come with being a woman, but placing gender dysphoria in that realm is a highly benighted comparison.

I was high anxiety. The only persuasion I had for her was my letter from my medical doctor. I was relieved when she prescribed hormone replacement therapy. She assured me my anxiety levels would diminish in a few days. She was right. I thought back to a time when I first asked my medical doctor for estrogen treatment, and how different my life would have been. Now I had a diagnosis of gender identity disorder which seemed so much better than severe personality disorder or cross-dresser. GID has since been changed to gender dysphoria to indicate that it isn't a disorder but can still cause severe emotional distress.

Then, on May 7, by the time I was really starting to appreciate the emotional benefits of transition, I got some bad news. A letter from the Department of Motor Vehicles indicated a female gender variance couldn't be approved, because I hadn't supplied sufficient information. I sent them copies of my prescriptions, indicated I had another appointment with my gynecologist, and asked what additional information they needed. Several weeks later I got a new license with Paula's picture, Paula's name, and Paula's gender, a big capital F.

Getting that license is a feeling that's hard to describe. If you can remember when you got your first driver's license then this is ten times better. I was a happy girl. I'd taken a very risky path, and it all worked out. I'd reached a place where I couldn't deal with another therapist, and I couldn't wait any longer.

At times, the bureaucratic issues of being transgender can be more complicated than the social ones. Some trans people will change all of their records, including things like grade school records and college transcripts. I never did, nor do I believe I ever could. I tried to change my name on the title to my house. What I get now is a statement addressed to Paul S. Overby c/o Paula M. Overby. It's nice to know I'm taking care of myself, but I'd rather be at the spa. Someday, I'll try again.

During all of this, I'm still trying to keep track of my son. It was snowing the night Tyler and I went to Adult Basic Education, orientation.

Does that vivid image portend its significance?

I wasn't happy about it. I'd worked so hard to ensure he graduated. Tyler said it was the best option for the few remaining credits he needed. He would still graduate with his class with a diploma from Eagan High School. The school counselor agreed it was a good option, even as I felt they were leaving something out.

I agreed, having no meaningful objection. Intuition tells me Marie never knew about it or surely Ms. Pitbull would have presented it as more proof of poor parenting. I did what I could to keep him on that path under the pressures placed on him by the divorce.

From the moment I became Paula, everything I had hoped to keep out of court records suddenly became the entire focus. In a letter to the court, Ms. Pitbull immediately insisted "she was a him," bolded and underlined. I wrote to the court, citing the action as abusive under the Minnesota Human Rights Act. They also invoked another popular tactic crafted to discredit transgender women. In simple terms, the claim goes that a man in an oppressive situation decides to become a woman to avoid harsh punishment. It's more antagonistic than Fay Weldon's assertion that we are men seeking female superiority. I start to like Fay's explanation better.

The most notable case I am aware of was Chelsea Manning after she was convicted of espionage. Much to my dismay, I've even heard trans women resort to the accusation. Trans women have a right to be terrified of men's prisons. They often end up in isolation. Transition has not kept them out. Transition is often accompanied by highly stressful situations.

Men in the sexual boundaries group experienced gender inequity in prosecutorial discretion. Women received therapy to be reunited with their children. Men went to prison. Equal rights can be a touchy subject.

When the case before the child support magistrate was dismissed, I amended the motion in district court asking to extend child support until Tyler was twenty, so he could attend community college. I offered to continue a decision on spousal maintenance for the same time period, which was actually a great offer. I was still pushing for some manageable solution. If I could focus on my career there was a chance it could work. There wasn't going to be any graceful exit.

Ms. Pitbull filed a motion to dismiss, asking the court to find me to be a frivolous litigant so she could collect her fees. This was, again, baseless, as I had already been granted permission from the court to file the motion. She submitted a responsive motion and more discovery requests. That too can be considered frivolous litigation. In my opinion, it's a strategy to exhaust the opposition emotionally and financially. The opinion is reinforced by remarks about how unfair it was I wasn't accumulating large attorney bills. In reality, I was. They were just being channeled through payments to Marie. I still had legal expenses. Printing costs alone were considerable.

And last, as always, there was another request for a continuance. As always, the hearing was continued. When the hearing was moved from May 14th to June 25th the date of the hearing was beyond Tyler's graduation date, which meant child support was no longer a consideration. I filed a motion to terminate spousal maintenance.

I was on the board of the Men's Center when I became Paula. At one of the board meetings, we received a request from *Girl Talk* for someone to appear on their show about the domestic abuse of men. We didn't seem to have anyone willing to do it so I agreed. Men don't want to acknowledge they are a survivor of domestic violence, just as women often don't want to admit they have been raped. I never did. I wasn't thrilled about appearing as a man, but all of the interpretations and actions against me were directed towards a man. The court case was predicated on the presumption that I was a man, a perpetrator, a deadbeat dad.

Continuing to define our relationship in terms of domestic violence I found equally uncomfortable, the issues Marie and I dealt with were far more complicated than simply deciding who abused who. These rules are defined for police, attorneys, child support services, prosecutors, and judges. They are not designed around healing families.

One of the participants I knew from the Domestic Abuse Project. Before the show was taped she was replaced by a woman from Cornerstone, who I'd later work with on the Open Door Project to expand domestic abuse services to LGBT partners.

Marie saw the show. Her attorney submitted a motion proclaiming it public harassment, asking the judge to prohibit me from public appearances and demanding I cancel any further appearances. There was only one appearance even though the show aired multiple times. It no longer exists in the station's archives.

It was a baseless assertion. They made their whole case on baseless allegations. There's no therapy in divorce court. With their petition, they sent transcribed statements I'd made during the show. I've reviewed the motion and show, but it remains unclear to me what they wanted to prove. I sent the judge a DVD of the entire show. I'm sure he never watched it, but I'm equally certain that if he had, he might have learned something from it.

Chapter Fifty: Last Stand

I wore a dress to Tyler's high school graduation. I wasn't the only one; other women wore dresses. Marie was finally realizing her worst nightmare. Tyler's whole class would see me there. The whole town would see me a couple of weeks later when I carried the rainbow flag in the Eagan Independence Day parade supporting one of our state candidates. I admire his courage, asking a transgender woman to be at the head of his parade, even in 2012, the year of marriage equality. He called me after the parade and said he'd gotten two comments on his website saying it was inappropriate for me to be at a family event. "Only two?" I said, "That's amazing." "I'm afraid I can't explain myself, sir. Because I am not myself, you see?"

I was happy for Tyler and a proud parent. It was a beautiful summer day and a pleasant ceremony. Marie agreed to a photograph of Tyler with both his parents.

I had a party for Tyler later at Cooper's. Ed was there. He was a loyal friend. He'd had good relationships with all of our children when they were growing up. The remaining guests were mostly political friends, including our representative. I was grateful to them. I know it made Tyler feel special.

Tyler's graduation also marked the start of the final episode in the divorce. Legally, he was no longer "an issue." I had custody of Tyler for a year and a half, same as Marie, but I only received child support for four months at half the rate.

According to the decree, spousal maintenance would be reviewed when Tyler graduated from high school. My motion asked for a termination of spousal maintenance. My argument again emphasized the ambiguity of the original order, but the deciding factors were more related to a significant change in circumstances resulting from the divorce and the transition.

Ms. Pitbull essentially repeated all of the same arguments about frivolous litigant and attempts to litigate the same issue. Once again, totally baseless, because the divorce decree already stated that spousal maintenance could be reviewed. They continued their allegations of abuse. I could see no pertinent justification for any of it. From my perspective, it was an indignant rage.

Ms. Pitbull repeatedly said she was helping Marie out of empathy for her struggle against an uncooperative husband. I saw it differently. First of all, she wasn't working pro bono. It's difficult to make a solid case that $150,000 in legal fees was somehow to the benefit of our son. Ms. Pitbull had lost a significant court decision to a pro se litigant and was defending her reputation. Right or wrong, that's my opinion. Despite Ms. Pitbull's own accolades about my legal talent, I'm not lauding it as a result of my amazing legal skills. I just believe that right finally prevailed over might. The enemy had exhausted themselves.

Following the harassment complaint about my appearance on *Girl Talk*, I responded with a request for an I25 assessment for Marie which is a chemical dependency and mental health assessment. The process disintegrated around discovery. After the fifth discovery request, I refused to respond without an order from the court. The June 24th hearing was continued again to Aug 6th.

The August 6th hearing largely focused on addressing the issue of harassment. The judge narrowed the issue list to child support, spousal maintenance, attorney fees, arrearages and frivolous litigation. It's a pretty long list.

I did empathize with the frustration of the court but again I didn't design the process. I find a particular quote from the August 6th proceeding expressed in a rather humorous way. "Make sure you have dates and times and specifics. I am not going to take twelve inches of information and turn it into another twelve inches." My own court file fills two file drawers.

They should have dropped the accusations. It wasn't relevant. The judge confirmed that at the hearing in August. He was clear about the fact it was history. Whether it was decided fairly or correctly was irrelevant. He repeated it multiple times. He also asserted that attorney misconduct was irrelevant. That was an issue for the Lawyers Board of Professional Responsibility (LBPR). The LBPR said it was the responsibility of the court. It was an air-tight defense for the attorney.

Even after clear and redundant instructions from the judge, Marie's attorney ended the hearing by accusing me of raping my wife. I wrote them a letter advising them that I wasn't the one who raped my wife and warning them not to rely on Dr. G's notes which were clearly speculative. I was moving to the offense. I don't know if that impacted a later decision to withdraw from the case.

A phone conference was scheduled for September 7th to follow up on the agreed exchange of discovery documents. They wanted all of my speaking engagements, which I said had no relevance. They again made an issue of the *Girl Talk* interview. The harassment claim was ambiguous from the start and never decided by the court. He simply said, "Don't harass Marie anymore." I said I wouldn't and that request was dismissed. They wanted names and dates and numbers for all the jobs I'd applied to. I was working, but I agreed to give them what I had which was nothing really. Marie was working as an apprentice for Fraidy Cats' and receiving no income.

The judge said he would limit a review of frivolous litigation to the past year, which I argued was insufficient, but he wouldn't change his position. I'd revise my argument about frivolous litigation around the definition: "A person who institutes and maintains a claim that isn't well grounded in fact" based on their claim for sole legal and physical custody. I agreed to pay Marie $2,500 per month in exchange for custody of my son. There was no other justification stated in the oral stipulation. The court couldn't possibly enter that into the record, so they created an explanation consistent with their view of a proper divorce decree leaving many deficiencies. Marie and I still own stock together.

The court did approve subpoenas for Mr. R, Dr. G, and detective McKnight. It illustrates how cost prohibits people from filing reasonable claims. Even as I was calling them to rebut their own false testimony, I'd still have to pay them their hourly rate for the time they were there, plus travel expenses. It could easily go to several thousand dollars.

On September 19th I met with attorneys at Gender Justice in St. Paul. They specialized in transgender cases. They couldn't represent me but did offer to write a letter for the evidentiary hearing in November. I'd also have letters from Dr. H and my gynecologist.

On September 28th Ms. Pitbull withdrew as Marie's attorney which also meant she wasn't going to pursue the frivolous litigant claim in an attempt to make me liable for her fees, which were well over a $100,000. I felt there was little chance of prevailing in my own frivolous litigation claim. The cost would be enormous and the return insignificant.

I wrote to Marie to ensure she had the most recent documents I had sent to her attorney. I also had to deliver to her all of the documents for the evidentiary hearing. She wouldn't accept them, so I set them in her car and advised her that she was the attorney now. It was a painful feeling, but there was nothing else I could do for her until Ms. Pitbull filed an intent to docket judgment against Marie for attorney's fees. I filed a request for a hearing and stay of judgment. I'd have challenged the validity of those fees on Marie's behalf, but the hearing never took place. Ms. Pitbull also attempted to attach loan payments from my daughter Jamie.

The final hearing came on November 16th, just Marie and me and the judge. I am thinking it should have started that way instead of ending that way. It was a brief hearing. I don't remember most of it. Marie testified to what she could earn working at Fraidy Cats'. I qualified how my average earnings should be calculated. It also showed my earnings were declining, which I attribute to the divorce proceedings, but there was little reason to believe my earnings would recover. A major factor was the transgender health care. Gender Justice provided the legal and medical reasons why that was necessary for me. Hormone replacement therapy can cost up to $500 a month without insurance. Sexual reassignment surgery can run $30,000 or more and isn't covered by most insurance plans.

When the judge asked me what would happen if I didn't transition I replied simply, "I'd be dead." That's the truth. But, as always, the facts don't matter. What matters is what the judge believes. I guess he must have believed me.

Final Chapter: Back to the Beginning

"Begin at the beginning," the King said, very gravely, *"and go on till you come to the end: then stop."*

–Lewis Carroll, Alice in Wonderland

I am back at the beginning. To know that I am a woman, even without the proof I need to satisfy the greatest skeptics, is only the beginning.

The final order of the court came on January 3, 2013. It was a curious epitaph to a four-year courtroom drama. According to the final order: "This court believes that the parties became inappropriately focused on the issue of the respondent's transgender identity at the onset of the litigation. This resulted in a significant source of difficulty in reaching finality in the case."

In that instant I was free, free of a four-year family court ordeal; free of my male gender constraints; free from the conflicts of my marriage; free of the responsibility. At the same time, everything else I had worked for most of my life lay in total ruin: my family, my home, my friendships, my career, my finances.

The family is still recovering, establishing new relationships in the context of a more open and more honest reality. According to the court, Marie and I had no one to blame but ourselves. We should have been less pretentious, more honest perhaps. "It wouldn't have ended this way if you had confronted your issues," as if we never tried.

There is no one to acknowledge the social pressures we experienced over things beyond our control. Marie and I may never speak again. It is a painful tragedy. It is far more than an indictment of our relationship, it is an indictment of our entire society. It is useless to blame the other side, we all have a part in it, and there are more than two sides.

The choices were not visible at the onset of the divorce. The choices are not easy or obvious when a powerful sense of who you are conflicts with what others might expect you to be. At the onset, I was convinced I could sustain a male presentation and that would be the least complicated means to an acceptable end

The Feminine Mystique advanced the idea that women were not adapted to the role of homemaker and caregiver by genetic disposition. Friedan presented the evidence that women were relegated to that position by a patriarchal model of masculine superiority and the hierarchical model of power, dominance, and wealth that accompanies it. They were seduced into that role by media and advertising dominated by male ideals of femininity, prodded and sedated by male doctors and therapists. Freeing women from the drudgery of utilitarian existence would enhance the relationship between men and women.

The patriarchy continues to reassert itself. The Violence Against Women Act advanced the adversarial relationship between men and women, creating billions of dollars in funding for the institutions that sustain the authority of a patriarchal society. I understood the extent of domestic violence from my own policing experiences in the seventies. I do agree that a response was necessary, but the approach has again crafted women as victim and provided few resources for early intervention or prevention. It has failed to provide intervention for men, the presumed denizens of violence, who themselves are victims of the same dysfunctional patterns of abuse.

Perhaps when Madeline Albright said there was a special place in hell for women who don't support each other[1], she should have added that there's a room next door for women who don't hold each other accountable. Marie's attorney was a woman. A good attorney would have helped Marie preserve her non-marital assets, obtain a reasonable settlement, and move on with her life. The average divorce costs about $15,000. I estimate ours at nearly a quarter of a million, more than our total assets at the start of the divorce. The vast majority of it was billed by one attorney. Marie's attorney exploited the bias of an authoritarian system of justice that has defined women as victim, men as perpetrator. It is at best a partial truth.

This gender bias is a significant challenge for modern day feminism. I hear those concerns in passing, working with professionals in the domestic abuse services, but I don't see it in mainstream media. What you hear about is "toxic masculinity:" socially-constructed attitudes that describe the masculine gender role as violent, unemotional, sexually aggressive. Taught on college campuses, it reinforces the victim/perpetrator model of male/female relationships.

Maybe it isn't coincidental that the concept seems to have been introduced by a man, in 1994, by the book, *Man Enough: Fathers, Sons, and the Search for Masculinity*, attempting to address men's issues. "Without a 'father in residence,' [men] may go through life striving towards an ideal of exaggerated, even toxic, masculinity," the author of the book, Frank Pittman, said on the topic of young men without fathers. This was also the year Congress first enacted the Violence Against Women Act.

I trust Fay Weldon recognizes the absurdity of describing transition as, "The only way men have of fighting back against the natural superiority of women is by becoming women themselves." Perhaps it does have some relationship to why men choose to identify as feminists. There is no opposite to transgender, just as there is no opposite to feminism. Transgender is an inclusive model of gender expression, whereas feminism remains exclusive. In the extreme, radical feminists believe that only pure-bred virgin females should be allowed to participate in any discourse about gender. They will point to the use of the word "virgin" as proof positive that a trans female author is really just a sexist male in feminist garb. Radical feminism is sexism, and it reinforces the transgender myth.

It certainly has bearing on the perceptions of transgender women. Transgender women often outperform men in many contexts in our efforts to conceal or even eliminate our female identity. Acting like a man around other women was exceedingly difficult. If not for my desire to have children, I may have chosen more male-dominated spaces, like the military, as many transgender women do, almost four times the rate of the male population.

Now, of course, living as a woman, the opposite is true. Being a woman around other women is easy. Around men, I feel more conspicuous because I know now I am acting like a woman without the perceptual veil of a man. I've been inside their clubhouse. In time, perhaps, this will feel more natural. Like any young girl, I am still discovering what type of woman I will be.

I have not experienced the full spectrum of female socialization that I know is inevitable. How much will I conform to the social expectations of my culture and how much will I challenge them. I will not be guided by the same hierarchical structures that shaped my male behaviors and perceptions of leadership. We don't ask girls what they want to be when they grow up. These hierarchical structures are more transparent to me than they are to many women.

More importantly, will my experience as a transgender woman contribute to a broader acceptance of the diversity of sexuality and gender? Will it empower both genders toward a broader range of options and opportunities, to an understanding of the differences, the similarities, and the high degree of intersectionality? Perhaps one day I will no longer feel coerced to support you because you're of the same sex. Perhaps one day I will choose to support you because of who you are as a person, how you have defined your relationship to society, and the nature of your accomplishments.

I am inspired and excited about this new beginning. Six months from the final order of the court, the opening headline will read: "Paula Overby, Eagan, could be state's first transgender congressional candidate." Most girls don't start out this way. I see so much uncharted territory ahead.

1 Rappeport, Alan, "Gloria Steinem and Madeleine Albright Rebuke Young Women Backing Bernie Sanders," *New York Times*, Web. Feb 7, 2016, http://www.nytimes.com/2016/02/08/us/politics/gloria-steinem-madeleine-albright-hillary-clinton-bernie-sanders.html.

Appendix A: Confessions of a Cross-dresser

CONFESSIONS OF A CROSS-DRESSER

Burlesque Performance in One Act – Patrick's Cabaret, August of 1999

By Paula Overby

Copyright © 2017

by Paula Overby

At Rise: PAUL OVERBY is standing, holding a letter he has just received from Santa's work shop at the North Pole. He is wearing a short flared skirt Santa's helper costume with fur trimming the skirt and bodice. He's had a complete beauty make over and he's wearing a wig with long auburn curls. He reads the letter aloud

Dear Paul,

We thank you for your recent application to the position of Santa's helper. While your many artistic talents are impressive we regret that we cannot offer this position. Everyone is welcome in our fantasy wonderland here at the North Pole, but Santa's helpers work with humans of a conservative nature. It is apparent that your particular ambition wouldn't be well received. Perhaps you would like to reconsider our sewing department.

Its signed Elf Resources but I can't really make out the signature. (Addressing the audience as she notes the signature on the letter)

Maybe I shouldn't have sent a photo. (is distressed by rejection)

Of course I was devastated. Rejection is never an easy thing for anyone. But when it's your dream job how is one to cope? Naturally, I penned a response right away and I am happy to recite it for you.

He brings holiday cheer but it comes with a price.

Leaving children to worry, were they naughty or nice.
And if you feel sad or so down and out.
You better not cry and you better not pout.
Cause even if mother and father have gone out.
Santa Clause may be lurking about.
Like so many beginnings I don't know the true start
Though I'm sure I can't blame it on math class or art.
I may have been eight, maybe nine, even ten.
I'm sure that it had to be sometime back then.
When I first started thinking about feeling pretty.
Instead of being class clown and trying to act witty.
One childhood memory of which I'm aware.
Is of catalog models wearing soft underwear.
So if there is blame that I can point toward.
It might have been Sears or Montgomery Ward.
Or maybe I should just give my parents the blame.
For living where each of my friends had some girls name.
But who could blame them for not wanting to see.
That when we played dolls I'd rather be Barbie.
Still somehow I knew even back then
That if boys play with dolls they better be Ken.
One day I just did it without knowing why.
Put on that cute nightie just to give it a try.
And that little nightie so colorful and frilly.
Made me feel pretty, and cute, even silly.
While turning about as I looked in the mirror.
I noticed my aunt in the hall to the rear.
She made it quite clear with a great deal of poise.
That nighties were for girls and definitely not boys.
But I saw in her eyes a real look of loathing.
And vowed never again to wear women's clothing.
That was the end of it. The end of that game.
And I put away that nightie along with my shame.
I made it through high school, and college, and began my career.
Went to plenty of parties and drank plenty of beer.
But in a dress or high heels I for sure wasn't seen.
Except for perhaps on a rare Halloween.

I later got married and had kids of my own
And don't stop the presses or wait by the phone.
Yes, I taught them about Santa and all of the joys.
He brings with the presents for good girls and boys.
But somehow years later I'd forgotten that vow
And I have to confess I'm a cross-dresser now.
So I put on some make up and slip on a dress.
Shave my legs and wear heels and all of the rest.
Like playing with my hair using ribbons and bows.
And painting the nails on my fingers and toes.
Once in awhile when the family is out.
And there really is nobody else there about.
I page through Fredrick's wondering how I might look.
Wearing just about anything from that little book.
Oh I'm not fooling myself cause I know how I'm seen.
Just a man in a dress not some prom beauty queen.
Then one night before Christmas alone in the house.
I happened to glimpse at a scurrying mouse.
There I was all dressed up in satin and lace.
Just relaxing a little in my comfortable place.
The sight of that mouse filled my mind with such chatter.
I knew I'd be forced to examine the matter.
I reached for the candle and snuffed out the wick.
But I knew in that instant I'd be seen by St Nick.
I ran to the bathroom and flicked on the light.
And went straight to my work in spite of my fright.
Removing foundation, eyeliner and shadow.
And untying my hair from that pretty red bow.
I took off my dress, my stockings, and heels.
Then paused at how sexy that silky bra feels.
Quickly I shook off that hesitant fit.
And reached round behind and quickly unsnapped it.
I let those lace panties just fall to the floor.
Then stuffed it all into a packed dresser drawer.
I took a quick shower and hung my towel on the rail.
Then saw the red polish shinning bright on my nails.
I searched through the cabinets and the closet too.

As I started to panic wondering what I should do,
In my rush from the shower I tripped on the hoover.
Knowing I had to find some kind of polish remover.
I grab my sore toe and I gave out a moan.
And went to my garage for some straight acetone.
Cross-dressers of course are really just men.
depend on their garage you know now and then.
I got rid of that polish all shinny and red.
Then rushed to my bedroom and went straight to bed.
I was nervous you might guess and I gave out a shiver.
You know that bit of doubt that Santa won't deliver.
But then I spoke words to myself like I never had.
Saying just feeling good can't really be bad.
I thought to myself as I began to retire.
That a big lump of coal makes a nice comfy fire.
As my apprehension faded and with it my fear.
I thought about Santa wearing satin next year.
And I heard him exclaim as he rode out of sight.
Merry Christmas to all and damn this bra is too tight.

Appendix B: Your Affiant Sayeth Not

STATE OF MINNESOTA DISTRICT COURT   COUNTY OF DAKOTA FIRST JUDICIAL DISTRICT

Court File No. 00XX-XX-00-00000

Re the Marriage of:

Marie Annette Taylor Overby, Petitioner

Paul Stewart Overby, Respondent

STATE OF MINNESOTA }

}ss.

COUNTY OF DAKOTA }

AFFIDAVIT of TYLER JENS OVERBY in support of respondent's request for sole physical custody.

Tyler Jens Overby, after being first duly sworn, deposes and says that he is the son of the parties in the above-entitled matter and makes this Affidavit in support of his father's request for sole physical custody.

My name is Tyler Jens Overby and my mom and dad are the petitioner and Respondent. I am making this Affidavit because I want the judge to hear my feelings and thoughts. I am 16 years old and was born August 5, 1993. My dad is a very important person in my life; he listens to me; he helps me with my homework, and teaches me many things. I want to stay in my house because I want to keep my dog and it's a great place for me and my friends to get together. The best chance for me to stay in my house is to live with my dad. Also staying in my house will help me keep stability and will allow me to continue doing well in school. With my dad in the house, he will allow my mom and I to do things there. My mom will not even let my dad in the house at all. Further your Affiant sayeth not.

Photos

On the following pages you can review the story in pictures: Before and After and In Between.

BEFORE
&
AFTER

Beauty Makeover by
Teri - Circa 1995

Costume for
confessions of a
crossdreser 1997

Courtney's Graduation
2008

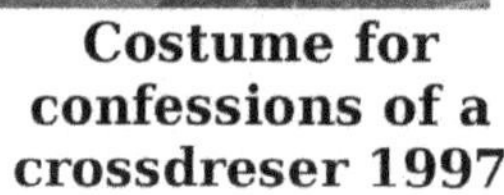

Tyler's graduation 2012

Weekend visitation with my
son 2009

In
Between

New girl in the office
2010

Pride parade during
the Minnesota Vote No
campaign 2012

Stonewall DFL Halloween
fundraiser 2013

Lightning Source UK Ltd.
Milton Keynes UK
UKHW041247280819
348710UK00006B/1074/P